What Teeth Reveal about Human Evolution

Over millions of years in the fossil record, hominin teeth preserve a high-fidelity record of their own growth, development, wear, chemistry, and pathology. They yield insights into human evolution that are difficult, if not impossible, to achieve through other sources of fossil or archaeological data.

Integrating dental findings with current debates and issues in paleoanthropology, this book shows how fossil hominin teeth shed light on the origins and evolution of our dietary diversity, extended childhoods, long lifespans, and other fundamental features of human biology. It assesses methods to interpret different lines of dental evidence, providing a critical, practical approach that will appeal to students and researchers in biological anthropology and related fields such as dental science, oral biology, evolutionary biology, and paleontology.

DEBBIE GUATELLI-STEINBERG is Professor of Anthropology, and Courtesy Professor of Evolution, Ecology, and Organismal Biology at The Ohio State University. She has conducted extensive research on fossil hominin teeth in Africa, Europe, and Asia, and has published widely in the fields of dental paleoanthropology and dental primatology.

What Teeth Reveal about Human Evolution

DEBBIE GUATELLI-STEINBERG
The Ohio State University, USA

CAMBRIDGE
UNIVERSITY PRESS

University Printing House, Cambridge CB2 8BS, United Kingdom

One Liberty Plaza, 20th Floor, New York, NY 10006, USA

477 Williamstown Road, Port Melbourne, VIC 3207, Australia

314-321, 3rd Floor, Plot 3, Splendor Forum, Jasola District Centre, New Delhi - 110025, India

79 Anson Road, #06-04/06, Singapore 079906

Cambridge University Press is part of the University of Cambridge.

It furthers the University's mission by disseminating knowledge in the pursuit of education, learning and research at the highest international levels of excellence.

www.cambridge.org
Information on this title: www.cambridge.org/9781107082106

© Guatelli-Steinberg 2016

This publication is in copyright. Subject to statutory exception and to the provisions of relevant collective licensing agreements, no reproduction of any part may take place without the written permission of Cambridge University Press.

First published 2016

A catalogue record for this publication is available from the British Library

Library of Congress Cataloging in Publication data
Guatelli-Steinberg, Debbie, 1961– author.
What teeth reveal about human evolution / Debbie Guatelli-Steinberg.
Cambridge ; New York : Cambridge University Press, 2016.
LCCN 2016015474| ISBN 9781107082106 (hardback) | ISBN 9781107442603 (paperback)
| MESH: Paleodontology – methods | Tooth – anatomy & histology | Anthropology, Physical | Odontometry | Biological Evolution
LCC GN209 | NLM GN 209 | DDC 599.9/43–dc23
LC record available at https://lccn.loc.gov/2016015474

ISBN 978-1-107-08210-6 Hardback
ISBN 978-1-107-44260-3 Paperback

Cambridge University Press has no responsibility for the persistence or accuracy of URLs for external or third-party internet websites referred to in this publication, and does not guarantee that any content on such websites is, or will remain, accurate or appropriate.

To my husband Daniel J. Steinberg and to Rose M. Guatelli, John L. Guatelli, Maria Catena (Zumbo) Sottile, and A. John Sottile

Contents

Acknowledgments		*page* ix
Introduction: The Convenient Tooth		1
PART I: TEETH AND AUSTRALOPITHS		9
1	March of the Bipeds: The Early Years	11
2	Dentally-Derived Dietary Inferences: The Australopiths	30
3	Curious Canines	59
4	Incisive Insights into Childhood	84
PART II: TEETH AND THE GENUS HOMO		111
5	March of the Bipeds: The Later Years	113
6	Dentally-Derived Dietary Inferences: The Genus *Homo* and Its Diminishing Dentition	137
7	Long in the Tooth: Life History Changes in *Homo*	157
8	Knowing Neanderthals through Their Teeth	177

9	Insights into the Origins of Modern Humans and Their Dental Diseases	211
10	Every Tooth a Diamond	232
	References	246
	Index	282

Acknowledgments

There are many people whose influence and direct assistance I would like to thank. I am indebted to my dissertation advisor, John Lukacs, for introducing me to the world of dental anthropology. I am also indebted to my most frequent collaborators: Donald Reid, Bruce Floyd, Joel D. Irish, Rebecca Ferrell, John P. Hunter, Paul Sciulli, Song Xing, and Patrick Mahoney. I thank Scott McGraw and Jeff McKee for reading and commenting on portions of the manuscript. I am grateful and fortunate to have worked with Alyssa Starrett, who drew many of the figures, and Tom Broa, who helped with research and referencing. I also thank Rob Scott for sharing his microwear texture images and Song Xing for the images of incisor shoveling in *Homo erectus*. The assistants and editors at Cambridge University Press provided much appreciated support, most especially Sarah Payne. Sources of ongoing inspiration are my current and former graduate students. Above all, I am thankful to my husband Dan Steinberg for his unflagging support of this project.

Introduction: The Convenient Tooth

A book about fossil teeth would have been unthinkable before 1669. Three years earlier, a group of Tuscan fishermen caught a colossal white shark. As Brian Switek tells the story in his engaging book, *Written in Stone: The Hidden Secrets of Fossils and the Story of Life on Earth*, that shark excited the imagination of Medici Grand Duke Ferdinando II, a great patron of the sciences (1).

The shark's body was too large to transport and had begun to decompose anyway, so its head was cut off and sent to the Grand Duke, who chose his most talented resident anatomist for the privileged job of dissecting it (Figure i). Danish-born Nicolaus Steno (aka Niels Steensen) turned out to be the man for the job (1). As he poured over his dissection, Steno was struck by the uncanny similarity of the shark's teeth to what were then popular triangle-shaped stones called *glossopetrae* or "tongue stones" (2, 3) (Figure 1).

At the time, *glossopetrae* were used for all sorts of purposes: as antidotes to snake venom, treatments for epilepsy, amulets, and when ground into a fine powder, as toothpastes (2, 3). Roman philosopher Pliny the Elder thought *glossopetrae* dropped from the sky on moonless nights (4). Inspired by his shark dissection, Steno published his own explanation in 1669. He suggested that the corpuscular theory, which held that matter was made of tiny corpuscles, could explain how shark teeth turned to stone (5). When the teeth were buried in sediments, the corpuscles of minerals gradually replaced the corpuscles that made up teeth, transforming them into stone. This explanation is not so far from our modern understanding of how fossils form. In the case of fossil teeth though, most of the original mineral remains while mineral from surrounding sediments fills in tiny pore spaces within them in the process of permineralization.

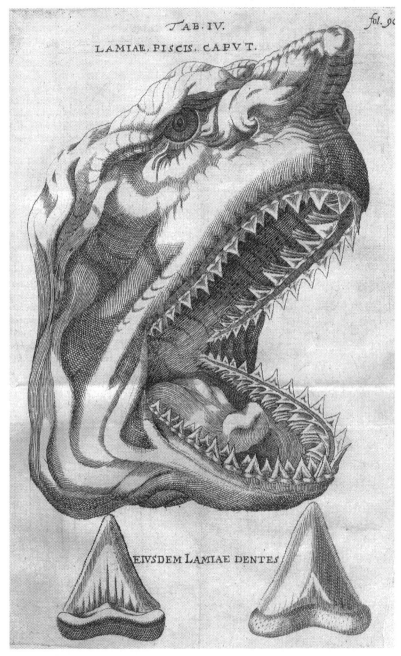

FIGURE 1: Shark head dissected by Niels Steensen (Steno). Image from Elementorum myologiae specimen, 1669.

That fossil teeth played such a starring role at the dawn of paleontology is no coincidence. To be sure, sharks lose a lot of teeth. But it is the fact that teeth are hard, compact, and composed of mineralized tissue that makes them prime candidates for preservation and fossilization. Indeed, most of the fossil record consists of teeth and that is also true of the human fossil record. This book is about what fossil teeth tell us about human evolution. Though they probably can't cure snake bites (I am not sure anyone has tried), the fossil teeth of our ancestors are surprisingly versatile in their uses for telling us about our past.

Teeth are the only parts of our skeleton that interact directly with our environments. Their direct interactions with food place them squarely in the path of evolutionary change. Thus, in large part, teeth tell us so much because they have evolved *directly* in response to our diets and changing ways of life. Our ancient ancestors had big teeth for processing hard and in some cases tough foods. Yet, over our evolutionary history, as we became increasingly dependent on cultural solutions such as tools and fire to break down food, our teeth dramatically reduced in size. The types of foods our ancient ancestors ate and how they ate them also left behind traces in their teeth during their lifetimes. These traces include distinctive microscopic marks on teeth produced by chewing different kinds of foods and tiny plant parts preserved in calcified plaque (dental calculus).

A less well-appreciated fact is that, as parts of our anatomy, teeth are affected *indirectly* by changes occurring elsewhere in our bodies, whether these changes occurred over evolutionary time scales or during the lifetime of an individual. Thus, evolutionary changes in a species' teeth tell us about evolutionary changes in the species as a whole. For example, like the rings of trees, growth lines in enamel (the outer covering of teeth) form at known intervals. But, instead of representing years of growth like tree rings, enamel growth lines represent *days* of growth and are preserved in enamel that is millions of years old. Because the growth of different parts of our body is generally integrated, the pace at which teeth grow, to a large extent, reflects the pace at which our bodies grow. We can track the evolution of extended juvenile growth periods, a hallmark of humanity, by tracing changes in tooth growth in our ancestors through time. Over individual lifetimes, tooth growth during childhood can be disrupted by malnutrition and disease, telling us about episodes of physiological stress our ancestors experienced as they grew.

Evolutionary changes in teeth took place in the broader context of human environments that included social relationships and culture. The direct and indirect responses of teeth to our physical, social, and cultural environments make teeth a model system for tracing the origins and evolution of our dietary diversity, extended childhoods, long lifespans, and other key features of our unique biology. These insights are made possible because over the millions of years of the fossil record, teeth preserve a high-fidelity record of their own growth, wear, chemistry, and pathology.

On top of this, the morphology of teeth – their shapes, cusps, and grooves – is highly heritable. This means that a great deal of variation in dental morphology is caused by variation in genes, rather than by the environment (6). For this reason, dental morphology can be used as a marker of species identities and relationships. It's no wonder that the eighteenth-to-nineteenth century French naturalist Baron George Cuvier is reported to have said "Show me your teeth and I will tell you who you are." Cuvier was referring to the distinctive features of vertebrate species' fossil teeth. He could just as well have made the same claim on a smaller scale for hominins, the taxonomic group of related species that branched off from our common ancestor with chimpanzees. (Figures ii and iii illustrate the morphology and names of the principal cusps of modern human molars. These principal cusp names will be used throughout the book.)

I have studied many of the teeth of fossil hominins, from *Australopithecus* to Neanderthals, and have conducted research on or related to several of the topics covered in this book. In doing so, I have grown to appreciate the importance of teeth in our evolutionary

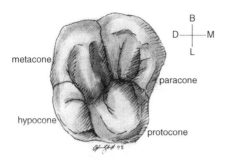

FIGURE II: Occlusal (chewing surface) view of upper right first molar with names of principal cusps. In the upper right of image is a direction key. "B" stands for "buccal," the side of the tooth facing the cheek; "L" for "lingual," the side of the tooth facing the tongue; M for "mesial," the side of the tooth facing the midline (and in the case of molars toward the front of the mouth); and D for "distal," the side of the tooth facing toward the back of the mouth. Drawn by Alyssa Starrett.

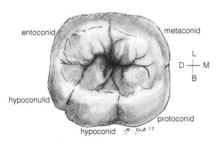

FIGURE III: Occlusal (chewing surface) view of lower right first molar with names of principal cusps. At the right of image is a direction key. "B" stands for "buccal," the side of the tooth facing the cheek; "L" for "lingual," the side of the tooth facing the tongue; M for "mesial," the side of the tooth facing the midline (and in the case of molars toward the front of the mouth); and D for "distal," the side of the tooth facing toward the back of the mouth.

history and the many clues about our past that fossil teeth hold. What prompted me to write this book was a desire to synthesize dental insights into human evolution. Here, I emphasize how evolutionary changes in human teeth are linked to key evolutionary trends in human evolution: the broadening of our diets, our increasing reliance on culture, our expanding brains, and the lengthening of our childhoods and lifespans. Because of these links, and because of the detailed information fossil teeth preserve, insights into human evolution are possible that are difficult, if not impossible, to achieve through other sources of fossil or archaeological data. Here, I further highlight how the evolution of teeth reflects human evolutionary dynamics, in which cultural adaptations shape and are also shaped by biological adaptations.

This book is meant to be an accessible account of many of the major insights into human evolution that can be gleaned from the study of teeth. In some instances these insights are about our teeth themselves, but more often these insights relate to larger evolutionary trends. The book is not about the detailed morphology of teeth but about the hard-earned insights into human evolution that dedicated researchers have extracted (excuse the pun) from fossil teeth. I intend the book for those who have a passion for human evolution in general and/or a particular curiosity about how human teeth inform us about our evolutionary history.

Intended readership also includes undergraduates in human evolution or dental anthropology courses. But the book is not meant to be a textbook for these courses. The book integrates dental findings with debates and issues in paleoanthropology, and in this respect, I hope that the book will be used to generate discussion in undergraduate classes. Most of the chapters (i.e., the nonintroductory ones, Chapters 1 and 5) would also work as starting points for discussion in graduate-level classes.

The book is divided into two parts: the first concentrates on the earlier time period of human evolution (primarily on Australopiths) and the second on the later time period (focusing on the genus *Homo*). (See Figure iv for a timeline of human evolution.) Most chapters emphasize particular species or lineages that are subjects of debate and/or extensive research activity. Part I covers the broad outline of early human evolution with special attention to teeth (Chapter 1), explores what various lines of dental evidence tell us about diet in our

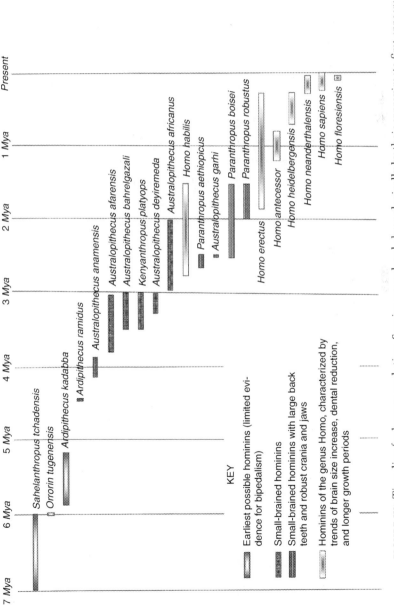

FIGURE IV: Time-line for human evolution. Species are ordered chronologically by their approximate first appearance dates. Drawn by author.

early (pre-*Homo*) ancestors (Chapter 2), considers whether sexual dimorphism in hominin canine teeth is related to levels of competition among males (Chapter 3), and synthesizes our understanding of what incremental growth lines in fossil teeth reveal about the length of juvenile growth periods in our earliest ancestors (Chapter 4).

Part II focuses on the genus *Homo*. Chapter 5 sketches the broad outline of evolution within the genus *Homo*, again with special attention to teeth. Chapter 6 explores interrelationships among changes in tooth size, culture, and diet in the genus *Homo* prior to Neanderthals and modern humans. Chapter 7 evaluates dental evidence for the evolution of childhood and longevity in the genus *Homo* before Neanderthals and modern humans. Chapter 8 highlights dental insights into Neanderthal phylogeny, behavior, diet, and life history. Chapter 9 emphasizes the contribution of teeth to understanding the origin of anatomically modern *Homo sapiens* and our dental diseases. Concluding, Chapter 10 recapitulates the book's main points and explores how an appreciation of our dental past can help us understand how we view and treat teeth today.

To pursue the insights that fossil teeth offer, we first need to discuss how evolutionary relationships among fossil species are assessed and to sketch the broad outlines of early human evolution.

PART I **Teeth and Australopiths**

1 March of the Bipeds: The Early Years

> It is, however, very difficult to establish the precise lines of descent, termed *phylogenies*, for most organisms.
>
> – Ayala FJ and Valentine JW
> *Evolving: The Theory and Process of Organic Evolution* (7)

As understood today, human evolutionary history involves some twenty species of fossil hominins, give or take a few depending on the taxonomic scheme to which one subscribes. In the field of paleoanthropology, taxonomic questions – how to classify fossil species – are famously contentious. As Richard Dawkins comments in the *Ancestor's Tale* (8), there is more than one paleontology book in print entitled *"Bones of Contention."* Names given to species carry implications for how species are related to one another. A species placed in the genus *Homo* for example, is recognized as sharing a more recent common ancestor with modern humans than a species placed in the genus *Australopithecus*.

Resolving species relationships is no straightforward task. That is one reason (among others) why there are so many different points of view about evolutionary relationships among hominin species. Such relationships are summarized in diagrams called *phylogenies* or *phylogenetic trees*. All methods of constructing phylogenies rely on comparing the characteristics of species, from their DNA sequences to their dental features to any aspect of their anatomy and even behavior. The most direct means of genetic comparison is through DNA, but, only in more recent hominins has it thus far been possible to extract adequately preserved DNA (see Chapter 5). For earlier species, the characteristics of teeth and bones must suffice for assessing evolutionary relationships. As noted, teeth figure prominently in such assessments: they are extremely well-preserved in the fossil record and much of the variation in their morphology is due to genes (rather than environment).

There are different ways to assess evolutionary relationships among species. According to the method of *phenetics*,[1] all available traits should be used to construct phylogenies. Species with greater similarity are considered more closely related. This method does not take into account two big problems. The first is the problem of *homoplasy*, when two species have similar traits but not because they inherited them from a common ancestor. One way that homoplasy can occur is when species independently evolve similar solutions to similar problems. The wings of dragonflies and seagulls were not inherited from their common ancestor but evolved independently as adaptations for flight in their separately evolving lineages. Another way homoplasy can occur is through reversal. In this instance, a trait that was present in an ancestor may be lost in some descendant species, but then evolve anew in one or more of them.

The second problem with phenetics is that even for traits that *are* inherited from a common ancestor, so-called *homologous traits*, not all are equal. If you were an alien landing on earth and happened across a dog, a baboon and a human, you might conclude that dogs and baboons share a more recent common ancestor than do baboons and humans. Dogs and baboons walk on all four legs and have very hairy bodies, while humans lack these features. But, these features that baboons and dogs share are *primitive traits* – walking on all four legs evolved in the first vertebrates to walk on land and the presence of hair evolved in the last common ancestor of all mammals. As soon as you looked around a bit more, you'd notice that these characteristics are present in nearly all living mammals. Dogs and baboons share these features not because they are particularly closely related to one another but because their distant mammalian ancestor had these features.

---

[1] The word "phenetics" comes from the Greek root *phainein*, "to show." It is the same root used in the word "phenotype," the observable features of an organism. (9. Tobin A, Dusheck J. *Asking about Life:* Cengage Learning; 2004.)

As you looked a bit further, you'd notice that baboons and humans share multiple traits to the exclusion of dogs and many other non-primate mammals. These traits include stereoscopic vision, nails instead of claws, bony eye sockets, fewer teeth, and larger brains. These characteristics shared by baboons and humans are *derived traits* that were present in their most recent primate common ancestor. Such *shared derived traits* would tell you that there is a branch of the mammalian evolutionary tree that includes baboons and humans but not dogs. Shared derived traits are the basis of a second method of reconstructing phylogenies known as *cladistics*.[2] Most paleoanthropologists prefer the cladistic method because it separates primitive from derived traits (among other advantages).[3]

The product of a cladistic analysis is a *cladogram* – a diagram that shows the branching sequence of a set of species from a hypothetical common ancestor. Strictly speaking, cladistic analyses do not tell you how species are linked to one another in ancestor-descendent lineages and do not have a time dimension. In this way a cladogram differs from other depictions of phylogenetic relationships. Among several and sometimes many possible cladograms that can be created from a set of trait data, those that would necessitate the greatest number of homoplasies are considered to be most improbable. The assumption is that a cladogram requiring a large number of independent evolutionary events to explain similarities among species is less likely than one requiring fewer of them. The most parsimonious cladogram, requiring the fewest homoplasies, is therefore preferred. The principle being applied here is Occam's Razor, that explanations requiring fewer assumptions are more likely to be correct than those requiring more.

But, there are problems with cladistics and the parsimony principle.[4] Sometimes there are several equally parsimonious

---

[2] The word "cladistics" comes from the Greek root *clados*, meaning "branch." (9. Ibid.).
[3] A third school, "evolutionary systematics," constructs phylogenies on the basis of branching sequences among species as well as on how much species have changed since they shared a common ancestor.
[4] A "maximum likelihood" approach can also be used in cladistic analysis. In this statistical technique, a mathematical model of trait evolution is applied to a set of

cladograms. Furthermore, parsimonious solutions may not always be correct ones. It is also sometimes difficult to determine the primitive state for a characteristic. We know that walking on all fours is a primitive state for mammals – this is obvious because the fossil record reveals that four-legged vertebrates predate two-legged ones. If we didn't have the fossil record to help us here, we could look around at a distantly related group – such as reptiles – to figure this out. Walking on four legs is clearly a very old trait if it is shared with reptiles. Distantly related groups, what are called *outgroups*, are used in cladistics to determine the direction of evolutionary change in a trait. But, using outgroups is tricky: whatever species you choose has its own unique evolutionary history and therefore may not always express the primitive condition. So, sometimes you arrive at different answers depending on which species you choose as an outgroup. With these problems, fragmentary remains for some species, and an incomplete fossil record, it is no wonder hominin species relationships are so vigorously debated.

THE EARLIEST HOMININS

Not surprisingly there is debate right from the start in determining exactly which fossil species is the first hominin. From DNA evidence, we know that our closest living relatives among modern primates are chimpanzees and bonobos. The last common ancestor we shared with them existed some 7–12 million years ago, according to a recent estimate[5] (10).

The anatomical similarities of humans to the African apes led Charles Darwin to predict that the fossil hominins would be found on the African continent. In 1924, a young woman named Josephine Salmons, a student at the University of Witwatersrand in South Africa, presented her anatomy professor Raymond Dart with the

species and their traits, and the phylogeny that best fits the data (the most likely one) is produced. This is a newer method that is increasingly being incorporated into hominin studies.

[5] Previous estimates had suggested a more recent divergence, around 5–7 million years ago.

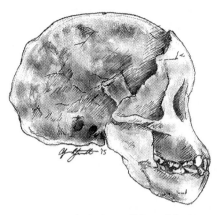

FIGURE 1.1: Artist's rendition of the Taung child. Drawn by Alyssa Starrett.

fossilized skull of a monkey that miners had blasted out of limestone (11). His interest piqued, Dart arranged to have additional fossils brought to him. When he opened one box of fossils, Dart found the remains of an endocast (cast of the interior of the cranium) together with the skeleton of a face cemented to the rock. Dart reportedly used his wife's knitting needles to painstakingly remove the rock (breccia) from the face of what is now known as the Taung Child (12) (Figure 1.1).

From the base of the endocast, Dart could tell that during life the child's head was held on an erect spine. Clearly the creature was bipedal, like humans today. Furthermore, the canine teeth were not the large and pointed variety that the African apes sport; they were far less impressive and similar in shape to those of modern humans. Yet, partly because the Taung Child's brain was small for a similarly-aged modern human and partly because up until this point fossil hominins had been found only in Europe and Asia, few of Dart's contemporaries believed he had found a human ancestor. Subsequent finds from South Africa, as well as the famous Lucy skeleton from Ethiopia dated to 3.2 million years ago, made clear that of our derived human traits, bipedalism arose first. Smaller, less pointed canine teeth than African apes were also present in our early ancestors, but large brains were not.

Today there are three contenders for the title of the earliest hominin, stretching back to 6–7 million years ago (Ma) in Africa. They are *Sahelanthropus tchadensis* (from Chad, dated to 6–7 Ma), *Orrorin tugenensis* (from Kenya, dated to 6 Ma) and *Ardipithecus kadabba* (from Ethiopia, dated to 5.2–5.8 Ma (13). The first species of hominin, evolving independently from the lineage that led to chimpanzees, may not have been bipedal. Yet, it is bipedalism that offers the clearest diagnostic clue as to the hominin status of a fossil species. Most of the debate regarding the hominin status of these three species therefore has to do with insufficient or ambiguous evidence of bipedalism (14). The first of these species, *Sahalanthropus tchadensis*, is a case in point: its skull was reconstructed from hundreds of pieces (15), so that details of the cranial base diagnostic of bipedalism have been disputed (16).

Still, the upper canine teeth of *Sahelanthropus tchadensis* are relatively small compared to a chimpanzee's and are worn at the tip as are those of humans today (17). Ape upper canines by contrast wear on the side facing the lower first premolar. Their projecting upper canines sharpen against their conical single-cusped first premolar in a *honing complex* (Figure 1.2). Honing creates wear on the back of the upper canine and front of the lower premolar. Ape lower canines also project beyond the tops of other teeth and are accommodated in the upper jaw by a *diastema* (gap) between the upper canine and incisors. But smaller canines with worn tips don't save the day for *Sahelanthropus* because some quadrupedal fossil ape canine teeth (probably those of females) that came before it in the fossil record appear to have had similarly sized canine teeth with similarly worn tips (16).

There is wider agreement that *Ardipithecus ramidus* (though see [18]), dated to 4.4 million years ago and from the Middle Awash area of Ethiopia (19), is a bona fide hominin. There are 109 specimens of this species, representing at least 36 individuals, including the individual represented by the famous *Ardi* skeleton. Standing 4 feet tall, *Ardi* had a pelvis with several key anatomical adaptations for bipedalism, a small brain, and smaller canines than a chimpanzee's.

THE EARLIEST HOMININS 17

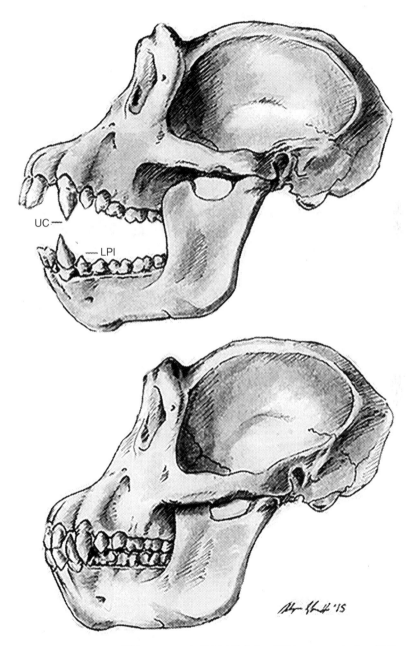

FIGURE 1.2: Chimpanzee skull highlighting UC (upper canine) and LP1 (lower first premolar). The distal edge of the UC hones, through jaw movements, against the mesial side of the LP1. Drawn by Alyssa Starrett.

But, *Ardipithecus's* mode of bipedalism was different from ours. Like an ape's foot, that of Ardi had a divergent big toe (Figure 1.3). Unlike modern humans, then, *Ardipithecus* could not push off the ground with its big toe while walking. Instead, *Ardi* seems to have propelled itself forward by pushing with the middle portion of its foot. *Ardi* also had longer arms (in relation to its legs) than modern humans do and may have combined bipedalism with above-branch climbing and clambering (19).

Whether *Ardipithecus ramidus* was a direct ancestor to modern humans or a member of an extinct side branch is a difficult if not impossible question to answer. After *Ardipithecus ramidus* appeared on earth, many other hominin species evolved, all clearly bipedal. They can be grouped into the genera *Australopithecus, Paranthropus,* and *Homo*. What follows is by no means a full accounting, but an introduction to: the species relevant to Part I of this book, some of their more salient dental attributes, and their possible phylogenetic relationships.

AUSTRALOPITHECUS

With the announcement of the Taung Child in 1925 in the journal *Nature*, Raymond Dart christened a new species: *Australopithecus africanus*. The literal translation of *Australopithecus* is "Southern Ape," reflecting Dart's view that he had found "... an extinct race of apes *intermediate between living anthropoids and man.*" (1925: 195).

The earliest representatives of this genus now known are from East Africa. The first to appear on earth was *Australopithecus anamensis* ranging in time from 4.2 to 3.8 million years ago, and represented by more than fifty dental, cranial, and postcranial specimens (13). Like great apes, *Australopithecus anamensis* had a rectangular dental arcade (Figure 1.4), canine teeth with large roots, lower first premolars with only one cusp (or sometimes with an incipient second cusp [20]), but a lower deciduous molar morphology (21) said to be "intermediate" between that of Ar. *ramidus* and *Australopithecus afarensis*.

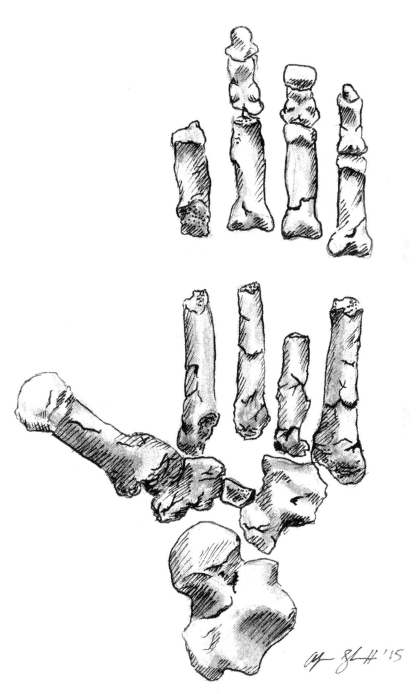

FIGURE 1.3: *Ardipithecus ramidus* foot. Redrawn by Alyssa Starrett from Figure 1a in Lovejoy CO, Latimer B, Suwa G, Berhane A, White TD, Combining prehension and propulsion: the foot of Ardipithecus ramidus. *Science.* 2009;326:72e2. Reprinted with permission from AAAS.

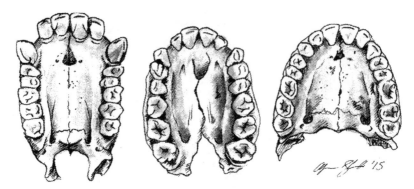

FIGURE 1.4: Artist's rendition of the dental arcades of a chimpanzee (left), *Australopithecus afarensis* (center) and a modern human (right). Drawn by Alyssa Starrett.

Au. afarensis, first appearing in the fossil record around 3.7 million years ago (22) was the next Ethiopian hominin in time, and likely evolved from *Au. anamensis* (23, 24). In 1974, Donald Johanson and his team discovered the famous Lucy, the nearly complete skeleton of an *Australopithecus afarensis* individual, whom President Barack Obama had the pleasure of "meeting" during his 2015 visit to Ethiopia. Small-brained and bipedal, but with long arms, Lucy stood about 3.5 feet tall, yet she was clearly an adult when she died as her wisdom teeth had already erupted and begun to wear. Since 1974, *Australopithecus afarensis* has become one of the most well-known early hominin species, with hundreds of remains from multiple sites along the East African Rift Valley (15). Like Ardi, Lucy also had long arms, and may have spent time in the trees (15). But with the big toe now in line with the other toes, Lucy's kind could "toe-off" while walking (15).

In *Au. afarensis*, as in *Au. anamensis*, the shape of the dental arcade (Figure 1.4) is somewhat rectangular, more like that found in Miocene and modern apes (although this is more true of *Au. anamensis* than of *Au. afarensis*). Both species had projecting jaws with large front teeth and nearly parallel-sided molar rows that created this rectangular form. Both also had more thickly enameled teeth than

Ardipithecus or its predecessors (15). Thick enamel is a derived feature of later hominins (25) presumed to be an adaptation to eating harder or more abrasive foods (see Chapter 2). In *Au. anamensis*, the upper canine and lower first premolar are more apelike, but along the evolving *Au. anamensis-Au. afarensis* lineage, these teeth became more derived in the direction of later hominins (20). Also along this lineage, molar teeth became larger (15).

Coexisting in East Africa with *Australopithecus afarensis* was a species that seemed so unusual that its discoverers coined both a new genus and species name for it: *Kenyanthropus platyops* (26). Fossil spanning 3.5 to 3.0 million years ago include a single cranium. The cranium has a much less projecting face than *Au. afarensis*: hence the name "platyops" meaning "flat-face" (26). The single well preserved tooth of the upper jaw is a second molar that falls below the known size range of *Australopithecus afarensis* second molars (26). These features appear to make it more humanoid. Yet, the fossilized face does not retain its original shape, as the over 1,000 tiny pieces of the face are separated by matrix-filled cracks of varying sizes (27). Given this distortion, paleoanthropologist Tim White (27) suggested that *K. platyops* may simply be a variant of *Au afarensis* – though one with smaller molars.

Two other middle Pliocene hominins should be noted. The first is *Australopithecus bahrelghazali* (28), from Chad, dated to between 3 to 3.5 Ma, and represented by a single mandible fragment with some teeth. The teeth have several similarities to those of *Australopithecus afarensis*, but with a few differences (e.g., both premolars with three separate roots). The second is the species *Australopithecus deyiremeda*, from Ethiopia, dated to between 3.3 and 3.5 Ma, and represented by a partial maxilla (upper jaw), two mandibles (lower jaws) and associated teeth (29). This species, announced in 2015 in the journal *Nature*, has molars that are generally smaller than those of *Au. afarensis*, but with different root structures. In a commentary accompanying the *Nature* article (30), paleoanthropologist Fred Spoor questions whether *Au. deyiremeda* and *K. platyops* are distinct species, given their gnathic (jaw-related) and dental similarities (including small first molar crowns).

It now also appears that stone tools may have made their first appearance in the east African middle Pliocene (31), though the species identity of their maker(s) is/are unknown. The evidence comes from a 3.3 Ma-site in Lomekwi, West Turkana, Kenya and consists of 149 stone artifacts, including stone cores and flakes that appear to have been struck from them.

Finally, late in the East African Pliocene is *Australopithecus garhi*, a hominin dated to 2.5 Ma, from the Middle Awash of Ethiopia (32). "Garhi" means "surprise" in the local Afar language, and the fossil remains of this species were a surprise for two main reasons. First, there are few *Australopithecus* remains from this time period in East Africa (13). Second, the skeletal remains of this species have a surprising combination of features, including premolar and molar teeth as large as those of *Paranthropus boisei*, the most "robust" of the robust australopiths (described below) and a humerus to femur ratio that is derived in a modern human direction (32).

Shifting the scene to South Africa, Raymond Dart's *Australopithecus africanus* species made its appearance in the fossil record a bit later in time, between 3 and 2 million years ago (13). Much is known about *Au. africanus* today, as hundreds of fossils have been recovered from South African limestone caves.

Relative to *Australopithecus afarensis*, *Australopithecus africanus* had a slightly larger brain. In some ways, its teeth were more derived in a human direction. In contrast to the more rectangular shape of many *Au. afarensis* dental arcades, those of *Au. africanus* more closely approach the parabolic dental arch seen in humans (13). *Diastemata* (pl. diastema) or gaps in the upper and lower jaws for accommodating canine teeth when the jaws are closed are present in great apes. Diastemata were also often present in *Au. afarensis*, while they were rarely present in *Au. africanus* (33). In *Au. afarensis*, upper canines generally have wear at the tip but there is often also wear on the side facing the lower first premolars, which are in some specimens (but not all) ape-like in bearing only a single cusp (34). Despite these more ape-like features, the first lower premolar of *Australopithecus afarensis* does not appear to have actually functioned as a whetstone for the upper canine (35). In *Au. africanus*, however, canines wear mainly at the tip and the lower first premolars are bicuspid (33), as are the lower first premolars of humans today. Yet *Au. africanus* has larger molars than both *Au. afarensis* (15) and early *Homo* (33) and in this respect, *Au. africanus* appears to be derived in the direction of species of *Paranthropus*, which had enormous molars.

Following closely on the (bipedal) heels of *Australopithecus africanus* in South Africa is the recently discovered *Australopithecus sediba* dated to 1.97 million years ago (36). Two partial skeletons and other fossil fragments currently represent this species (36). Like other *Australopithecus* species, it retained long arms with strong hands and had wrists that would have enabled it to climb (37). Also like other *Australopithecus* species, it had a small cranium. But, in some features it seems more derived in the direction of humans than *Australopithecus africanus*. These features include a more human-like pelvis and smaller molars (36, 38).

Overall, then, species of the genus *Australopithecus* were small-brained bipeds that retained climbing abilities and had canines and lower first premolars that became more humanoid over time. That is not the case for molars, which do not exhibit such a temporal trend, with some later species having small, more human-like, molars (e.g., *Au. sediba*, and others having extremely large ones (e.g., *Au. garhi*). That much seems clear. The more detailed picture of the phylogenetic relationships among *Australopithecus* species, to our own genus *Homo*, and to the genus *Paranthropus* is, however, not at all clear, as the next section explores.

PARANTHROPUS AND EARLY HOMININ PHYLOGENY

The genus *Paranthropus* includes three "robust" hominin species, so-called because they have faces and crania with large bony attachments for chewing muscles, bony buttresses for resisting large bite forces, huge molars, and square premolars that are often called "molarized." South African paleontologist Robert Broom gave the genus its name (39), announcing discovery of a *Paranthropus robustus* skull in 1938 in *Nature*. "*Paranthropus*" literally means "beside man." Broom remarked on the human-like qualities of the skull's relatively flat face, broad and short palate, and diminutive canine teeth. He also noted that its large premolars, which he estimated to be twice the size of those of humans, were completely different from those of other South African *Australopithecus* hominins found to date. To Broom, the distinctiveness of these premolars justified naming both a new genus and species. *Paranthropus robustus* is estimated to date from 2.0–1.5 Ma (15).

Similar robust forms were later found in East Africa, the most famous of which is "Nutcracker man," discovered by Mary and Louis Leakey at Olduvai Gorge in Tanzania in 1959 after they had spent nearly thirty years searching for hominin remains (40). The sobriquet seemed apt at the time given that this skull is robust in the extreme and has huge back teeth (Figures 1.5 and 1.6). Nutcracker Man is joined by many other similar finds from the East African Rift valley dating from about 2.5 to 1.4 million years ago into the genus *Paranthropus boisei* (15). Figure 1.6 illustrates a *Paranthropus boisei* mandible (Peninj) beside that of the African *Homo erectus* specimen WT 15000. The huge molars and premolars of *Paranthropus boisei* are larger than those of any other hominin. These teeth have extremely thick enamel on both their chewing surfaces and sides (41, 42). Immediately preceding *Paranthropus boisei* in the East African fossil record is the earliest of the robust species – *Paranthropus aethiopicus* – dating from 2.7–2.5 million years ago (15). It differed from *Paranthropus boisei* mainly in having more primitive characteristics, such as a more projecting face and a smaller brain (15).

What do paleoanthropologists make of this plethora of early hominin species, each with a unique combination of primitive and derived traits? Most introductory paleoanthropology texts include multiple possible phylogenies, outlining the arguments for and

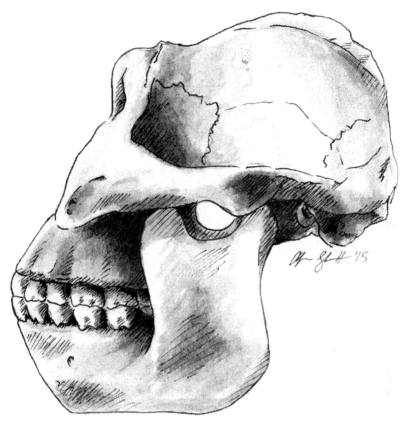

FIGURE 1.5: Artist's rendition of Nutcracker Man. The first skull of *Paranthropus boisei* ever found. Drawn by Alyssa Starrett.

against them. Unfortunately, even cladistic analyses, which are currently the most objective and replicable methods for reconstructing phylogenies, are not in strong agreement.

Consider four cladistic analyses that use different data sets, though with some overlap among them. The first is an extensive analysis published in 2004 by Strait and Grine (43) using 198 cranial and dental characters. As in most cladistic analyses, in this study traits were treated as having discrete states: traits are either absent or present with different levels of expression. Figure 1.7a (redrawn

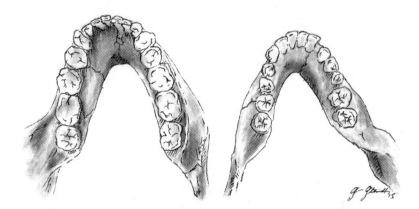

FIGURE 1.6: On the left is the Peninj mandible, belonging to the species *Paranthropus boisei*. On the right is the mandible of the Nariokotome Boy (WT15000) of the species *Homo erectus* (or *Homo ergaster*). The proportions of the two mandibles are to scale. Drawn by Alyssa Starrett.

from their Figure 10) shows a consensus of their most parsimonious cladograms. Note that many species branch off separately but that the top half of the cladogram consists of two multispecies branches: one that includes *Paranthropus* and *Kenyanthropus* and the other consisting of *Homo* species.

Compare and contrast this figure with Figure 1.7b, a simplified version (omitting the relationships among later *Homo* species) of the 2008 analysis of González-José and colleagues (44). These researchers used a novel approach, measuring and treating cranial size and shape variation as continuous. In so doing, they captured biological variation more realistically than previous analyses that divided it into discrete states of expression. Furthermore, these researchers performed their cladistic analysis with respect to functional or developmental modules, instead of treating every trait as an independently evolving unit. This is important because traits used in cladistics analyses are assumed to be independent, each providing a unique piece of data included in the analysis. In the resulting cladograms from this

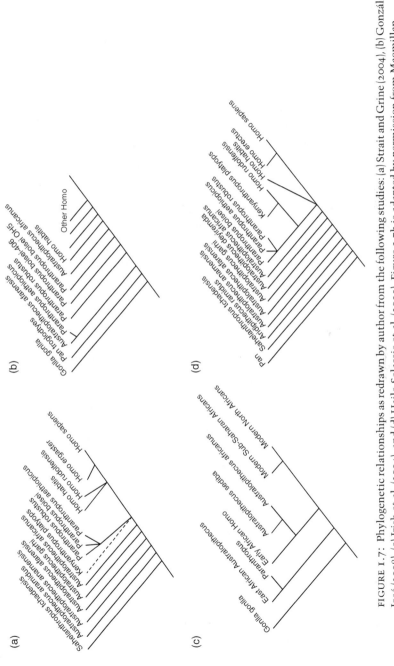

FIGURE 1.7: Phylogenetic relationships as redrawn by author from the following studies: (a) Strait and Grine (2004), (b) González-José (2008), (c) Irish et al. (2014), and (d) Haile-Selassie et al. (2015). Figure 1.7b is adapted by permission from Macmillan Publishers Ltd: Nature: González-José R, Escapa I, Neves WA, Cúneo R, Pucciarelli HM. Cladistic analysis of continuous modularized traits provides phylogenetic signals in Homo evolution. *Nature*. 2008;45 3:775–778. Figure 1.7d is adapted by permission from Macmillan Publishers Ltd: Nature: Haile-Selassie Y, Gibert L, Melillo SM, Ryan TM, Alene M, Deino A, et al. New species from Ethiopia further expands Middle Pliocene hominin diversity. *Nature*. 2015;521:483–488.

approach (one derived from the method of maximum parsimony, the other from the other of maximum likelihood), the closest species to *Homo* is *Australopithecus africanus*. Figure 1.7b shows the cladogram resulting from their maximum parsimony analysis.

Next, consider the maximum parsimony cladogram shown in Figure 1.7c from 2013 and 2014 studies by Joel Irish, myself, and our colleagues (45, 46), which included the recently discovered *Australopithecus sediba* and used only dental traits, such as root number and the number and degree of expression of cusps on premolars and molars. We analyzed a particular set of dental traits whose outward expression is known in living humans to be highly heritable (i.e., variation in these traits is largely due to variation in genes rather than environment [6]). We also tested for correlations among these dental traits, using only those that were not strongly (statistically) correlated with one another. In our strictly dental analysis, *Australopithecus africanus* and *Australopithecus sediba* are the closest species to *Homo*, sharing several derived dental features. This was true whether we used gorillas or chimpanzees as outgroups.

Lastly, with their 2015 announcement of *Australopithecus deyiremeda*, Haile-Selassie and colleagues presented a consensus cladogram (of seventeen equally parsimonious trees) shown in Figure 1.7d. Their analysis included nineteen traits of teeth and jaws of these species. The newly named *Australopithecus deyiremeda* branches off just before *Australopithecus africanus*, which is then followed by a multispecies *Paranthropus* clade, a clade including *Kenyanthropus platyops* and *Homo rudolfensis*, and a clade containing the remaining *Homo* species.

These four studies, including one focusing specifically on crania and one focusing exclusively on teeth, differ in many ways, but have a few things in common. They all indicate that East African *Australopithecus* species (not including *Kenyanthropus*) are more distantly related to *Homo* than are South African *Australopithecus* species. Those that include multiple species of *Paranthropus* also find that these species are closely related to one another. The different approaches at least converge on these points. But, exactly which species are most closely related to *Homo* varies in these studies, as well as in many other studies not reviewed here. Beyond this inconsistency, it turns out that the dental and cranial traits commonly used in paleoanthropological cladistics studies do not always give the same answers about phylogenetic relationships among living species that their DNA does (47)! Given these problems, we have some clues about the origin of our genus, but do not yet (and may never) know exactly where it came from. In the understated words of Ayala and Valentine in the quote that heads this chapter, establishing "precise" lines of descent for most organisms is "very difficult."

This brief overview sets the stage for exploring the insights teeth provide into early hominin evolution. These insights begin with what teeth reveal about the evolution of hominin diets, a fundamental adaptation affecting multiple facets of species biology and therefore intertwined with all of the topics in Part I.

2 Dentally-Derived Dietary Inferences: The Australopiths

> The diet of *Paranthropus* appears to have been primarily vegetarian, while that of *Australopithecus* seems to have been omnivorous and to have included a fair proportion of flesh.
>
> – Robinson JT
> *Prehominid Dentition and Hominid Evolution*

Australopiths were not likely to have gone *on* diets but they certainly had them. Diets provide the energy and nutrients that enable survival and reproduction. Natural selection favors those individuals who are best at transforming their diets into surviving offspring, who will, in turn pass on the genes that made them and their parents successful. For this reason, diets fundamentally shape species' biology, from how they distribute themselves in relation to resources to the contours of their molar cusps.

Because what a species eats is a keystone adaptation, scenarios of human evolution often begin with changes in diet. In the 1950s, the South African paleoanthropologist John T. Robinson (1923–2001), presented an argument about early human evolution (48, 49), now referred to as the "Dietary Hypothesis." According to Robinson, the cranial and dental differences between South African hominins *Paranthropus robustus* and *Australopithecus africanus* pointed to a major dietary difference between them. Robinson reasoned that the large muscles of mastication (as inferred from bony anatomy) and expanded molars of *Paranthropus robustus* were adaptations to a tough vegetarian diet, including roots and bulbs, that required a great deal of chewing. His analysis of craniodental morphology in *Australopithecus africanus*, however, led him to conclude that this species was the founder of a new line of more omnivorous, tool-using hominins that could respond more flexibly to changing environmental conditions. This is the line, he argued, that eventually gave rise to us.

Raymond Dart's ideas (50) about early human evolution were likely to have influenced Robinson. Dart's study of South African cave sites led him to believe (incorrectly, it turned out [51]) that hominin hunting was responsible for the animal bones accumulated there. In his view, hunting transformed our peaceful ape-like ancestors into intelligent, weapon-wielding, blood-thirsty predators. More recent ideas about the importance of meat in human evolution de-emphasize the act of hunting as a prime mover of human evolution, focusing instead on the nutritive benefits of meat in facilitating human evolution. Humans and chimpanzees do differ in their meat-eating habits. Per year, chimpanzees are estimated to consume only 10% of the amount of meat that African hunter-gatherers do (52), so, anthropologists' seeming obsession with meat as having to do with human origins makes some sense.

Aiello and Wheeler's (53) "Expensive Tissue Hypothesis" contends that the incorporation of increasing quantities of meat and decreasing quantities of plant foods over human evolutionary history made the evolution of large brains possible. Because leafy plants, which are rich in fiber, are difficult to digest, animals who specialize in eating them have evolved complex stomachs and long intestines. These digestive tissues are energetically expensive to maintain, and any reduction in their size frees up energy for other purposes. According this hypothesis, the increasing proportion of meat and decreasing proportion of plants in the line that led to modern humans relaxed the selective pressure to maintain large guts. Energy was now available to sustain another energetically expensive organ: the brain. This hypothesis has been questioned though, on the basis of a test across 100 mammals (54) showing that brain size is not negatively related to the size of the digestive tract – in other words there doesn't seem to be an energetic trade-off between the two, at least on this large scale.

Still other dietary hypotheses have de-emphasized the importance of meat in human evolution, focusing instead on gathered plant foods (55, 56). The argument here is that plant foods comprise the bulk of modern-hunter-gatherer diets. In addition, even though meat may be an important dietary component (providing protein), it is not as reliably acquired as are plant foods, which are more abundant and evenly distributed in space and time. For these reasons, the importance of meat in human evolution has been doubted. World-renowned primatologist and chimpanzee authority Richard Wrangham (and colleagues) (52, 57) propounded the view that it was *cooking* plant foods that was the critical adaptation. Cooking released nutrients locked in otherwise indigestible plant parts and improved the digestibility of other parts, fueling the evolution of large brains in the genus *Homo*. The kinds of plant parts Wrangham and colleagues had in mind were underground storage organs (USOs): tubers and other root vegetables that are staples of some modern African hunter-gatherer groups.

These ideas, however, get a little ahead of the present chapter. This chapter focuses on the diets of the australopith species that preceded and coexisted with the genus *Homo*, and from whose ranks the genus evolved. Based on the study of teeth, what do we think we know about the diets of the earliest australopiths? Do their diets suggest a fundamental adaptive shift that differs from the diets of modern chimpanzees and bonobos, our closest living relatives? How different *were* the diets of *Australopithecus africanus* and *Paranthropus robustus* and how much meat were these species likely to have consumed? How variable (i.e., flexible) were australopith diets? And, with such huge and thickly-enameled back teeth, did Nutcracker Man really eat nuts or at least foods that were very hard? These questions are explored in this chapter, the answers to which differ depending upon which paleoanthropologists you talk to.

A case in point is the *Viewpoints* section of the July 2013 issue of the *American Journal of Physical Anthropology*. In it is a debate from two groups of paleoanthropologists, one led by David Strait from the University at Albany SUNY (58) and the other by David Daegling from

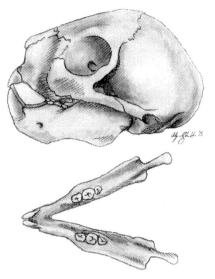

FIGURE 2.1: Skull of an Aye-Aye, a lemur of Madagascar that, like rodents, has ever-growing incisors. Aye-Ayes consume a variety of food types yet have a reduced number of teeth. Drawn by Alyssa Starrett.

the University of Florida (59). Both Davids were PhD students of paleoanthropologist Fred Grine at Stony Brook University. Both of them agree that australopiths were dietary generalists, in not being limited to eating items within one or two specific food categories. Primates, as a whole are dietary generalists. So, although robust australopiths appear morphologically specialized in having large faces and back teeth, it would seem unlikely that they were highly restricted in their dietary proclivities. The most specialized primate, the aye-aye of Madagascar, has rodent-like ever-growing incisors (unlike any other primate), that it uses to gouge tree bark and expose grubs that it stabs with its elongated bony middle finger. Despite these specializations and the loss of permanent second incisors, canines, and most of its premolars (Figure 2.1), the aye-aye nevertheless consumes several different kinds of foods including seeds, nectar, fruits, and fungi (60).

On the other hand, the two Davids most definitely do not agree about the role of hard foods in selecting for australopith craniodental morphology. *Hard* foods are those that are "stress-limited" in that high forces are required to initiate cracks in them. Strait and his colleagues contend that the consumption of hard foods (e.g., hard nuts and seeds) can explain the masticatory adaptations of australopiths: enlarged chewing muscles provided the force necessary to fracture hard foods while reinforced facial bone and thick enamel were selectively advantageous in preventing fracture of bone and enamel, respectively, under high force.

Daegling et al. point out that these features of australopiths do not necessarily signal that australopiths were eating hard foods but could result from other causes. For example, enlarged chewing muscles and buttressing of the facial skeleton in australopiths could also have resulted from selection for the repeated chewing necessary to break down *tough*, fibrous plant foods. These are foods that fracture when they are subject to high displacements (i.e., movements in the direction of force). It doesn't necessarily take a lot of force to induce a crack in tough foods, but it does take a sustained force in one direction – by tearing or slicing– to propagate the initial crack. The disagreement over hard vs. tough foods stems from the kinds of evidence the two different groups of paleoanthropologists believe provide the most reliable evidence for reconstructing hominin diets.

There are two broad categories of fossil evidence. The first category consists of morphological or structural features of fossil crania, faces, and dentitions that are inferred adaptations to eating different kinds of foods. Such inferences are usually based on associations between these features and diet in living primates. For example, modern primates that frequently eat hard foods or eat them as "fallbacks" when their preferred foods are unavailable (62), typically have low, blunt cusps and thick enamel (63). Those that eat tough foods, such as leaves, either frequently or as "fallbacks" (42), tend to have thinner enamel (at least on their chewing surfaces) with taller cusps and shearing crests (61). As the thin enamel of the cusp wears, it exposes patches of softer dentine underneath. Because dentine wears away more quickly than enamel, a sharp edge of enamel is maintained along these dentine patches that can slice through tough foods (61). The inferential reasoning is that if specific morphological features are adaptations to specific dietary items, then fossils with these features probably attest to the presence of these items in fossil species' diets, at least during their evolutionary histories if not in their actual lifetimes. The limitations of such inferences are explored below.

The second category of evidence consists of physical and chemical traces of ingested food. This category includes such evidence as chipped enamel, food particles trapped in dental calculus, microscopic wear on chewing surfaces, and the chemical composition of enamel. I will first review the strengths and weakness of these different kinds of evidence. Then, I will explore the questions raised at the beginning of this chapter emphasizing what arguably provides the most reliable source of evidence coupled with the greatest number of insights – the chemical signatures of food in tooth enamel.

DIFFICULTIES OF DIETARY INFERENCE FROM ANATOMICAL FEATURES

While aspects of craniodental anatomy and morphology exhibit strong correlations with dietary variation in primates, inferring the diets of fossil species based on these correlations is complicated by several factors. First, similar selection pressures may result in multiple solutions. Although hard object feeding is associated with thick enamel in primates (61), Lawrence Martin and colleagues (64) note that there is a group of new world monkeys, the Pitheciini (Pitheciins), that feed on fruit protected by hard husks but have thin molar enamel. These monkeys use their robust and splayed canine teeth to puncture through the hard husks of these fruit but use their molar teeth to process the soft seeds inside. As these authors point out, their observations reveal that thick molar enamel is not always associated with hard-object feeding. They suggest that the morphology of both anterior and posterior dentition should therefore be considered when inferring the diets of fossil species.

Perhaps more problematic than the existence of multiple solutions to similar adaptive problems is the situation in which different selection pressures result in similar adaptations. A good example of this problem is once again enamel thickness. Joanna Lambert and colleagues (62) (2004) drew the attention of physical anthropologists to the fact that grey-cheeked mangabeys from the Kibale Forest Uganda, which have very thick enamel, do not subsist on hard foods year-round. When soft fruits are available, they prefer to eat those. It is only when their high-quality preferred soft fruit are not available that they rely on hard seeds and bark. These authors suggest that although seeds and bark are consumed infrequently, these are critical "fallback" resources for grey-cheeked mangabeys. In these authors' view, natural selection favored thick enamel in grey-cheeked mangabeys because it allowed them to make use of these resources during "crunch" times, when high-calorie and easier-to-process fruits were not available. Thus, there is a "mismatch" between grey-cheeked mangabey enamel thickness and the soft fruits they prefer and eat most frequently. This mismatch is often referred to as Liem's paradox, after Karel F. Liem who demonstrated (65) that cichlid fish of the East African Rift valley lakes often have specialized jaws for accessing specific food types but nevertheless are dietary generalists in eating a wide variety of food items.

Fallback foods are generally considered to be low quality, mechanically challenging foods (i.e., foods that are difficult to break down physically) that animals resort to only when their preferred high calorie and softer foods are unavailable. The association between fallback foods and specialized morphology has suggested to some that fallback foods have had a primary role in selecting for specialized dental adaptations. However, that this is not necessarily the case is indicated by another mangabey, the sooty mangabey of the Tai Forest in the Ivory Coast. Sooty mangabeys have very thick enamel, among the thickest in the primate order. Analyzing two years of feeding data, Ohio State University primatologist Scott McGraw and colleagues

(66) found that the hardest item in the sooty mangabey diet is eaten year round.

The tale of the two mangabeys – grey-cheeked and sooty – tells us that thick enamel can be an adaptation to hard foods that are eaten either as fallbacks or as regularly consumed items. It also tells us that "preferred" food items are not always soft. Furthermore, thick enamel is not associated with only hard foods. Evolutionary anthropologist J.D. Pampush and colleagues (67) analyzed the relationship between enamel thickness and diet across seventeen primate species. They pointed out, as have others before them, that thick enamel could be an adaptation to abrasive particles in primate diets that come either from grit adhering to their foods or from phytoliths. The latter, literally "plant stones," are formed when plants take up silica from the soil and deposit it in within their cells. In the first portion of their analysis, Pampush and colleagues found an association between hard food items in the diet and enamel thickness, just as others had before them (61, 63). But, in the second portion of their analysis they omitted the hard-object feeding species and analyzed only the ten remaining species. In the remaining portion, they found a relationship between enamel thickness and the interaction between dietary abrasives (measured in terms of the phytolith content of plants) and lifespan. It seems that species with longer lifespans, whose teeth must function for longer time periods, and who have abrasive diets tend to have thicker enamel on their chewing surfaces.[1]

Pampush and colleagues note that most mammals whose teeth are subject to high wear from abrasion – for example, horses – have evolved other solutions, such as hypsodonty, which appears in many

---

[1] In their In vitro experiment at the nano level, Peter Lucas and colleagues suggest that phytoliths do not actually remove enamel but instead simply scratch it. (68. Lucas PW, Omar R, Al-Fadhalah K, Almusallam AS, Henry AG, Michael S, et al. Mechanisms and causes of wear in tooth enamel: implications for hominin diets. *Journal of the Royal Society Interface.* 2013;10(80):20120923.) If this is also the case *in vivo*, then an adaptive association between enamel thickness and phytolith load in terms of wear resistance becomes implausible. Yet, a more recent papers suggests otherwise – that phytoliths can indeed remove enamel and cause tooth wear (69. Xia J, Zheng J, Huang D, Tian ZR, Chen L, Zhou Z, et al. New model to explain tooth wear with implications for microwear formation and diet reconstruction. *Proceedings of the National Academy of Sciences.* 2015;112(34):10669–72.)

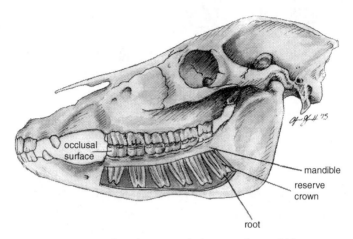

FIGURE 2.2: Hypsodont dentition of a horse with mandible cut away to show reserve crown and root. Drawn by Alyssa Starrett.

grazing mammals (70). Hypsodont teeth are tall with reserve crown embedded within the jaw (see Figure 2.2). The reserve crown gradually erupts at a rate that is about equal to the rate of wear. For unknown reasons, hypsodonty did not evolve in primates, but thick enamel may be an analogous adaptation to abrasive foods in some primates. So, thick enamel in australopiths may be an adaptive response to hard foods or to dietary abrasives and it would be difficult to tell simply on the basis of the thickness of the enamel (although microstructural details of enamel prism orientation might provide a way to discriminate between these two possible causes (71).

Finally, adaptations such as thick enamel tell you most clearly about what animals ate in their evolutionary past that selected for these adaptations. They do not provide evidence of what animals eat currently. Translated into the fossil record, features of morphology such as low relief on the chewing surfaces of teeth and thick enamel tell you something about the kinds of foods the ancestors of these fossil species ate. Morphological change may lag considerably behind changes in diet. An example of such a time lag is found in fossil bovids and suids from East Africa (72). Analysis of tooth enamel (see below for discussion of these methods) suggests that these lineages experienced a rapid change in their diets around 2.8 million years ago, when they began consuming large quantities of tropical grasses. Their rapid dietary shift, however, is not matched by a rapid change in dental morphology. Instead, the teeth of these lineages change very gradually over the Plio-Pleistocene, becoming more hypsodont over time, presumably in response to their more abrasive diets.

Because of the issues associated with dietary inference from anatomy, data derived from the physical and chemical traces left by foods eaten during the lifetimes of the fossil individuals themselves provide more direct evidence of diet, as explained next.

INTERPRETING PHYSICAL AND CHEMICAL TRACES OF DIET

For dietary inference in fossil hominins, three physical sources of evidence have proven most informative. These are plant-specific and plant-part-specific phytoliths trapped in dental calculus, distinctive microscopic wear on chewing surfaces, and the size of chipped areas of enamel on chewing surfaces. Each of these methods provides different kinds of information and each has its limitations.

Dental calculus is calcified plaque, a slime (or biofilm) containing thousands of bacteria that bathes your teeth. If you don't brush your teeth for a few days, a yellowish plaque can build up, and if you don't brush them for a couple of weeks of so, the plaque will calcify, becoming dental calculus (which dental hygienists spend a lot of time scraping off of teeth). Luckily for us, australopiths had no dental hygienists, and it has so far been possible to analyze phytoliths in dental calculus from one *Australopithecus sediba* individual. Different plants and different plant-parts have differently shaped phytoliths, so it is possible to gain very specific information about diet from identifying phytoliths. Unfortunately, the presence of distinctive phytoliths in dental calculus cannot tell you how *frequently* the items containing them were consumed.

The analysis of dental microwear has a long history and has been studied in multiple early hominin individuals of diverse species. During the 1970s, several studies established associations in living primates between microwear pitting and hard object eaters and between microwear striations and leaf-eaters (70). Primates that primarily eat soft fruit were found to have intermediate microwear patterns (70). These studies involved scanning electron microscopy at magnifications of 500x and painstaking identification of pits vs. striations in micrographs. In addition to being time-consuming, this method involved subjectively assessing whether microwear features were pits or scratches, which in some cases was not so clear and can vary with slight differences in the angle at which the electron beam hits the tooth surface. Although microwear on enamel surfaces could have been produced while fossils were lying in the ground for thousands or millions of years, methods were developed in the 1980s to distinguish such "artifacts" from true dental microwear associated with chewing during life (73). The specific regions of enamel surfaces studied microscopically are those involved in the crushing and grinding of food trapped between molar cusps (74).

In more recent times, automated techniques have transformed microwear studies, making it possible to quantify microwear objectively (75). In "microwear texture analysis" the surface of molar facets are scanned with a confocal imaging system to obtain three dimensional images of the enamel surface. These images are then analyzed using "scale-sensitive fractal analysis" to quantify different characteristics, such as surface *complexity* and *anisotropy* (76). The consumption of hard plant foods is associated with microwear textures with high complexity values (owing to pitting) while the consumption of tough plant foods is associated with high anisotropy, meaning that there is strong directionality to the scratches. Species such as brown capuchins who eat hard seeds have microwear textures with high complexity and low anisotropy (77). By contrast, species like howler monkeys who eat large quantities

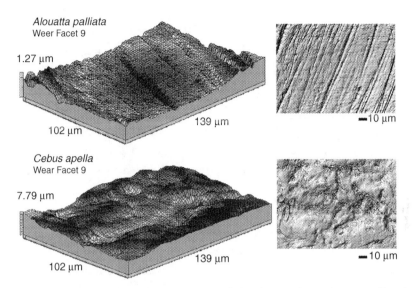

FIGURE 2.3: Microwear textures of a howler monkey (*Alouatta palliata*) and a capuchin monkey (*Cebus apella*). Notice the high directionality of scratches on the howler monkey wear facet (high anisotropy) and the uneven and pitted surface of the capuchin monkey wear facet (high complexity). These images were kindly provided by Professor Robert Scott, Rutgers University.

of leaves, have microwear textures with high anisotropy and low complexity values (77) (Figure 2.3).

These important technical advances in microwear analysis, however, do not address other limitations of this approach. Experimental studies have shown that microwear features have high rates of turnover (78). Some features can be formed and then erased within twenty-four-hour periods. Striations of average size observed in microwear studies can be worn away less than one week after they have formed. So, microwear observed on fossil teeth represents what was eaten in the few days before death, in what is often called the "Last Supper" effect (79). Given the likelihood of dietary variability owing to seasonal or interannual food availability, microwear therefore gives us a limited view into what individuals ate during their lifetimes.

Another problem may have to do with what exactly produces microwear. In 2013, physical anthropologist Peter Lucas and colleagues published *in vitro* experimental evidence that rocked the microwear world (literally actually, because quartz was involved). These researchers slid individual particles of quartz dust, phytoliths, and enamel chips across flat enamel surfaces, but it was only the quartz dust that was hard enough to actually remove enamel (68). Much softer phytoliths and enamel chips formed nanowear in the form of grooves or troughs in the enamel but did not cause enamel loss. A question that remains unclear, however, is how well this experiment corresponds to what actually happens during chewing in the mouth and to microwear patterns above the nano level.

These researchers further suggest that pitted enamel surfaces found in microwear studies are not likely to be *caused* by hard foods which are softer than quartz dust or phytoliths. Instead, they argued, quartz dust may cause this pitting, and although phytoliths may create microgrooves in enamel, phytoliths themselves reveal nothing about whether hard or tough foods were eaten. They point out that there are several examples of living primates with very different diets but similar microwear and that it is likely that such inconsistencies reflect the fact that quartz dust and phytoliths have more to do with microwear than do food particles themselves.

Microwear researchers countered that they had been misunderstood (59, 77), that they never contended that food particles themselves create microwear. Instead, they explained, it is the phytoliths or other silica-based structures in plants that leave distinctive microscopic marks on enamel chewing surfaces *depending* on the material properties of foods (77). Hard plant parts require that upper and lower molars are brought together in direct opposition in order to crush them. As the molars press against one another, silica-containing particles are driven into the enamel creating pits in the enamel surface. Tough plant parts require molars cusps to slide past each other in order to tear them, creating directional striations on the enamel surface where silica-containing particles are dragged across it.

This explanation is reasonable and very likely explains why there *are* associations between microwear textures and the toughness vs. hardness of plant foods, as Rob Scott and colleagues showed in their analysis of twenty-one anthropoid species (77). Yet, it does not rule out the complicating factors of quartz dust or exogenous grit adhering to foods as causes of microwear. David Daegling and Fred Grine (80) found that grit adhering to plant underground storage organs (USOs), such as tubers and corms, resulted in microwear pitting in chacma baboon enamel similar to that of primates who eat hard foods. What all this means is that microwear can be influenced by more than food properties and therefore can be a somewhat noisy dietary signal.

Recently, molar enamel chipping has emerged as a potential source of information about hominin diets. John Robinson of the "Dietary Hypothesis" noted chips in the molar enamel of *Paranthropus robustus* and *Australopithecus africanus* (48). Because the boundaries of these chipped areas were not sharp but were dulled by subsequent wear, Robinson inferred that the chips had been created during life. But, it is only in the last few years that meaningful information has been extracted from enamel chips.

Paleoanthropologist Paul Constantino and colleagues (81) showed by experiment that the sizes of chips along the edges of molar crowns (more precisely, the scar left behind after a chip was removed) are mathematically related to the force used to create them. Essentially, large molar edge chips imply strong bite forces. The presence of large chips with worn boundaries on the edges of fossil molars may indicate that some kind of hard food, requiring a strong bite force was chewed. Yet, a hard piece of gravel ingested along with tough food that required a strong bite force could theoretically produce a similar enamel chip. What can be concluded for this type of analysis, then, is that large molar enamel edge chips *may* signal the consumption of hard foods that required high bite forces.

In support of the association between enamel chips and hard foods, Constantino and colleagues (82) showed that within the great apes, the highest frequencies of chipping are found in orangutans who are frequent consumers of hard seeds and nuts. But, frequencies of enamel chipping are difficult to interpret because, as Daegling and colleagues point out (59), they may be affected by the size of the molar crown and the period of time a molar has been in use, both of which are likely to affect the chances of chip formation.

In sum, the least controversial physical evidence of hominin diets derives from the analysis of particles trapped in dental calculus. Microwear and enamel chip analysis also provide useful information but have some limitations that must be considered when interpreting what these sources of evidence signal about hominin diets. Chemical evidence of hominin diets, specifically the analysis of stable carbon isotopes[2] and trace elements locked within dental enamel, provide a rich source of information that has yielded important insights into hominin diets.

Chemical evidence rests on the principal that you are what you eat (83). The analysis of stable carbon isotopes in tooth enamel reveals whether certain types of plants were eaten during the period of tooth formation. Plants using different enzymatic pathways during photosynthesis incorporate into their tissues different proportions of the stable carbon isotope C-13 in relation to C-12, the most common form of carbon. These differing proportions are incorporated into the tissues, including the enamel, of animals that eat these plants (and the animals that eat the animals that eat these plants). Enamel forms only during a limited time frame: when teeth are developing during infancy and childhood. Enamel is also the most mineralized tissue of the body consisting of 96% mineral with the remaining 4% consisting of water and some protein. With these attributes, enamel essentially locks the ratio of ingested C-13 to C-12 into its dense mineral structure which can be preserved with minimal chemical alteration for millions of years (83).

The different photosynthetic pathways are C3, C4, and CAM (crassulacean acid metabolism) (84). Plants that use the C3 pathway

---

[2] Stable isotopes are nonradioactive versions of atoms.

initially incorporate carbon dioxide into a three-carbon molecule, while those that use the C4 pathway initially incorporate carbon dioxide into a four-carbon molecule (84). Both pathways discriminate against C-13 in favor of C-12, but to a different extent, resulting in their having different C-13 to C-12 ratios in their tissues.[3] C3 plants have less C-13 relative to C12 than do C4 plants. The majority of plants use the C3 pathway. Trees, shrubs and bushes all use the C3 pathway but tropical grasses and sedges (e.g., papyrus) use the C4 pathway. Without going into great detail, the C4 pathway makes it possible for plants to fix carbon dioxide quickly, and so minimizes the time that stomata (pores in plants that allow gas exchange) are open. With stomata open for shorter periods, the evaporation of water is minimized. For this reasons, C4 plants, such as tropical grasses and sedges, are believed to be well-adapted to the warm environments in which they are found.

CAM plants are similar in their enzymatic pathway to C4 plants (84), but they open stomata only at night, and are also adapted to dry conditions. Such plants include succulents such as cacti and are found primarily in desert or semidesert environments. Since living primates rarely make use of CAM plants which are, in addition often toxic (84), stable carbon isotope ratios in hominin tooth enamel are likely to reflect only the proportions of C4 vs. C3 plants (or the animals that eat them) in their diets.

The stable carbon isotope signal in enamel reflects the percentage of C3 vs. C4 food sources eaten during the juvenile phase of growth, when tooth formation is occurring. The dietary signal therefore reflects a longer span of time than does the signal from microwear. It is even possible to gain insight into variability in the proportion of C3 vs. C4 foods in the diet over the time span of enamel formation (see below). Clearly, however, the information obtained is quite general – C3 vs. C4 plants are broad categories. Furthermore, eating the animals

---

[3] By convention, C13 composition is reported as percent per thousand as $\delta^{13}C = [(^{13}C/^{12}C_{sample})/(^{13}C/^{12}C_{standard}) - 1] \times 1000$, where the international standard is the Vienna Peedee Belemnite (VPDB).

that eat plants from those categories (or some animal/plant combination) can produce similar signals.

Trace elements can, however, provide insight into animal vs. plant matter in the diet. Mammalian digestive systems discriminate against Barium (Ba) and Strontium (Sr) (trace elements) relative to Calcium (Ca) (84). Thus, herbivores have higher levels of Ba and Sr relative to Ca in their tissues than do the animals that eat them and so on, up the food chain. It is possible to compare, for example, the Sr/Ca composition of dental enamel in fossil teeth to that of modern herbivores, and if it is similar, to deduce that the fossil tooth came from an individual who ate a large quantity of plant matter during the period of enamel formation.

WHAT EARLY HOMININS ATE

The carbon isotope signal of our closest living relatives, the African apes, reflects the predominantly forested environments they inhabit. Chimpanzee and gorillas are said to have nearly "pure" C3 signatures (85). Even where chimpanzees inhabit savanna woodlands, their strong C3 signals are nearly unvarying, suggesting that chimpanzees do not make use of C4 resources even when they are available. Yet, modern humans do, and hominins such as *Australopithecus africanus* and *Paranthropus robustus* did, incorporate substantial quantities of C4 foods in their diets. Physical anthropologist Matt Sponheimer and colleagues (86) suggested that the ability to make use of C4 foods provided australopiths with critical dietary flexibility, allowing them to survive in the more arid and open habitats that increasingly characterized the African Plio-Pleistocene. If flexible diets that incorporated C4 plants represent a fundamental hominin shift, then how early does this adaptation appear in the hominin fossil record?

Stable carbon isotope analysis on the tooth enamel of *Ardipithecus ramidus* (19) from Aramis Ethiopia dated to 4.4 million years ago suggests a diet focused on C3 plants. Most of the *Ardipithecus ramidus* individuals from which enamel was sampled had $\delta^{13}C$ values that were slightly elevated relative to savanna-woodland chimpanzees, but were much less than the values of later hominins (19). Such a diet is consistent with the reconstructed environment of *Ardipithecus ramidus*. The many kudu, colobine monkeys, and other faunal as well as floral remains suggest a forest-woodland environment, dominated by C3 plants. Savanna resources may have been nearby, which may explain the slightly elevated $\delta^{13}C$ levels relative to savanna-woodland chimpanzees (87).

Two hundred thousand years later, between 4.2 and 4.0 million years ago, *Australopithecus anamensis* from the Kenyan Turkana Basin has $\delta^{13}C$ values quite similar to that of *Ardipithecus ramidus* (88), indicating that it too had a diet dominated by C3 resources (either C3 plants or animals that ate them or some combination). That these were likely to be C3 plants rather than animals that ate C3 plants is likely because most of the contemporary herbivores in this region were C4 plant consumers.

Like modern chimpanzees, both *Ar. ramidus* and *Au anamensis* avoided C4 resources even though these resources were becoming increasingly available in the Pliocene. The microwear of neither of these hominins is characterized by the high complexity or pitting associated with the consumption of hard foods or foods with exogenous grit (89, 90). Despite these similarities, *Au. anamensis* had considerably thicker molar enamel that did *Ardipithecus ramidus* (84). Furthermore, *Au. anamensis* had enamel that was "decussating" in having enamel prisms that cross one another. Decussating enamel is thought to be an adaptation that stops cracks from propagating (91). Opposite to the suid case discussed earlier, here there is no direct chemical evidence of dietary change from one species to another over time. Anatomical changes in tooth enamel have nevertheless occurred.

A marked dietary shift toward the incorporation of significant quantities of C4 based foods occurred by 3.5 million years ago in *Australopithecus bahrelghazali*, *Australopithecus afarensis*, and *Kenyanthropus platyops*. In the first of these, *Au. bahrelghazali* from Chad, the teeth of three individuals were sampled, and these

FIGURE 2.4: Plant corm: an underground storage organ. Drawn by Alyssa Starrett.

indicate diets composed of 55–80% C4 food sources (92). Environmental indicators, such as the fossils of open-country grazing bovids, attest to the likelihood that C4 plants were dominant in the environment of *Au. bahrelghazali*. But whether they were eating C4 plants or animals that ate these plants or some combination is not clear. Because the low-cusped and thickly enameled teeth of *Au. bahrelghazali* do not seem well-adapted to slicing through grass blades (nor do they appear well adapted to slicing through tough meat), Julia Lee Thorp and colleagues (92) suggest that some of the C4 plant resources that *Au. bahrelghazali* ate might include fleshy tubers or corms (Figure 2.4). Or perhaps they ate rhizomes of the most abundant C4 sedge plants surrounding Lake Chad today – papyrus. The latter suggestion prompted Nathaniel J. Dominy to title his commentary on this paper "Hominins living on the sedge" (93).

In *Australopithecus afarensis*, there was wide variability in $\delta^{13}C$ levels in a sample of twenty Ethiopian specimens spanning the time frame of 3.4 to 2.9 million years ago (94). Four of them had low $\delta^{13}C$ levels, comparable to those of chimpanzees, but the rest had much higher levels, some indicating consumption of up to 50% C4 plants. This variability likely reflects the diverse habitats that *Au. afarensis* occupied, from more open grasslands to closed woodlands (84) (Grine, 2012). Surprisingly, no temporal trends in C4 plant consumption were detected over this time period. Dental microwear of *Au afarensis* also indicates no change over time. Both *Au afarensis* and its hypothesized predecessor, *Au. anamensis*, had microwear with low complexity as well as low anisotropy, which microwear expert Peter Ungar and colleagues (90) believe is consistent with "milling" tough foods on relatively flat molars. Meanwhile, twenty-one *Kenyanthropus platyops* specimens, from 3.4 to 3.0 million years ago, show a level of variability along the C3-C4 spectrum equivalent to that of *Au. afarensis* (95). Thus, by 3.5 million years ago, hominins in different regions of east Africa had begun to incorporate levels of C4 based resources in their diets that are not seen in today's African apes. The question now becomes whether similar dietary shifts were afoot in Pliocene southern Africa.

DIETARY PATTERNS IN SOUTHERN AFRICA:
AUSTRALOPITHECUS AFRICANUS, PARANTHROPUS ROBUSTUS, AND AUSTRALOPITHECUS SEDIBA

Environmental conditions appear to have changed considerably over the periods in which *Australopithecus africanus* and *Paranthropus robustus* roamed southern Africa. In the limestone caves of Makapansgat South Africa, where the oldest (96) *Australopithecus africanus* remains have been found, the mammalian fossil fauna assemblage consists predominantly of browsing species (97). Browsers tend to eat leaves and fruit from trees and shrubs, while grazers mostly feed on grasses. The dominance of browsers as opposed to grazers at Makapansgat suggests dense vegetation, although study of the full mammalian fossil community suggests a mosaic habitat with bushland, riparian woodland, and grasslands (97, 98). The presence of C4 grasses is also indicated by isotopic studies of mammalian tooth enamel (99). The Sterkfontein cave site where hundreds of *Australopithecus africanus* fossils have been recovered appears to have also been a mosaic habitat, consisting of woodland, bushland, riverine forest (100), and open savanna (101).

Like *Australopithecus africanus*, *Paranthropus robustus* seems to have lived in a mosaic environment, but analysis of the mammalian faunal community from the cave sites Swartkrans and Kromdrai (from which a majority of the *Paranthropus robustus* specimens derive) indicates a significant expansion of the grassland component (97). Further analysis of stable carbon isotopes in the enamel of fossil mammals from South African cave sites corroborates this finding and suggests a major expansion of open, grassy environments around 1.7 million years ago, parallel to that occurring in East Africa at this time (99). A shift in environments from *Australopithecus africanus* to *Paranthropus robustus* is consistent with Robinson's dietary hypothesis if the latter, living in drier more open conditions, had to increasingly rely on hard foods or tough roots and tubers (aka underground storage organs) to find sufficient food.

Direct evidence from teeth, however, suggests differences as well as similarities in the diets of *Australopithecus africanus* and *Paranthropus robustus*. In 1986, using a scanning electron microscope, microwear pioneer Fred Grine found a marked difference in microwear between *Au. africanus* and *Pa. robustus* (79). The latter exhibited a much higher frequency of pit features than the former. Subsequent microwear texture analysis supported his analysis. Of all the australopiths, *Paranthropus robustus* has the most complex microwear textures. Daegling and colleagues (59) calculated means and confidence intervals around complexity values of australopith species reported in various studies. Only *Paranthropus robustus* had confidence intervals around its mean that overlapped with those of the habitually hard-object feeding sooty mangabeys of the Tai forest

(*Cercocebus atys*). Although microwear may not distinguish species of differing diets (see above), in this case a clear microwear complexity difference between *Paranthropus robustus* and other australopiths species is evident. Whether this difference indicates that *Paranthropus robustus* consumed harder foods (at least for its last suppers) and/or underground storage organs along with a lot of grit, however, remains unclear. But relative to other hominins, *Paranthropus robustus* has higher variation in complexity values, suggesting dietary variability (90).

Despite these microwear differences, *Australopithecus africanus* and *Paranthropus robustus* are alike in the stable carbon isotope composition of their enamel. In both species, mean carbon 13 values are similar (84), suggesting diets composed of some 35–40% C4 resources (plants or the animals that ate those plants). Teeth of *Australopithecus africanus* from Sterkfontein (102) of *Paranthropus robustus* from Swartkrans (103) show high variability in the $\delta^{13}C$ composition of their enamel over the period of tooth formation. They were clearly neither specialized grazers nor browsers, but instead were flexible foragers, at times relying almost exclusively on C4 resources, while at other times consuming nearly entirely C3 resources. For *Paranthropus robustus*, in a study to which I contributed data on enamel formation, such wide dietary swings occurred over the course of less than two years' time (103). These data weaken the notion that the extinction of *Paranthropus robustus* can be attributed to dietary rigidity.

Adding a wrinkle to this dietary picture of South African hominins is *Australopithecus sediba*, at 1.9 million years ago. In 2012, Amanda Henry and colleagues published data on the first-ever phytoliths extracted from the dental calculus of an early hominin. These included phytoliths of shade and water-loving C3 grasses and sedges and well as fruit, leaf, or wood/bark phytoliths. The carbon isotope composition of the teeth of both *Au. sediba* individuals (MH1 and MH2) is unusual for hominins in this time period – it is similar to that of giraffes, who are C3 specialists, and to that of savanna chimpanzees. Like the much older East African *Ardipithecus ramidus* and *Australopithecus anamensis*, *Australopithecus sediba* seems to have consumed C3 foods even though C4 foods were available. It will be interesting to see if these findings are replicated in additional *Australopithecus sediba* finds.

Returning to *Australopithecus africanus* and *Paranthropus robustus*, in Robinson's view, the absence of meat in the diet of *Paranthropus robustus* was the critical component. His point was that *Australopithecus africanus* and *Homo* became omnivorous while *Paranthropus robustus* remained stubbornly *vegetarian*, leading to its demise. Data on Sr/Ca and Ba/Ca ratios help to address this question. Unexpectedly, initial studies on bone yielded low Sr/Ca ratios in *Paranthropus robustus* (104) similar to those of carnivores. Yet, as mentioned, fossilized bone is highly susceptible to chemical alteration, while the enamel of fossilized teeth is much more stable. Accordingly, Matt Sponheimer and colleagues (105) analyzed Sr/Ca ratios in the enamel of *Australopithecus africanus*, *Paranthropus robustus*, as well as of modern and fossilized mammalian teeth. They found that both hominin species had higher Sr/Ca ratios than contemporaneous baboons or browsing mammals. Given these results, there is no support for either of these species having consumed more meat than do today's baboons.

More recently, Balter and colleagues (106) measured both Sr/Ca and Ba/Ca ratios in the teeth of *Australopithecus africanus*, *Paranthropus robustus* and early South African *Homo*. For early *Homo*, both ratios were indistinguishable from those of carnivores while for *Paranthropus robustus*, both ratios were similar to those of browsing mammals. *Australopithecus africanus* had values that spanned a wide range, indicating a more complex diet. Variation in the Sr/Ca and Ba/Ca ratios over the course of enamel formation was also much higher in *Australopithecus africanus* than it was in *Paranthropus robustus* or in early *Homo*. These findings are quite consistent with Robinson's contention that *Australopithecus africanus* included more meat in its diet than did *Paranthropus robustus*, the latter of which it seems was more focused on plant foods. From the broader omnivorous diets of *Australopithecus africanus*, then, came the more narrow diets of the later species *Paranthropus robustus* and early *Homo*, who appeared to have gone in different directions with respect to meat vs. plant eating. This is similar to what was happening in East Africa with *Paranthropus boisei* and *Homo habilis*, except that the diet of *Paranthropus boisei*, aka "Nutcracker man," was quite different from that of its robust South African cousin.

DID NUTCRACKER MAN CHEW NUTS OR ESCHEW THEM?

"Nutcracker man" has a slightly better ring to it than "C4-resources-man," but C4 resources are what *Paranthropus boisei* predominantly ate. Somewhere between 75–80% of the *Paranthropus boisei* diet consisted of these resources (95). Based on a sample of twenty-two *Paranthropus boisei* individuals (a large sample for these kinds of studies), Thure Cerling and colleagues (95) argued that *Paranthropus boisei* was eating a large amount of the C4 grasses and sedges themselves, rather than the animals that ate those plants, because to accumulate such high $\delta^{13}C$ in enamel by only eating animals, *Paranthropus boisei* would have had to have consumed an unrealistically large amount of animal food. Grasses and sedges don't produce nuts. (There are such plants called nutsedges, but the "nuts" are actually underground tubers, not true nuts.)

It seems that the percentage of C4 grasses and sedges in the *Paranthropus boisei* diet was comparable to that of a zebra or warthog (59). As Julia Lee-Thorp noted (107), such high dependence on C4 resources in monkeys and apes is not seen today. The percentage of C4 foods in the *Paranthropus boisei* diet even exceeds that of the extinct gelada baboon *Theropithecus oswaldi*, a presumed grass and/or grass-seed eater. Furthermore the $\delta^{13}C$ values indicate little variability in C4 consumption among the twenty-two individuals sampled. With such apparent dietary mono-focus, *Paranthropus boisei* has been labelled a "C4 specialist" (83).

These isotopic findings square nicely with the microwear data on *Paranthropus boisei*. Alan Walker first noticed an absence of pits in the microwear of *Paranthropus boisei*, yet for many years it was simply assumed that *Paranthropus boisei* must have eaten hard foods (84). Fred Grine points out (84) that the reason for this assumption is that his 1986 study of *Paranthropus robustus* revealed heavily pitted microwear, indicating the consumption of hard foods. By anatomical analogy to *Paranthropus robustus*, it made sense to consider *Paranthropus boisei* a hard-object feeder, though no *Pa. boisei* teeth had yet been sampled.

Then, in 2008 Peter Ungar and colleagues (108) conducted a microwear texture analysis on a sample of *Paranthropus boisei* teeth. Surprisingly, the teeth had very low complexity and anisotropy: in other words the surfaces were nearly featureless. There is no evidence for hard food eating here, yet there is also no evidence for leaf eating. Aside from Jell-o™ (not a likely dietary candidate), featureless microwear could have been produced by milling grasses and/or sedges between opposing teeth. Dental anthropologist Gabrielle Macho notes that the flatly worn and polished surfaces of *Paranthropus boisei* premolars and molars attest to repetitive chewing of tough, abrasive foods which, by analogy with baboons, she thinks may have been corms. Reliance on C4 plants is consistent with the paleoenvironments in which *Paranthropus boisei* remains have been recovered. These range from riverine forests and woodlands to grasslands, but include an increasing number of drier grassland habitats over time (84).

The repetitive chewing of such C4 plant parts may explain *Pa. boisei's* perplexing combination of a C4 diet consisting of tough foods, and teeth with low, blunt cusps that are conspicuously *un*adapted to shearing such foods. With low and blunt molar cusps, *Paranthropus boisei* would have had to engage in repeated chewing to break down these tough foods. In line with the "tough foods" idea, analysis of *Pa.*

boisei's temporomandibular joint indicates that its mandible moved transversely (109), as it would have if its teeth were used in repetitive chewing of tough foods. Yet, there is a problem with the idea that these tough foods were primarily corms. The outer surfaces of corms are usually gritty with particles of quartz – these would tend to produce pitted microwear that *Paranthropus boisei* simply doesn't show. Nathanial Dominy (93) suggests that *Pa. boisei* could have peeled the corms before eating them, removing most of the grit. Or, as Sponheimer and colleagues suggest (83), perhaps *Paranthropus boisei* concentrated on the kinds of C4 plants that the gelada baboons include in their diets – grass blades and grass seeds, which do not leave much microwear pitting on gelada baboon teeth (77).

If *Paranthropus boisei* was a C4 specialist, then this raises the question of whether its diet was too narrow to allow it to flexibly respond to the vacillating environmental conditions of the Plio-Pleistocene. In living primate species, specialized diets appear to increase the risk of extinction (110). It might seem tempting then, to blame *Paranthropus boisei's* extinction on dietary inflexibility. But if *Paranthropus boisei* was so limited in adaptability, it seems difficult to understand how it persisted in East Africa during a period of widely fluctuating environmental conditions for over 1 million years. That is 800,000 years longer than anatomically modern humans have managed to exist so far. By analogy with baboon dietary ecology, Gabrielle Macho estimates that *Paranthropus boisei* could have met 80% of its caloric requirements and all of its protein requirements just by spending about 40% of its feeding time on C4 resources (111). Life on the "sedge" does not appear to have been life on the edge.

At several locations, *Paranthropus boisei* appears to have lived near seasonally wet areas where C4 sedges and grasses flourished (112). These areas provide a home to huge numbers of microorganisms and tiny crustaceans, that Kathlyn Stewart believes *Paranthropus boisei* would likely have eaten as well. Furthermore, *Paranthropus boisei* teeth, like those of several other australopiths, exhibit large edge chips suggesting at least the occasional presence of hard foods in the diet (81), so there was probably more to *Paranthropus boisei* diets than sedges and grasses. Given that even the most dentally specialized primate today – the aye-aye – eats a variety of foods with very few teeth, it seems plausible that *Paranthropus boisei*, with its complete set of very large teeth, did the same.

CONCLUSIONS

Here, I have emphasized the difficulties involved of drawing conclusions about the diets of fossil species based on known links between dental morphology and diet in extant primates. The causes of these difficulties are several. Morphological change may be gradual and lag considerably behind dietary change, as is the case of the bovids and suids of East Africa who began eating more C4 foods 2.8 million years ago, but whose teeth became more hypsodont only gradually over the Plio-Pleistocene.

In addition, there may be different adaptive solutions to similar problems. Indeed, Matt Sponheimer and colleagues found that the increasing consumption of C4 resources from *Australopithecus anamensis* to *Australopithecus afarensis* to *Paranthropus boisei* is associated with a trend to larger and larger premolars and molars over time, most likely for processing these tough foods (83). It is not clear why the consumption of these foods did not select for the thin enamel and sharp cusps with shearing crests present in today's primates who eat tough foods. Thick enamel may have provided a selective benefit in maintaining tooth longevity, as Pampush and colleagues (67) suggest is the case for the longer-lived extant primates that subsist on tough, phytolith-containing abrasive plant foods. Consistent with this idea, it has been noted that in some nonprimate herbivores, the chewing surfaces of teeth are flat despite their tough food diets – a different solution from that of modern primates (67). In addition, of course, it is entirely possible that thick enamel and large posterior teeth evolved in response to eating hard foods as fallback resources. Unfortunately, this possibility is not easily tested.

Matt Sponheimer and colleagues (85) consider the incorporation of C4 resources into australopith diets to reflect a "fundamental hominin trait" that enabled hominins to adapt to the increasingly open and grassier environments in which they lived. Chimpanzees living in savanna environments today spend the majority of their feeding time on fruits, giving them their strong C3 dietary signal (85). Judging from their predominantly C3 signals, the early east African hominins *Ardipithecus ramidus* and *Australopithecus anamensis* were probably like chimpanzees in this regard. Beginning with *Australopithecus afarensis* in east Africa, hominins began adapting to changing resource availability, making use of C4 resources in a way that modern savanna chimpanzees do not. In the case of *Paranthropus boisei*, with its highly elevated C4 signal, it is likely that sedges and grasses themselves were predominantly eaten, rather than the animals that ate those plants. But as Kathlyn Stewart suggests (112), tiny freshwater shrimp and copepods living in seasonal C4 wetland environments could easily have been consumed along with these plants.

Meanwhile, in southern Africa, *Australopithecus africanus* and *Paranthropus robustus* incorporated sizeable percentages of C4 resources in their diets, though not nearly at *Paranthropus boisei* levels. One source of South African australopith C4 resources could certainly have been tropical grasses and sedges themselves, although it is possible that animals that ate these resources also contributed to their C4 signals. Termites have been suggested as one potential animal food *Paranthropus robustus* may have consumed. Microscopic wear on experimental bone tools used to poke into termite mounds matches the wear on bone tools recovered from Swartkrans cave where *Paranthropus robustus* remains have been found (113). Chimpanzees are well known to use tools in "termite fishing." Some termite species consume C3 plants, while others consume C4 plants, so it is possible that termites could have contributed to C3 or C4 signatures, or both (114). Oddly, *Australopithecus sediba* maintained a C3-rich diet despite wide availability of C4 resources.

The analysis of this species dental calculus nevertheless attests to diverse foods in its diet, including fruits, leaves, grasses, and even bark.

Australopiths were therefore flexible foragers. In terms of meat consumption, *Australopithecus africanus* appears to have had the most variable diet of the South African australopiths. Appearing later in time, *Paranthropus robustus* and early South African *Homo*, seem to have survived drier conditions by taking divergent adaptive paths, *Paranthropus* becoming more herbivorous and *Homo* including more meat in its diet. This situation points to evolutionary niche divergence, which results when members of coexisting species are able to access more food if they avoid competing with one another over the same resources. As explored further in Chapter 6, *Homo* in East Africa also seems to have included more meat in its diet than did its contemporary robust cousin, *Paranthropus boisei*. Proffered in 1954, John Robinson's Dietary Hypothesis continues to gain empirical support today. But, before turning to what teeth tell us about the diets of early and later *Homo*, the next chapter considers whether the uniquely reduced canines of hominins are related to their diets, mating habits, or both.

3 Curious Canines

> He who rejects with scorn the belief that the shape of his own canines, and their occasional great development in other men, are due to our early progenitors having been provided with these formidable weapons, will probably reveal by sneering the line of his descent. For though he no longer intends, nor has the power, to use these teeth as weapons, he will unconsciously retract his "snarling muscles"... so as to expose them ready for action, like a dog prepared to fight.
>
> – Darwin CR
> *The Descent of Man and Selection in Relation to Sex*, Vol. 1

Charles Darwin's analysis of the size and shape of human canine teeth convinced him that at some point, human male ancestors possessed large and projecting canines, similar to those of male gorillas or orangutans. In Darwin's view, male canine teeth, like other male armaments such as horns in mammals or spurs in birds, were the result of sexual selection: the advantage that members of the same sex have over one another in "exclusive relation to reproduction."

Darwin conceived of sexual selection happening in two ways: first, through competition among males for mating opportunities with females, and second through differences among males in their ability to attract females. These two sides of the sexual selection coin are called *intrasexual* and *intersexual* selection, respectively. In the first case competition occurs among males and in the second, females select males who they find most attractive (or on the basis of other traits that would presumably enhance the survival of their offspring). Thus ensues the evolution of armaments, like the large curved horns of male bighorn sheep, and ornaments, like the peacock's tail. Slashing canine teeth, in Darwin's view, were a male armament which evolved through time because males with larger and sharper teeth were able to win more contests for females and thus pass these traits to their offspring.

Darwin unfortunately did not have a satisfactory answer for why there is a general pattern in nature of male-male competition for mates and female choice of them, but later work (116, 117) offered an explanation in terms of sex differences in investment in offspring. In mammals, it is usually females that make an enormous investment in offspring through gestation and lactation. Males, who by comparison invest much less, compete with one another for access to females. The pattern of male-male competition and female choice has been attributed more fundamentally to anisogamy—the difference in size of eggs and sperm. Males whose individual sperm cells are "cheap" in comparison to the much larger egg cells of females, can maximize offspring number by increasing the number of females with which they mate, while females maximize their reproductive success by "ensuring" the quality of their offspring through being choosy about their mating partners.[1]

While Darwin believed that our remote ancestors must have had intimidating canine teeth, he also believed that once our ancestors began to walk bipedally, males could have used their free hands to throw stones or to wield "clubs or other weapons." Assuming that males won more fights in this way rather than by using their slashing canines, selection for maintaining large canines would be relaxed.

---

[1] As evolutionary anthropologist Michael Plavcan and colleagues point out, sexual dimorphism should not be assumed to result from selection acting only on male traits. (118. Plavcan JM, van Schaik CP, Kappeler PM. Competition, coalitions and canine size in primates. *Journal of Human Evolution.* 1995;28(3):245–276.) A tendency to make that assumption arises from Darwin's conception of competition among males as the cause of intrasexual selection and female choice of mates as the mechanism of intersexual selection. In both cases, male traits – armaments and ornaments – are being selected. To be sure this is the general pattern in nature that Darwin observed, later understood to result from the generally greater investment in offspring made by females. In primates it is now clear that there are situations in which females compete with other females, potentially resulting in intrasexual selection among them, as well as situations in which males may be choosy about mating partners, potentially resulting in intersexual selection for female traits (119. Dixson AF. *Primate Sexuality: Comparative Studies of the Prosimians, Monkeys, Apes and Human Beings,* 2nd ed. Oxford: Oxford University Press, 2012.)

Darwin explained that like other anatomical structures which are no longer of use to animal, canines would, over generations, diminish in size (owing, most likely, to selection for energy economy). In ruminants, Darwin reasoned, canine teeth are either absent or are vestigial because horns took over their function as weapons; so too did human canine teeth reduce in size as males could now use their hands to deploy weapons. Darwin did not explain why canine teeth did not become vestigial or disappear altogether. Yet, he saw human canines as "perfectly efficient instruments for mastication" (1871:126). He might therefore have envisioned that no longer under selection as weapons, canines could have been maintained by selection for their contribution to food processing, as some anthropologists would later propose.

Darwin's view of canine evolution in humans ties together defining human features – bipedalism, tool-making, and small canine teeth – in a tidy evolutionary scenario. Indeed, to Darwin, one of the key selective benefits of bipedalism was that it freed the hands for other uses, including making tools and weapons. As many have noted, evidence of stone tools in the fossil record postdates the evolution of bipedalism, casting some doubt on this explanation. But of course, it remains possible that early hominins could have begun to use unmodified stones or wooden clubs to a greater extent than chimpanzees do today. Such objects would be difficult to recognize in the archaeological record as tools in the first instance, and in the second instance, would be unlikely to be preserved over millions of years.

Nevertheless, if *Ardipithecus ramidus* is ancestral to later hominins (19), then the link between small canines and bipedalism breaks down. Analysis of this species' skeleton suggests *facultative* bipedalism – Ardi had the ability to walk on two legs when necessary but still spent a significant portion of time spent in the trees as an arboreal quadruped. Yet, the canines of *Ardipithecus ramidus* are considerably smaller than those of modern chimpanzee, gorilla, or orangutan males (Figure 3.1).

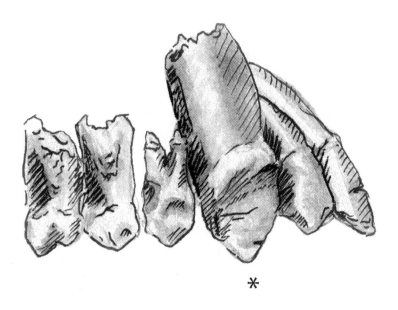

*

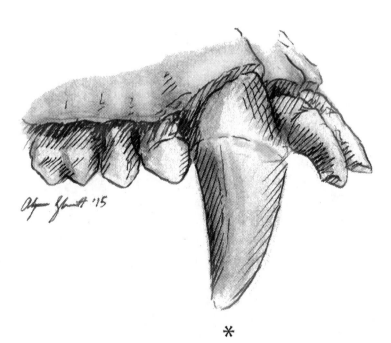

*

FIGURE 3.1: Comparison of upper canine teeth of *Ardipithecus ramidus* and *Pan troglodytes* (chimpanzee) males. Redrawn by Alyssa Starrett from the Author Summary figure in Lovejoy CO., Reexamining human origins in light of *Ardipithecus ramidus*. *Science*. 2009;326:74. Reprinted with permission from AAAS.

Paleoanthropologist and *Ardipithecus*-discoverer Tim White (19) described canines from twenty-one *Ardipithecus ramidus* individuals. These canines are all similar in size and shape to those of female apes and derived in the direction of those of later hominins. The upper canines and lower first premolars do not show signs of functioning as a "honing complex": sharpened edges on the upper canine are not present and there are no wear facets on the lower first premolar. There is minimal variation in the size and shape of these canines, and, assuming that some of the twenty-one individuals were males, this limited variation suggests little difference in the canines of males and females. Finally, *Ardipithecus ramidus* maxillary canines were shorter than their mandibular canines, while in chimpanzee, gorilla and orangutan males, maxillary canines are longer, reflecting their use as weapons. This canine sample provides evidence that in *Ardipithecus ramidus*, substantial changes in canine teeth toward the modern human condition preceded the evolution of either the more habitual bipedalism of later australopiths or the obligate (committed) bipedalism of *Homo erectus* and later *Homo*.

In 1925, when South African anatomist Raymond Dart introduced the name *Australopithecus* to the world, he considered one of its defining human-like features to be its small canine teeth. If the connection between bipedalism and canine reduction envisioned by Darwin breaks down with *Ardipithecus ramidus*, then what explains the curiously small canine teeth of hominins, including modern humans? Although many different ideas have been proposed, they primarily fall into two classes of explanation. The first suggests that the selection pressure maintaining large canines would diminish if males were no longer competing for mates as much as their ancestors did. The second suggests that changes in diet may have brought about hominin canine size reduction.

These classes of explanation are not mutually exclusive, but there is substantial debate as to which of them had more influence and at what point during human evolution they may have come into play. For example, if one can rule out changes in diet as a factor leading to the initial reduction of canines, then does this suggest that there was comparatively little physical competition among early hominin males, or even a monogamous mating system (120)? On the other hand, if dietary changes are primarily responsible for the initial reduction in canine size, then the presence of small canines in hominins implies little if anything about their mating habits.

Hominin canines are distinctive not only in their small size relative to those of most other primates but also with respect to their minimal *sexual dimorphism* – differences between the sexes other than those related to the sex organs themselves. In the case of canines, sexual dimorphism refers to the differences between the sexes in the size and shape of these teeth. It is possible to have large and projecting canine teeth with minimal sexual dimorphism, as occurs in gibbons. In gibbon species, monogamously paired males and females defend their territories. With both males and females engaged in territorial defense, selection has presumably favored enlarged canines in both sexes. So, for humans and earlier hominins, the question is: why are canine teeth small and nonprojecting as well as minimally sexually dimorphic?

Here I will first explain that given available evidence, a reasonable case can be made for relating diminution in canine size and sexual dimorphism to reduced competition among males for mates in *Ardipithecus ramidus,* as White and colleagues (19) and Lovejoy and coworkers (121) contend. Reduced male-male competition, however, does not necessarily imply monogamous social organization or mating. I will then argue that in some later hominins species, even though evidence of skeletal sexual dimorphism may suggest more intense mate competition (or female choice for large males), the incorporation of canines into food processing functions and/or changes in jaw architecture would have acted to *constrain* the evolution of canine size and sexual dimorphism. This argument relies entirely on Leonard Greenfield's analysis of canine function in early hominins and Peter Lucas' (122, 123) and William Hylander's (124) biomechanical analysis of canine size and jaw gape in nonhuman primates.

But first, to explore the contribution of sexual selection and diet to canine size and sexual dimorphism in hominins, it is necessary to examine what we know about the causes of canine variation in living primates and about how canine size and shape changed over primate evolutionary history.

ULTIMATE AND PROXIMATE CAUSES OF CANINE VARIATION IN MODERN PRIMATES

Causes of canine variation in modern primates can be sought at "proximate" and "ultimate" levels. Evolutionary causes and influences constitute an ultimate level of explanation in biology, while genetic, developmental, and physiological causes constitute proximate explanations (125). The primary focus here is on ultimate causes of canine variation in modern primates. Yet, elucidating proximate causes are of interest as well because they may illuminate evolutionary events. For example, if different developmental mechanisms are associated with a shared feature among species, then it is likely that this feature evolved in these species independently and therefore constitutes homoplasy. Shared developmental mechanisms may suggest common evolutionary origins or the lack of alternative developmental pathways for the evolution of an anatomical feature.

Insight into both categories of causes can be gleaned by examining patterns and correlates of canine size and sexual dimorphism in living primates. First, taxonomic patterns are clearly evident. In prosimians, upper (maxillary) canines are generally similar in size for males and females (118). Where there are differences, male canines are larger than those of females, with some exceptions (e.g., the diademed sifaka whose canines are larger in females than they are in males). In some prosimians upper canines may be somewhat large and projecting (e.g., in ring-tailed lemurs), yet they do not reach the size – either absolutely or in relation to their body sizes – of those of some anthropoids (118). Similarly, sexual dimorphism in body size in prosimians is limited (119). In anthropoids, and especially in some Old World monkeys, males have maxillary canines that are up to four times larger than those of females (126–128) and are very tall in relation to their other dimensions. Body size dimorphism reaches an extreme in Old World monkeys as well.

In great apes, neither canine nor body size sexual dimorphism reaches such extremes, with male maxillary canines approaching twice the size of that of females (gorillas and orangutans), and with similar differences in body size (128). The proportions of great ape canine teeth are different from those of Old World monkeys in being wider and thus appearing stouter than those of older world monkeys (128).

From the standpoint of human and hominin canine size and sexual dimorphism, it is interesting that in great apes, our closest primate relatives, canine dimorphism size and shape does not approach the extremes seen in some old world monkeys. And, as anthropologist Michael Plavcan points out (128), in bonobos and common chimpanzees, to whom we are most closely related, canine size in both sexes as well as canine sexual dimorphism are rather modest by anthropoid standards. Relative to body size, bonobo male canines even appear to be "reduced" to a degree comparable to *Australopithecus afarensis* male canines (129). Bonobos are no more closely related to hominins than are chimpanzees, so either reduction occurred in parallel in hominins and bonobos or the ancestors of the hominin-chimpanzee-bonobo clade had modest canines to begin with, and these evolved to larger size in chimpanzees.

A second pattern in primates is that sexual dimorphism in both canine and body size is related to body size (130–133). The relationship between sexual dimorphism and body size extends beyond primates to a wide array of animals, and is known as *Rensch's rule* (134). Exactly why sexual dimorphism should be more pronounced in larger-bodied species is debated (128), but Rensch's rule suggests that it may be useful to compare the degree of sexual dimorphism among species in a way that takes into account their differences in body size.

In anthropoids, not only is sexual dimorphism in canine size correlated with body size, but so is absolute canine size itself (131, 135). Canine size dimorphism is also correlated with body size dimorphism (132, 136–138). Yet, it is important not to overstate these relationships because canine size and body size as well as dimorphism in the two can clearly be dissociated. For example, in living humans, there is greater body size dimorphism than canine size dimorphism (139). The opposite is true of most colobine monkeys, in which high sexual dimorphism in canines is coupled with minimal sexual dimorphism in body mass (128). Selection pressures can therefore act independently on canine size and body size and on sexual dimorphism in both.

Just as Darwin anticipated, a sizeable portion of the variation in primate canine sexual dimorphism and male canine size relates to male-male competition for mates. Observation of primates makes it clear that males in some species inflict slashing wounds with their canines on their competitors and may use them in threat displays (119). (Not all canine exposure appears to relate to threat displays, however [140].) Females too can inflict harmful wounds with their canines in some species (141).

Early studies found ambiguous associations between canine sexual dimorphism and intrasexual selection because they relied on social organization as a proxy for male competition. For example, Harvey and colleagues (131) proposed that in monogamous primate species, where each male has a mate, there should be minimal competition among males and canines should be least dimorphic. They argued that species that form "harem" or single-male polygynous groups (one adult male, several adult females and their offspring) would have the greatest degree of sexual dimorphism because in these species, bachelor males would frequently challenge "harem" leaders for access to their females, and "harem" leaders would in turn be required to defend them. Finally, multimale groups (several adult males and females and their offspring) were expected to exhibit intermediate levels of canine dimorphism, because, in such groups males cannot maintain exclusive access to females.

These early investigations did find that monogamous species had the least sexually dimorphic canines, but there was no statistically significant difference in canine dimorphism between single-male and multimale groups, lending only partial support to the hypothesis that the degree of male-male competition in primate groups is related to canine sexual dimorphism. Harvey and colleagues (131) also found that terrestrial species had greater canine sexual dimorphism than arboreal species, supporting the notion that selection has also acted on males as protectors of their groups against predators in open environments. (Tree-living species can more easily hide.)

What was needed to adequately test the intrasexual selection hypothesis was a more accurate measure of male-male competition. To see why social organization is not a reliable proxy for male-male competition, consider baboons and woolly spider monkeys, both of which form multimale groups. Baboons form multimale groups in which males vigorously compete for dominance rank year-round and are highly sexually dimorphic in both canine and body size. Woolly spider monkeys have a much more relaxed mating system, in which many males mate with many females (142) and canine sexual dimorphism is minimal. In the latter case, competition has gone "underground" in the form of sperm competition—male woolly spider monkeys have very large testes in relation to their body sizes (143) as do other species in which females mate with multiple males during their peri-ovulatory periods (119).

Owing to such problems with using social organization as a proxy for male-male competition, Richard Kay and colleagues (144) devised a four-point rating scale to investigate the relationship between degree of male-male competition and canine sexual dimorphism, and in so doing found an unambiguous positive association between the two. Building and expanding on this analysis, Plavcan and van Schaik (138) created a rating scheme reflecting both the frequency and intensity of male-male competition and applied it to a wide range of primates. These authors too found a clear relationship between male-male competition and canine sexual dimorphism (and later with body mass sexual dimorphism [139]). The relationship held within substrate type (arboreal vs. terrestrial), taxonomic groups and dietary categories (e.g., folivore vs. frugivore vs. insectivore and their combinations), meaning that when "controlling for" these other factors, male-male competition is independently associated with canine sexual dimorphism.

A recent study further demonstrated that male canine size is not simply a reflection of male body size (145): males of sexually dimorphic species with large body sizes had larger canine sizes than expected on the basis of scaling their canines to their body sizes. Selection therefore appears to be acting specifically on male canine size. Consistent with this conclusion is an innovative study by Steve Leigh and colleagues showing that male mandrills sired most of their offspring during the period of maximum canine height – after the canine was fully erupted and before the canine began to wear. Adult male mandrills join groups of adult females and their offspring only during the mating season, when they must establish dominance and relationships to females in a limited period of time. Thus, sexual selection is thought to be intense in this species, which exhibits extreme sexual dimorphism in body and canine size as well as coloration (119) (Figure 3.2).

An important point to keep in mind, though, is that variation in *female* canine size is associated with the degree of competition among females (usually for food and other resources) (118). This means that canine sexual dimorphism should be viewed as a result of selection acting not only on males but also on females, as Michael Plavcan often emphasizes. The fact that gibbons have large canines but minimal sexual dimorphism reflects selection on both sexes for large canines in intra sexual competition. Plavcan and colleagues (118) found reduced female canine size in species in which females compete in coalitions, as in macaques, baboons, and mandrills. This finding suggests that

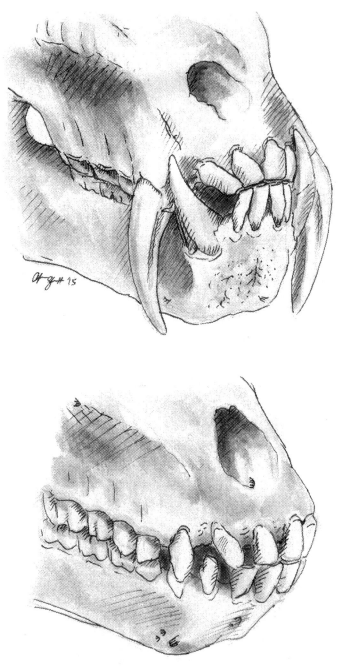

FIGURE 3.2: The dentitions of a mandrill male (top) vs. that of a female (bottom) showing strong sexual dimorphism in upper canines. Drawn by Alyssa Starrett.

part of the reason why canine sexual dimorphism is so great in these species may be not only because selection is acting to increase male canine size but also because there is minimal selection for large canines in females.

Although much of the variation in canine size and canine sexual dimorphism in anthropoids (monkeys and apes) relates to sexual selection (146), there is evidence for relationships to diet as well. For example, in marmosets, lower canines are small and are used, in conjunction with lower incisors, to gouge tree bark in obtaining gums. In the pithecine New World monkeys (a subfamily including saki monkeys and uakaris), both upper and lower canines are used to crack open hard fruit. Both males and females have tall canines with a "chisel-like" morphology that appears to be adapted for this specific use (147, 148).

Leonard Greenfield (149, 150) suggested that in primates, primary (deciduous) canines and the canines of females are often incorporated into incisal functions. He further argued (150), in his "dual selection hypothesis," that primate canines are under competing selection pressures for use as incisors in acquiring food and for use as sexually-selected weapons. Much of the evidence for these ideas came from Greenfield's observation that female canines often had blunted tips as compared to male canines. Greenfield argued that blunted wear in the lower canine is produced by contact with the upper lateral incisor. Blunted wear in the upper canine, he explained, is produced by tip-to-tip occlusion (contact) with the lower canine as well as by the functional use of the upper canine in puncture-crushing.

Plavcan and Kelley (151) questioned whether tip-to-tip occlusion could actually occur, given the ways in which jaws typically move during chewing. They also countered that "incidental contact" with food during food gathering may be an alternative explanation of such blunted wear and that it is not necessarily indicative of "tip-to-tip" occlusion between upper and lower canines, functional use of upper canines in "puncture-crushing," or functional contact between the lower canine and upper lateral incisor. These points are important to bear in mind, yet they do not negate the possibility that the higher frequency of blunted canine tip wear in primate females that Greenfield found (150) reflects the functional use of canines in food acquisition.

Diet may also have an indirect role in constraining the evolution of canines as weapons. This idea has its roots in the work of Peter Lucas and colleagues (122, 123), who showed that the size of primate males' canines appears to be related to their gape. The use of tall canines to inflict a wound requires that the jaw be opened widely. These authors found that the length of the mandible and the height of the jaw joint relative to jaw length – variables that affect gape – were strongly related to canine size in male primates. This finding suggested that the size of male canines may be limited by their gapes.

William Hylander and coworkers (124) actually measured gape in living subjects and showed, across twenty-seven species of Old World monkeys and apes, that jaw gape is closely linked to canine crown height. Going a step further, these authors made the point that evolutionary adaptation to diet can affect gape. A forward shift in the position of jaw muscles makes it possible to increase bite force without adding muscle mass because this is a position of greater mechanical advantage for the jaw muscle lever system. Thus, an energetically efficient solution to chewing hard and/or tough foods that require high bite force is to shift the chewing muscles forward, but this has the effect of decreasing gape. Thus, in species that solve the problem of chewing hard or tough foods by shifting the chewing muscles forward, the evolution of the canine is constrained by the reduction in gape.

Research into proximate causes of canine size and sexual dimorphism has thus far focused primarily on the Y-chromosome, testosterone and the developmental processes that lead to sex differences in male versus female canine crown height. The work of Alvesalo and Verrela suggests that forty-six X,Y females with androgen insensitivity syndrome have teeth as large as those of males (152). This syndrome is characterized by lack of receptors for androgens (including testosterone) indicating that independent of testosterone, there are genes on the Y chromosome affecting tooth size. On the other hand, of all tooth types, canines were least affected in size in forty-seven, XYY males (153), suggesting that the additional Y chromosome had a disproportionately *smaller* effect on the canine than on other tooth types.

Other evidence suggests a direct influence of testosterone on canine size. Prenatal administration of testosterone propionate (an injectable form of testosterone) to female rhesus macaque fetuses resulted in taller canines than were present in control females (154). More recently, Ribeiro and colleagues (155) measured dimensions of deciduous and permanent canine teeth of human opposite-sex dizygotic (fraternal) twins and same-sex dizygotic twins. They hypothesized that females in opposite-twin pairs would have larger canine teeth if testosterone from the male twin had an influence on the female twin's canine development *in utero*. Their results supported their hypothesis, suggesting that testosterone *in utero* affects the size of both deciduous and permanent canines. In opposite-sex twins, the female twin's canine eruption timing is also "masculinized" in the sense that canine eruption occurs later in childhood than is normal for females, approaching the time when male canines normally erupt (156). In humans, boys erupt their canines approximately one year later than females do, in part because their canine teeth take longer to form.

The longer development of canine teeth in males relative to females is even more pronounced in primates with strong sexual dimorphism than it is in humans. For example, on average male orangutan lower canine crowns take approximately three years longer to form than do those of females (157). My colleagues and I showed that in both Old and New World monkeys, the primary mechanism by which males achieve their greater canine crown heights is through prolonging their periods of crown formation, rather than by increasing their speeds of crown formation (158). The common ontogenetic pathway of anthropoid primates suggests that the alternative pathway of speeding up crown formation in males was, for some other reason, not favored within this group of primates. It appears, however that the 50-million-year-old Eocene primate *Cantius* (not an anthropoid), did achieve canine sexual dimorphism by speeding up crown formation in males, rather than by extending the period of male canine crown formation (159).

The ultimate and proximate influences on variation in canine size and sexual dimorphism in living primates reviewed in this section provide important context for evaluating hypotheses about the evolution of hominin canines. Yet, these hypotheses must also be evaluated with respect to the fossil evidence, which we turn to next.

THE EVOLUTIONARY TRANSITION TO HOMININ CANINES: FOSSIL EVIDENCE

Sexual dimorphism of the Eocene primate *Cantius* dates to more than 50 million years ago, yet because the developmental pathway by which *Cantius* grew large male canines was by speeding up growth, its canine sexual dimorphism probably evolved independently from that of anthropoids. Canine sexual dimorphism is also present in early anthropoids (*Catopithecus* and *Proteopithecus*) in the fossil record of Egypt, dating to 36 million years ago. These early anthropoids had small bodies (less than the size of a guinea pig), yet they had pronounced canine sexual dimorphism in apparent defiance of Rensch's rule.

But it is the fossil apes of the Miocene that are the immediate predecessors of hominins and living apes, and are therefore more likely to provide insight into hominin canine evolution. Many of the fossil apes of the Miocene (of which there were a great many species) exhibited canine sexual dimorphism in both size and shape (160). One of them, *Lufengpithecus* from China may, have even been more sexually dimorphic than any of the living apes (161). From which of these Miocene apes the African ape and human clade descended is not clear. Cladistic analysis suggests it may be the "Greek Ape,*Ouranopithecus macedoniensis*," dating to 9.6 to 8.7 million years ago. Synapomorphies linking *Ouranopithecus* to this clade include in part its facial morphology (162) and several dental traits: minimally sexually dimorphic canines (though this has been questioned, as explained below), the lack of a honing facet on the lower premolar (163), and molarized deciduous premolars (164).

Miocene ape expert David Begun and coauthors (164) contend that reduction in canine size, change in the upper canine-lower premolar honing complex, and postcanine megadontia characterize *Ouranopithecus* and some other Miocene apes including *Sivapithecus* and *Gigantopithecus* (though these two Asian genera exhibit affinities to Asian great apes). The authors suggest that these are interrelated characteristics consistent with selection for powerful chewing and so could represent homoplasy in these Miocene genera as well as in the hominin *Paranthropus*. The co-occurrence of these characteristics would be consistent with Hylander and colleagues (124) explanation of the trade off between canine size and gape that would accompany a forward shift in jaw musculature. The presence of these features in *Ouranopithecus* raises the possibility that the common ancestor of the African-ape human clade had relatively small canines that were inherited by early hominins, with larger canines subsequently evolving in the chimpanzee and gorilla lineages. This idea is challenged by other analyses suggesting that the canines of *Ouranopithecus* were not so small relative to their estimated body sizes and may have been rather sexually dimorphic after all (129).

If *Ouranopithecus* had sexually dimorphic canines comparable to those of great apes of similar body size (129), then in addition to weakening the possibility that early hominins inherited their small canines from *Ouranopithecus*, the association between large back teeth and relatively small, minimally dimorphic canines breaks down. Incidentally, sooty mangabeys habitually eat very hard nuts and have enlarged premolars and molars, but they also maintain a wide gape (165) and quite sexually dimorphic canines. Clearly eating mechanically challenging foods doesn't *necessitate* small canines, a point which Hylander and colleagues (124) make when they note that the forward movement of jaw muscles is only one solution to

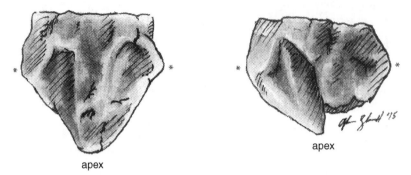

apex   apex

FIGURE 3.3: Lingual (tongue-side) view of *Australopithecus anamensis* canine on left, and *Australopithecus afarensis* canine on right. Note that in *Australopithecus afarensis*, the shoulders of the canine (marked by asterisks) are closer to the apex of the crown. The *Australopithecus afarensis* canine is therefore said to be more "diamond-shaped." After Ward CV, Plavcan JM, Manthi FK. Anterior dental evolution in the Australopithecus anamensis–afarensis lineage. *Philosophical Transactions of the Royal Society B: Biological Sciences.* 2010;365: 3333–3344 by permission of the Royal Society. Drawn by Alyssa Starrett.

a mechanically challenging diet. Another solution would be enlarging the muscles themselves with no change in position.

The very strong evidence of reduced canines and minimal canine sexual dimorphism in *Ardipithecus ramidus* was reviewed earlier. *Ardipithecus*, however, retained a canine with large roots (similar to those of chimpanzees) and had a crown shape that was similar to that of its presumed descendent *Australopithecus anamensis*. In the *Australopithecus anamensis-Australopithecus afarensis* lineage, there were further changes in canine size and shape. In their analyses, Carol Ward and colleagues (166) and Fredrick Manthi (167) and coworkers showed that although there was no reduction in crown height along this lineage, there were shape changes in upper canines, lower canines and lower first premolars. The upper canine crown became more diamond-shaped as the "shoulders" of the crown shifted toward the crown apex (Figure 3.3), the lower canine crown became less "blade-like," and the lower premolars "less unicuspid." Modern humans have canine teeth with a similar diamond shape, although they are of smaller size (166, 167). In addition, there was a strong reduction in the size of the canine root with the transition to *Au. afarensis*, a change that is also in a modern-human direction.

The canine crown shape changes, according to Ward and colleagues (166) would increase the area of contact between upper and lower teeth and are therefore the likely result of selection for the increased use of the canine in acquiring food (i.e., functioning like an incisor) and also perhaps for an expanded role of the lower first premolar in mastication. The authors further suggest that changes in jaw structure as well as in molar crowns (which become taller) denote dietary changes that would have affected premolar use.

HYPOTHESES FOR HOMININ CANINE REDUCTION

It is not yet possible (and may never be) to conduct definitive tests of the various hypotheses for hominin canine reduction. It *is* possible to evaluate some of the strengths and weaknesses of these hypotheses in light of what we know about canine variation in living primates and fossil hominins. Darwin's ideas about the link between canine reduction and bipedalism are questionable based on what we know from the fossil record today. But, the idea that hominin canine reduction is related to changes in sexual selection pressures remains a plausible one.

In an influential 1981 *Science* article entitled "The Origin of Man," Owen Lovejoy (120) proposed a complex scenario for the evolution of distinctively hominin traits. Ecological changes during the Miocene (greater seasonality and variability) combined with long periods of infant dependency were suggested to have intensified selection for adaptations that increased both offspring survival and adult reproductive rate. These adaptations included bipedalism and monogamy. Bipedal males who could use their free hands to "provision" their families would, in so doing, enhance the survival of their offspring as well as hasten the return of their lactating mates to reproductive condition. This situation could only evolve under the condition of monogamously mated females – males who provisioned the offspring of *other males* would simply not pass on the genes that predisposed them to provisioning behavior. Males would also be selected to mate monogamously because by doing so they would devote their energies to the survival of their own offspring rather than to competition with other males. Monogamous mating would then result in relaxed selection pressure on maintaining large male canines, as intermale competition diminished.

In a footnote (120), Lovejoy pointed out that he did not mean to imply that monogamy was the "cause" of canine reduction, but that it simply relaxed selection pressure on canines, which then evolved to smaller size by positive selection "... most likely to be found in the concurrent dentognathic changes of greater molar dominance and general anterior tooth reduction" in hominins (1981:350).

Lovejoy's scenario raises the possibility that the reduced canines and minimal canine sexual dimorphism of the earliest hominins is a signal of monogamous mating. The reason that this is not *necessarily* so, is that there is no clear link between mating system and canine size or sexual dimorphism in living primates (see above). Michael Plavcan explains that even his competition level categories that *have* been linked to canine sexual dimorphism in living primates account for only 48% of the variation in canine sexual dimorphism in 128 species. Some of that variation also has to do with selection on female canine size as well as on selection for dietary uses of canines in some species. Thus, small male canines and reduced canine sexual dimorphism are in and of themselves ambiguous evidence of a low level of male-male competition in fossil forms.

In the case of *Ardipithecus ramidus*, however, there is evidence of minimal canine sexual dimorphism and reduced canine size relative to great apes coupled with minimal skeletal sexual dimorphism (19, 121). The combination of both skeletal and canine sexual dimorphism strengthens the possibility that there was relaxed sexual selection for large male canines in *Ardipithecus*. It does not appear that *Ardipithecus ramidus* was eating mechanically challenging foods to the same extent as *Australopithecus afarensis* and later hominins were – it was not incorporating C4 plants to the extent that these later hominins did, and it had not yet evolved the enlarged molars of these species, nor had it evolved enamel as thick as that of later australopiths (see Chapter 2). For these reasons, it would be difficult to support the view that canine reduction in *Ardipithecus* and reduced canine sexual dimorphism was in some way a consequence of adaptation to mechanically challenging diets (either through reduced gape or by some other connection).

But what about other possible explanations for canine reduction in *Ardipithecus ramidus* as well as in later hominins? Several other ideas have been proposed, although many early ideas appear less plausible today. One older idea was that large interlocking canine teeth might interfere with "rotary" chewing of mechanically challenging foods (169). But as Jungers (170) pointed out years ago, male baboons, which have very large canine teeth, are quite capable of rotary and lateral chewing movements. Experimental studies on male anthropoids with extracted canines showed that there was no change in molar occlusal relationships following extraction of the large canine (171, 172). Canine reduction in *Ardipithecus ramidus*, in any case, occurred prior to the incorporation of significant quantities of C4 foods that may have been milled between upper and lower molars.

Another influential idea was that of developmental dental crowding (170). This idea held that molarized premolars in early hominins limited the space available to later-erupting canine teeth, thus limiting their size. This idea has difficulty accounting for the reduced canines of *Ardipithecus ramidus*, which did not have molarized premolars. Yet one more idea was that canine reduction might have simply been a by-product of incisor tooth reduction in hominins (i.e., genes affecting incisor reduction simultaneously affected canine reduction). While this is possible for *Ardipithecus*, which had smaller incisors than modern chimpanzees, it is difficult to see why this would necessarily be so because there are living primates with relatively small incisor teeth (leaf-eating colobines) that nevertheless have very large canines. Lucas Delezene (173) recently showed that across anthropoid primates, there is no evidence that canine tooth size covaries with incisor tooth size (or with postcanine tooth size either).

Against the backdrop of these earlier ideas, Leonard Greenfield (150) applied his "dual selection" hypothesis to hominin canine reduction. At the time of Greenfield's writing, the earliest hominin canines known were those of *Australopithecus afarensis*. Greenfield argued that *Australopithecus afarensis* canines exhibited "incisor-like traits" and were therefore probably under selection to function as incisors. For example, the lower canines had enlarged "mesial cristids" or ridges which would have contacted the lateral incisors when the incisors were used to bite, and on some of *Au. afarensis* specimens, the mesial cristids and points of contact with the lateral incisors were worn. Not all showed such wear, indicating to Greenfield that the mandibular canines were not yet functioning as fully as incisors as they would be in later hominins and modern humans.

Plavcan and Kelley (151), in questioning various aspects of the dual selection hypothesis, did not argue against the possibility that these changes reflected a change in canine function, but rather disputed that this change was the *cause* of canine reduction. The recent analysis of changes in canine size and shape from *Ardipithecus ramidus* to *Au. anamensis* to *Au. afarensis* reveal an initial reduction in upper canine size that remained constant from *Ardipithecus ramidus* to *Au. anamensis* to *Au. afarensis*. Both upper and lower canines only changed shape, toward the derived human condition with more incisor-like traits, *after* this initial reduction (167).

Thus, a good case can be made that with *Ardipithecus ramidus*, canine reduction and minimal canine sexual dimorphism may have had less to do with changes in diet and more to do with diminished male/male competition and/or with female choice of males with smaller canines. Yet, because of the tenuous links between canine sexual dimorphism and mating systems, it would a leap to conclude on this basis that the mating system of *Ardipithecus ramidus* was monogamy. Diminished competition among males would also be consistent with a relaxed multimale-mutifemale mating system like that of woolly spider monkeys.

It would be an even greater leap to suggest that modern humans inherited monogamous tendencies (which are debatable anyway) from *Ardipithecus ramidus*. That is both because direct descent of modern humans from a line extending back to *Ardipithecus ramidus* is unclear and because in several later hominin species (with some question about *Australopithecus afarensis* (174, 175), there appears to have been substantial body size dimorphism (128), potentially indicating elevated male-male competition and/or female selection for large males. Among characteristics deemed consistent with monogamous ancestry for humans are their relatively small testes, low sperm motility, and lack of penile spines (176). But, these traits do not specifically point to monogamy. In living primates, these traits are associated with minimal sperm competition, which occurs when females mate with only one (or few) males during their periovulatory periods (119). Minimal sperm competition occurs not only in today's monogamous primates but also in those that live and mate in polygynous groups (one male, several females). In both groups, females mate with only one (or a very limited number) of males, so that a female rarely has the sperm of multiple competing males in her reproductive tract at one time.

What is interesting, and the crux of the problem, is that despite body size sexual dimorphism in some later hominins, including early *Homo* (177), canine sexual dimorphism continued to decrease. It seems possible that, as per Greenfield's "dual-selection" hypothesis (150), the increasing incorporation of the canine into incisal functions in *Au. afarensis* onwards might partly explain this continued reduction. In addition, in the evolution of *Paranthropus* species, the zygomatic root shifted forward and prognathism decreased – the result would have been improved mechanical efficiency of the jaw muscles but with a reduction in gape. Prognathism decreases in the *Homo* lineage as well. Hylander and colleagues' (124) biomechanical analysis suggests that even if male-male competition had been high in these species, such changes in the face and jaw would have constrained the canine from evolving to greater size. And finally, returning to Darwin, since *Paranthropus* and *Homo* were more consistent bipeds than *Ardipithecus ramidus*, the ability to use hand-held weapons may have precluded selection for large canines anyway.

CANINE CONCLUSIONS

Overall then, what can we conclude about the curiously small size of human canines? First of all, it is clear that small, sexually monomorphic canines have been part of our evolutionary history since the time of *Ardipithecus ramidus* 4.4 million years ago. Secondly, it is difficult to see how the evolution of these diminutive canines in *Ardipithecus ramidus* could be related to changes in jaw architecture associated with chewing mechanically challenging foods, given what we think we know about the predominantly C3 diet of this species and its relatively thin enamel. On the other hand, changes in the morphology of *Australopithecus afarensis* canines hint at the incorporation of these teeth into incisal functions. Furthermore, the greater incorporation of C4 foods in the diet of *Australopithecus afarensis* and most later australopiths (especially *Paranthropus*) suggest that adaptive changes in jaw architecture associated with chewing mechanically challenging foods would have limited gape. Gape limitation in *Paranthropus* and minimally prognathic early *Homo* species in turn would now have acted as constraints on canine size, even if males began to compete more vigorously with one another.

None of this means, of course, that sexual selection was not operating during our evolutionary history, but simply that it did not result in much of sex difference in canine size. It has been suggested (178) that across primates there appears to be a "trade off" in sexual selection for large male canines vs. wide male faces. The evidence comes from a study of fourteen species of anthropoid primates, in which there is a negative correlation between sexual dimorphism in canine height and sexual dimorphism in the width of the face across the cheekbones. The authors of this study point out that male cheekbones become larger under the influence of testosterone during puberty and that several studies have demonstrated that human females have a preference for wide male faces. While the number of species in this study is small, it is nevertheless an interesting possibility that wide faces in both human and nonhuman primates may serve as a signals to females of male quality when canines lose their signaling function.

Leaving behind the question of our small canines, the next chapter considers dental evidence for another unique aspect of human biology – our prolonged periods of growth that are unmatched by any other primate. The question this next chapter looks into is whether any of the australopiths show signs of extending their growth periods beyond those of modern great apes.

4 Incisive Insights into Childhood

> Although a prolonged period of juvenile helplessness and dependency would, by itself, be disadvantageous to a species because it endangers the young and handicaps their parents, it is a help to man because the slow development provides time for learning and training, which are far more extensive and important in man than in any other animal.
>
> – Dobzhansky T
> *Mankind Evolving: The Evolution of the Human Species (179)*

Humans, along with their teeth, take a very long time to grow. A puppy does not stay little for long, and her first adult teeth come in around five to six months of age. Contrast this puppy with a human baby, who will not get her first adult teeth until she is around six *years* of age.

A protracted growth period is considered one of humanity's uniquely derived features relative to other primates. One view is that over the course of our evolutionary history, human juvenile growth was extended by the insertion of a novel developmental phase – childhood – which has been defined as a period after weaning during which a juvenile continues to depend on others for survival (180). Whether or not human childhood is unique, it is clear that subadult growth spurts begin at much later ages in humans than they do in African apes (181). Humans reach sexual maturity at comparatively later ages as well (181).

Viewed through the lens of "life history" theory, the scheduling of key life benchmarks such as age at weaning, age at sexual maturity, age at first reproduction, intervals between births, and natural life span, is shaped by natural selection. For different species experiencing different environments and ecologies, natural selection will result in different life history solutions – or adaptations – to the problems of survival and reproduction. Natural selection is thought to have optimized the amount of energy organisms devote to growth *versus* reproduction at different points in their lives. There is a trade off between the two because energy is limited and so can be devoted to either growth or reproduction, but usually not simultaneously to both (182).

According to life history theorists and biologists Eric Charnov and David Berrigan (182), the optimal age at which a primate species reaches sexual maturity is largely determined by adult mortality – the risk of death due to "extrinsic factors" such as predation, disease, or accidents. If that risk is high, the earlier a primate species can start reproducing, the better for leaving lots of offspring. If that risk is low, then the selective pressure to mature early is relaxed. But, that leaves open the question of whether there are actually selective advantages to prolonging juvenile growth periods and delaying reproduction, as primates tend to do in comparison to many other mammals, and humans do in the extreme.

One school of thought is that slower rates of growth are favored when juveniles face the risk of starvation. According to Janson and Van Schaik's "ecological risk aversion hypothesis" (183), extended juvenile periods with slow rates of growth in primates evolved as an adaptation to avoid feeding competition with adults, with whom juveniles must maintain close proximity for protection. In species that face uneven resource availability where the risk of starvation is greater, even slower growth rates are favored. For example, frugivorous primate species that rely on seasonally available fruits tend to have slower rates of growth that folivorous ones, who face less fluctuation in their food supplies (184).

Anthropologist Steve Leigh (181) points out that "ecological risk aversion" might help to explain the evolution of the extremely slow growth of humans. Leigh notes that human brains are energetically expensive. Slower rates of body growth would prevent starvation when so much energy is being devoted to brain growth and development. It is surprising how much energy the brain guzzles during childhood. Using PET scan and MRI data, human biologist Chris Kuzawa

(185) and colleagues recently found that the brain's use of glucose rises to a lifelong high during childhood, corresponding to 66% of the body's resting metabolic rate and 43% of the body's daily energy use. These researchers further found that rates of body growth during the period from infancy to puberty are slower when the brain is consuming glucose at its highest levels, potentially explaining why large-brained humans take so long to grow up. The selective benefits of large brains, such as greater success in obtaining food, avoiding predators, and acquiring mates, are the key to this scenario. Slow growth rates *permit* the diversion of energy to brain growth and development when larger brains make a substantial contribution to reproductive success.

A related idea is that slow human growth rates are related to *maternal* energetics. Primate females, and especially humans, make use of fat stores as body "capital" to supply the energy needed to gestate and nurse offspring. By growing for longer periods, human females may have been able attain the large body sizes required to support their offspring's energetically expensive brains (186). According to this idea, human mothers with delayed maturation would have had a selective advantage in being able to support offspring with large and complex brains.

Evolutionary theorist Theodosius Dobzhanksy, in the 1962 quotation that heads this chapter, encapsulates a long-held explanation for the evolution of childhood, namely that it provides necessary learning time (187). In this view, extended association with mothers affords children time to master complex cultural adaptations that will greatly enhance their survival and reproduction. The large evolutionary payoff of learned skills and knowledge offsets the cost of the reproductive delay that prolonged growth periods entail.

To what extent these different possible influences on our protracted growth periods came into play over the course of human evolution is not clear. That brains are in some way related to the pace of life history seems quite likely. There is a strong correlation between brain weight and gestation time across placental mammals (188). Similarly, there are strong correlations between brain weight and various aspects of life history across the primate order (187, 189–191). We may never know whether selection initially favored prolonged growth *because* of the increased learning time it provided, or whether increased learning time was a by-product of the slow growth that our energy-consuming large brains required. Nevertheless, through the study of fossil dental growth and development, great insight has been achieved into the question of whether early hominins shared this defining feature of our biology.

Published in 1981, Lovejoy's scenario of human evolution (discussed in Chapter 3) tied together monogamy and male provisioning of females and their young with a decrease in interbirth intervals that would have allowed early human ancestors to speed up their reproductive rates. Lovejoy's perspective was that these greater reproductive rates made possible "... protraction of the subadult (learning) period" (1981:348) with its consequent delay in age at first reproduction. Based on Anthropologist Alan Mann's studies of dental development in South African autralopiths, Lovejoy felt that there was "... strong evidence that a major demographic shift was fully developed 2.0 to 2.5 million years ago which included an extended period of sub-adult dependency" (1981:350).

Dean and Lucas (192) note that the idea of prolonged juvenile growth in australopiths goes back to Raymond Dart (193), who believed that the Taung Child's greatly worn deciduous teeth evinced a delay in the eruption of the first permanent molars. Long periods of childhood dependency in australopiths would mean that they had taken a "giant biological and cultural leap toward 'humanness,'" as science writer Bruce Bower put it (194). But, the view that early hominins had human-like childhoods was about to change dramatically over the course of the 1980s, as research on dental development increasingly focused on growth increments in teeth that represent absolute time.

Today it seems clear that early hominins tended to develop more quickly than do modern humans. However, today most researchers also recognize that not all aspects of dental development are equally informative about the length of juvenile growth periods, that not all aspects of dental development in early hominins can be characterized as either ape-like or human-like (195, 196), and that growth periods in early hominin species may have been rather variable (196). As this chapter recounts, such advances in understanding were made possible by much work–on clarifying the strength and nature of relationships between dental development and life history, on documenting ranges of variation in great ape and human dental development, on understanding enamel growth processes, and on applying innovative technologies.

HOW STRONG ARE THE LINKS BETWEEN DENTAL DEVELOPMENT AND JUVENILE GROWTH PERIODS?

In 1935, anatomist Adolph H. Schultz published a pioneering comparative study (197) of dental eruption in fifteen primate genera on 2,908 skulls from various laboratories and museums. His data on dental eruption sequences revealed a pattern today known as "Schultz's Rule." The idea rested on differences in eruption between molars, which have no deciduous predecessors, and the eruption of incisors, canines, and premolars, which do. Schultz noticed that in species with rapid growth periods, first and second molars are the first teeth to erupt into the oral cavity. But in slower growing species, the permanent successors of deciduous teeth – the permanent incisors, canines, and premolars – erupt early *relative* to molars.

In lemurs, for example, first and second molars erupt in advance of the permanent replacing teeth. This is not so in chimpanzees, for whom first molar eruption is followed by eruption of permanent incisors, and only after that do the second molars erupt. Humans are even more extreme in this regard, with permanent central incisors generally erupting before or together with first molars (198), and lateral incisors, canines, and premolars erupting before the second and third molars do. Schultz's Rule is a generalization about the sequence of permanent tooth eruption. According to this rule, longer-lived species shift the eruption of their replacing teeth to earlier in the sequence of dental eruption. The evolutionary reason for this has to do with tooth wear. If a species prolongs growth, it will be necessary to replace the deciduous teeth relatively earlier in the sequence of dental development because the deciduous teeth will simply wear out before the first molar erupts.

As Schultz put it, "... in man the tremendous and unique lengthening of postnatal growth, accompanied by corresponding increases in the ages of dental eruption, has brought about a dangerously long period of functioning for the deciduous teeth without any improvement in the durability of the substance of these teeth" (1953:543). Why didn't larger deciduous teeth evolve instead? Anthropologist B. Holly Smith points out (191) that this may not have been an option. In placental mammals, deciduous teeth begin to form *in utero* and are often already present at birth, when the small size of the face and jaw would limit the size of the deciduous teeth they could accommodate.

Beyond noting patterns of dental development, Schultz (199) found that the absolute ages at which teeth erupt tend to increase across the primate order in relation to the "pace" of life history. Schultz superimposed dental eruption ages over a diagram of life stages across different grades of primates (Figure 4.1, based on Schultz [199]). He used tooth eruption ages as a relatively stable marker of development associated with life stages. He defined infancy as the period between birth and the eruption of the first permanent tooth and juvenility as the period of time between this and the eruption of the last permanent tooth. Dental eruption could be used in this way because, as B. Holly Smith explains, teeth are developmentally integrated with the development of the organism as a whole. Teeth must be present for weaning to occur, permanent teeth must replace deciduous ones before they wear out, and the face and jaw must grow large enough so that there is space for the molars to erupt.

Building on Adolph Schultz's work, B. Holly Smith established a comparative primate context of great utility (191, 200). She found that across primate species, brain size, body size, and life history

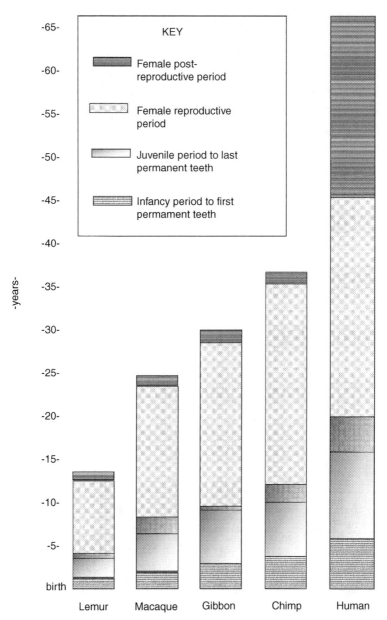

FIGURE 4.1: Approximate primate life history phases, based on Schultz (1960). Schultz defined the period of infancy as the period of time prior to the eruption of permanent teeth. He defined the juvenile period as the span between the eruption of the first and last permanent teeth. Dental eruption provided Schultz with a stable marker of development with which to define these phases. Approximate time periods in Schultz's diagram were retained here, with the exception of the postreproductive period, which is shown here to be much longer in humans than in other primates. Drawn by author.

variables were highly correlated with the age at which first molars erupt. For twenty-one primate species, the correlation between brain weight and M1 eruption was highest, at 0.98 (a correlation of 1 is a perfect correlation), supporting the view that the brain acts as a "pacemaker" for life history. The second highest correlation was to weaning age, at 0.93 (fifteen species), which in Smith's view reflects a functional tie: having first molars in occlusion at weaning facilitates the processing of solid food. Holly Smith's work suggested that first molar eruption ages determined for fossil forms could be used as a proxy for the paces of their life histories, and might be particularly informative about weaning age.

Today, most researchers on dental development in fossil hominins realize there are limitations to such inferences. Correlations among living species do not necessarily hold for fossil species that are millions of years old, as relationships may have changed over time. Furthermore, a correlation across a broad taxonomic range of species does not guarantee that at finer scales the correlation will hold true. Indeed, much of the variation in life history present in mammals occurs at higher taxonomic levels, i.e., it is associated with the evolution of major clades (201). More specifically, the idea that molar eruption age is related to life history variables within the great ape clade has recently been challenged (202). Even so, Kelley and Schwartz showed that ages at first reproduction in great apes are consistent with their ages at M1 eruption, with the earliest ages for both in gorillas, followed by chimpanzees, orangutans and lastly, humans (203).

Still, it isn't clear that the presence of first molars is functionally related to weaning. First molar eruption in wild chimpanzees does not appear to dictate when mothers introduce solid foods to their young (204). Modern humans are themselves a challenge to the notion that first molar eruption predicts weaning age. Although first molar eruption occurs at around five to six years of age in different human groups, weaning age is usually much earlier than this (205). These modern understandings of the limits of life history inference from teeth leave us with the recognition that first molar eruption may not be a specific indicator of weaning age. But, first molar eruption age nevertheless appears to be associated with ages at first reproduction within the great ape clade (203). Because this clade includes hominins, the association between age at first molar eruption and age at first reproduction may be usefully applied to them – assuming, of course, that the association has not changed over time.

OTHER ASPECTS OF DENTAL GROWTH AND DEVELOPMENT IN RELATION TO LIFE HISTORY VARIATION

Beyond first molar eruption, other aspects of dental growth and development have been studied for their potential relationships to the pace of life history in a comparative primate context. Gabrielle Macho (206) found that adult brain size, body size, weaning age, age at reaching sexual maturity and lifespan were strongly correlated across a broad taxonomic range of primates with the length of time it takes for first molar crowns to form. Her result makes sense if the time it takes to form first molar crowns affects the time at which first molars erupt. Yet, once again on a smaller scale, it has been noted (207) that the first molar crown formation times of humans, gorillas, and orangutans are essentially the same (202, 207), even though ages at first molar eruption differ among them. This finding suggests that first molar crown formation time is not a useful indicator of variation in growth periods within the great ape clade.

Another dental growth variable that may have some relationship to the pace of life history at a broad taxonomic level is the rate of enamel formation in the tips of tooth cusps. This variable shifts from faster to slower from monkeys to apes to humans (208). The possibility of relationships between other microstructural dental growth variables and life history variation has also been explored, but they are only weakly-to-moderately correlated with the scheduling of life history (209). Such relationships may be tenuous because process is not the same as outcome. For instance, while there is a strong link between first molar eruption age and life history variation across a broad taxonomic range, different processes or factors may contribute to different ages at eruption in different species. If natural selection acts on first molar eruption (an outcome) and there are many different processes or developmental stages that species alter to achieve that outcome (e.g., changing rates of crown or root formation, or changing their overall formation periods without altering their formation rates), then there is no reason to think that relationships between these processes and stages to life history variation will be strong.

Nevertheless, in recent years, one dental growth variable has been shown to be rather strongly associated with life history variation across the primate order. This variable is the length of time between "long-period" growth lines in enamel. To describe what we currently know about this relationship requires a digression into how enamel forms.

Enamel begins to form at the cusp tip of a developing crown (Figure 4.2). *Ameloblasts,* which are enamel-forming cells, secrete an organic matrix of proteins, primarily composed of *amelogenins,* which serve to "accept" mineral. As ameloblasts differentiate from their epithelial cell precursors, they move away from the boundary between enamel and dentine (the enamel-dentine junction or EDJ) and toward what will eventually become the enamel surface. During this *secretory stage* of enamel formation, enamel becomes 30% mineralized. In the following *maturation stage,* ameloblasts alternate between adding mineral to the matrix and removing water, amelogenin proteins, and other organic materials until the enamel attains a state of 96% mineralization.

During the secretory stage, as ameloblasts migrate away from the EDJ secreting the enamel matrix, ribbon-like mineralized structures known as "enamel prisms" or "enamel rods" form in their wake. In thin sections of enamel viewed under a transmitted light microscope, fine lines called *cross-striations* can be seen cutting across the diameter of each enamel prism at regular intervals (Figures 4.2 and 4.3). Studies dating to the early 1900s (210, 211) first suggested that cross-striations form according to a circadian rhythm. Mimura

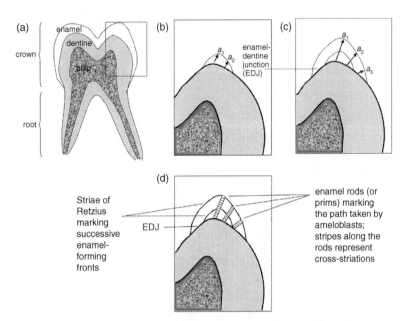

FIGURE 4.2: Diagram showing the process of enamel formation in a section through the middle of a tooth. The area in B is an enlarged portion of the cusp of the tooth, just as the first two ameloblasts, a_1 and a_2, have differentiated from the inner enamel epithelium and begun to move outward, secreting enamel matrix. The area in C shows the process of enamel formation at some later point in time, as a third ameloblast, a_3, has differentiated and has begun to move outward, secreting enamel matrix in its wake. The area in D diagrams mineralized structures known as enamel rods (or prisms) that mark the paths of ameloblasts. Along the rods are *cross-striations* or *short-period lines* that reflect daily fluctuation in the secretion of enamel matrix. Every few days, a slowing of enamel formation occurs at and is marked by dark lines called *striae of Retzius*. These lines represent the enamel-forming front at successive time periods. striae of Retzius are also called *long-period lines* and the number of days between straie is called the stria *periodicity*. All of the permanent teeth of an individual have the same stria periodicity, although periodicities range from six to twelve days in modern humans (see text for further explanation). Drawn by author.

confirmed this rhythm in 1939 by injecting growing mammals with lead acetate and sodium fluoride (212). These chemicals marked the enamel forming in their teeth at the time of injection. The number of cross-striations between these marking corresponded exactly to the number of days between injections.

Anthropologist Timothy Bromage used a similar experimental design to confirm the daily formation of cross-striations in enamel in a primate (simultaneously confirming the daily formation of analogous structures in the underlying dentine). More recently Rodrigo Lacruz and colleagues showed that mouse ameloblasts not only express "circadian clock" genes, genes required for generating circadian rhythms, but also produce amelogenin proteins according to a 24-hour rhythm (214). Cross-striations are therefore now well accepted as growth lines that form according to a daily rhythm.

Cross-striations also go by the name of "short-period increments" to differentiate their 24-hour formation period from that of "long-period increments" in enamel. Microscopically, long-period increments appear as dark lines traversing a series of enamel rods at an angle (Figure 4.3). They are also called *striae of Retzius*, after their discoverer Anders Retzius, a Swedish anatomist of the nineteenth century (74). Striae of Retzius are actually a series of growth layers in a three-dimensional tooth that form when all the ameloblasts along the enamel-forming front (Figure 4.2) simultaneously slow their secretion of the enamel matrix (215).

The simultaneous slowing of secretory ameloblasts occurs at regular intervals throughout all of the teeth of an individual (215, 216), which suggests a common cause. The interval, however, varies among individuals. In humans, the average interval for permanent teeth is eight or nine days, ranging from a minimum of six days to a maximum of twelve (217). To determine the interval for an individual's teeth, one counts the number of cross-striations falling between striae of Retzius. For the virtual (synchrotron-imaged) tooth section shown in Figure 4.3, striae of Retzius repeat with a periodicity of eight days.

Exactly what causes the regular periodicity of Retzius striae is not clear. There are metabolic (218) and cardiovascular rhythms with similar periodicity in humans and other animals (219), possibly suggesting that a systemic rhythm produces the periodicity of Retzius striae.

96 INCISIVE INSIGHTS INTO CHILDHOOD

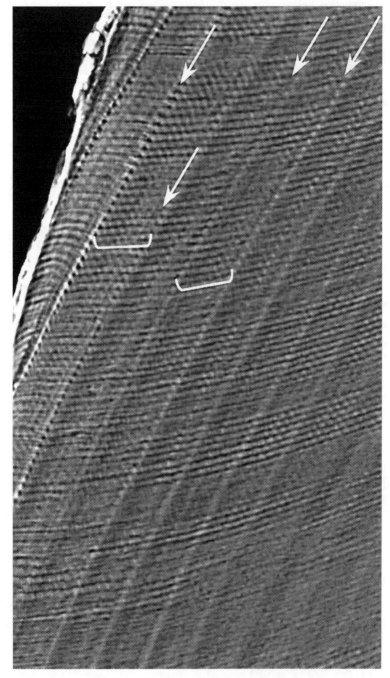

FIGURE 4.3: Synchrotron image of striae of Retzius (white arrows).
Eight short-period increments (white brackets) can be seen between the

Recently, anthropologist Timothy Bromage and colleagues developed the idea of systemic growth rhythms further (220, 221). They found that mean periodicities in mammalian species range from one to fourteen days, with small-bodied mammals (e.g., mice) having low periodicities and large-bodied mammals (e.g., elephants) having high periodicities. They also found that across primates, species' mean periodicities correlate with life history variables, mean body masses, mean basal metabolic rates and the mean rates at which bone-forming cells (osteoblasts) proliferate. These associations led them to conclude that "some aspect of metabolism" regulates "... cell proliferation rates and growth, thus controlling the pace, patterning, and co-variation of life history traits" across primates" (2012:131). In their view the periodicity of striae is a result of a species-specific metabolic growth rhythm, which they named the Havers-Halberg Oscillation (in reference to scientists Clopton Havers, hard tissue anatomist, and Franz Halberg, chronobiologist who pioneered the investigation of long-period rhythms).

Whether Bromage and colleagues are correct in the entirety of their explanation – that the periodicities of striae represent species-specific metabolic growth rhythms that control the pace of life history – there are moderate to strong correlations between mean periodicity and such aspects of life history variation as weaning age, age at sexual maturity, age at first breeding and lifespan. These associations, however, are not strong within the great ape clade, as lowland gorillas have higher periodicities than common chimpanzees, but are weaned and begin to reproduce at earlier ages than do chimpanzees. Stria periodicities along with other aspects of dental growth and

---

CAPTION FOR FIGURE 4.3: (cont.)

striae of Retzius. This tooth therefore has an eight-day periodicity. This is a fossil hominin tooth (DNH 67). The image is modified from (196) Figure 1 in Smith et al. (2015) *PLoS ONE*, reprinted here under the terms of the *Creative Commons Attribution License*, https://creativecommons.org/licenses/by/4.0/.

development discussed above clearly vary in their reliability as indicators of juvenile growth periods. It may be informative to study as many aspects of dental growth and development as possible in fossil species to determine if they give the same signal. Do they all, for example, indicate more rapid rates of development? Of course, when they don't give the same signal, that makes the problem of interpretation a lot more tricky.

DENTAL GROWTH AND DEVELOPMENT IN AUTRALOPITHS: HUMAN-LIKE OR APE-LIKE?

Alan Mann's pioneering study (222) suggested human-like patterns of development in four specimens of *Paranthropus robustus* from the site of Swartkrans. He noted, for example, that in the SK-64 mandible, the unerupted first permanent molar is close to completion, the second deciduous premolar root is almost complete, and there is no development as yet of the second permanent molar. This pattern of relative dental development is similar to a human at this stage of development, and not to a chimpanzee, in which the second permanent molar would have already begun to form. Because the teeth of autralopiths appeared to progress through the same stages of development relative to one another as those of humans, Alan Mann argued that they all likely erupted according to the same schedule as well.

Of course (and Alan Mann noted this), the whole sequence of tooth formation and eruption could have been accelerated in australopiths even if they maintained the same pattern of relative dental development as modern humans. What was needed here was an estimate of the absolute timing of development, and that is what Bromage and Dean's (223) innovative study, published in 1985, offered. These researchers counted enamel surface manifestations of striae of Retzius – perikymata (Greek: *peri* = around; *kymata* = waves) – to obtain such estimates. The wavelike "crests" and "troughs" of perikymata encircle the lateral enamel, enamel on the sides of teeth (Figure 4.4). As long as they haven't been worn or eroded away, perikymata can be directly observed and counted on fossil teeth under low

DENTAL GROWTH AND DEVELOPMENT IN AUTRALOPITHS

FIGURE 4.4: Synchrotron image of fossil hominin incisor DNH 71. The virtual section of the tooth shows the striae of Retzius (oblique dark lines) cropping out onto the enamel surface as perikymata (marked with asterisks). The image is modified from (196) Figure 1 in Smith et al. (2015) *PLoS ONE*, reprinted here under the terms of the *Creative Commons Attribution License*. https://creativecommons.org/licenses/by/4.0/

magnification (around 20x or so). Perikymata are simply surface manifestations of striae of Retzius so, the periodicity of an individual's striae is exactly the same as the periodicity of his or her perikymata. By counting all the perikymata from the tip of the tooth to its cervix (the "bottom" of the tooth) and then multiplying by the mean periodicity for a species, an estimate of their lateral enamel formation time can be made. Bromage and Dean's counts of perikymata on incisor teeth from *Australopithecus* and *Paranthropus* suggested abbreviated periods of lateral enamel formation in these teeth (223).

More to the point, Bromage and Dean estimated age at death in six immature australopith individuals. These individuals died when their incisor crowns had just completed forming. To estimate their ages at death, Bromage and Dean assumed that the incisor teeth had begun to form three or four months after birth. They added to this "initiation time" an estimate of the amount of growth that had occurred in the cusp of the tooth. In the cuspal region of the tooth, the striae of Retzius cover one another like layers of an onion and so do not emerge as countable perikymata on the crown surface. This period they estimated to be about six months, bringing the total to nine months of life so far. The crucial step was to add to this nine-month estimate the count of perikymata in the lateral enamel multiplied by the periodicity of seven days (then assumed to be the mean periodicity for both humans and hominins).

For example, for *Australopithecus afarensis* specimen LH2, the perikymata count of 130 was multiplied by seven days. Added to the nine-month estimate for growth prior to this, the age at which the incisor crown completed formation works out to about 3.25 years of age. Yet, previous estimates for the age of death based on modern human charts of dental development suggested the individual had died at 4.45 years of age. Indeed all of the hominins in their sample had a "... biological equivalence to modern man at roughly two-thirds the chronological age, demonstrating that they had growth periods similar to modern great apes" (1985:326).

Bromage and Dean's study broke new ground and many supporting studies based on growth increments followed. Despite the huge size of *Paranthropus boisei* molars, they appeared to form in shorter time periods than do those of modern humans (224). *P. boisei* molars appeared to accomplish this feat through increasing the rate at which ameloblasts secreted enamel matrix as well as by increasing the rate at which the crown grew in height. For immature individuals who died while their first molars were erupting (or had recently erupted), Beynon and Dean (225) estimated age at death by using growth increments on incisors, just as Bromage and Dean had done. (See Figure 4.5, which shows the LH 2 mandible, in which the incisor has just completed crown formation as the first molar is erupting.) This gave ages at M1 eruption for *Australopithecus* at 3.5 years and even slightly

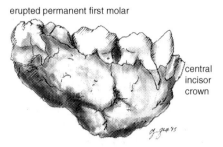

FIGURE 4.5: Artist's rendition of right side of LH 2 mandible (*Australopithecus afarensis*) in which lower the central incisor crown has just completed formation and the first molar has just erupted. Using growth increments (perikymata) from the incisor crown, it was possible to estimate the age at death of the LH2 juvenile and to therefore estimate the age at which the first molar erupted into occlusion. See text for additional explanation and discussion. Figure 4.5 is a drawing by Alyssa Starrett adapted by permission from Macmillan Publishers Ltd: Nature: Beynon AD, Dean MC. Distinct dental development patterns in early fossil hominids. *Nature*. 1988;335:509–514.

earlier in *Paranthropus*, within the known range of M1 eruption ages for apes but well outside the known range of M1 eruption in modern humans. Ape-like eruption times for australopths made sense given that their brain sizes were comparable to those of chimpanzees and first molar eruption ages are highly correlated with brain size across the primate order (190, 200).

Continuing along this line of investigation and using a large modern human comparative sample, Dean and colleagues (226) demonstrated that counts of perikymata on australopith anterior teeth were lower than those of *Homo sapiens*. They were especially low for the small anterior teeth of *Paranthropus*. Rates of cuspal enamel formation were also faster in australopiths than they are in modern humans. Both of these findings point to faster developmental rates in australopiths. Dental biologist and anthropologist Rodrigo Lacruz and colleagues (227) used a confocal microscope to obtain periodicities from naturally fractured teeth. This method allowed them to make serial "optical sections" from the fractured planes.

Overall, the periodicities they obtained for eight *Australopithecus africanus* teeth and seven *Paranthropus robustus* teeth centered around seven days. If periodicities bear some relationship to the pace of life history, these results too suggest a faster pace in australopiths than in modern humans, whose periodicities center around eight to nine days (217).

In parallel with this work on incremental growth lines in teeth, work on patterns of dental development in fossil hominins continued to progress. As long ago as 1951, Broom and Robinson had suggested that the eruption patterns of *Paranthropus* were more similar to those of *Homo* than to *Australopithecus* (228). Using radiographs, Christopher Dean (229) seemed to find evidence of this in the nearly simultaneous eruption of the first molar and first incisor in both *Homo* and *Paranthropus*. *Australopithecus afarensis* and *Australopithecus africanus* were more like modern apes in erupting their first permanent molars well before erupting their incisors. Following Schultz's logic, *Australopithecus afarensis* and *africanus* would be assumed to have had abbreviated growth periods compared to both *Paranthropus robustus* and to modern humans. Modern humans have to erupt their permanent anterior teeth relatively early in order to replace their long-functioning and worn out deciduous precursors. This explanation however, did not seem to fit *Paranthropus robustus*, whose deciduous teeth did not show excessive wear. Dean therefore suspected that the similarity between *Paranthropus robustus* and modern humans was superficial—that it represented homoplasy rather than a shared derived feature. Further analysis based on CT scans suggested that *Paranthropus* may not have been like modern humans in the simultaneous eruption of the M1/I1 (230) after all, but that it did have a more human-like M1/I1 developmental pattern (231).

Follow-up studies also suggested a more ape-like overall pattern of dental development in australopiths. In 1986, Holly Smith (195) plotted stages of dental development of fossil hominins on developmental charts for apes versus humans. *P. boisei*, *P. robustus*, *Au. africanus* and *Au. afarensis* all were more similar in their relative states of dental development to apes than to modern humans. The following year, Conroy and Vannier (232) CT-imaged developing teeth inside of the Taung Child's jaw, whose first molar had erupted. They compared the developmental state of the Taung Child to that of a 3–4-year old chimpanzee and a 5–6-year old modern human, both of whose first molars had just erupted. Like the chimpanzee, the Taung Child's anterior teeth had not yet developed much of their roots. The modern human, by contrast, had more advanced anterior tooth development, in line with Schultz's rule.

These studies of incremental growth and patterns of dental development did not go unchallenged. Chief among the critics were Alan Mann and colleagues, whose analyses helped move this entire area of research forward. With respect to studies of incremental growth, Mann and colleagues (233) questioned whether cross striations or striae of Retzius were truly markers of time in enamel, whether the latter consistently emerged onto the enamel surface as perikymata, whether comparisons had been made to a sufficient number and range of modern humans as well as apes, and whether anterior tooth formation times reliably indicated the length of juvenile growth periods.

The first of these criticisms spurred Bromage's (213) demonstration of the circadian rhythm of cross-striations. The second criticism spurred work demonstrating a close correspondence between striae and perikymata counts on anterior teeth (234). The third was partly addressed by later studies that broadened the range and number of modern humans to which hominins were compared. But, even today, we lack complete knowledge of the extent to which ape and human dental development can vary, and as this knowledge trickles in, interpretations can and do change. As for the fourth criticism, this is still valid. Ape anterior teeth are larger than those of modern humans – their crowns take absolutely longer to form than those of modern human teeth (235) – yet their life histories are certainly faster paced. That fact suggests it is unwise to rely on anterior teeth as an indicator of life history variation within hominoids, including fossil hominins.

Up until just the last few years, the consensus has been that hominins correspond more closely to apes than to modern humans in the pace and pattern of their dental development, and by extension in the length of their juvenile growth periods. Yet, it was also clear that they were not identical to modern apes in their dental development. For example, early fossil hominins had abbreviated anterior tooth crown formation times relative to great apes (196) as well as to most humans (226). Another difference is that robust australopith crowns have perikymata that are more uniformly distributed along their enamel surfaces than do either modern humans or chimpanzees, which show greater compaction of perikymata toward the cervix (236). The specific enamel formation processes underlying this difference are not clear from examining the enamel surface, but clearly the robust australopiths were forming their enamel differently in some way than do either apes or humans. While such observations hint at hominin uniqueness, the most recent research gives hominins their dental developmental due.

DENTAL DEVELOPMENT IN AUSTRALOPITHS RE-ENVISIONED: NEITHER HUMAN NOR APE-LIKE?

As teeth erupt, they move from their bony crypts through the jaw bone (specifically the alveolar bone), then break through the gingiva (gums), and finally come to rest in their functional positions in the jaw. It has been pointed out that the event of M1 eruption in fossil hominins is assessed from bones and teeth, yet correlations between M1 eruption, brain size, body size, and life history features in living primates are based on M1 emergence through the gingiva, soft tissue which does not preserve in the fossil record (203). It has also been pointed out that estimates of first molar eruption in fossil hominins using growth increments are based on a mix of actual data from the fossils (e.g., counts of perikymata) and estimates of unknown variables (e.g., periodicity, initiation of crown formation, cuspal enamel formation)

(196, 203). With these points in mind, two sets of researchers have recently conducted new assessments of australopith dental development.

Just how similar australopiths are to apes or humans in dental development requires knowledge of variation within and among species of great apes as well as among different human population groups. M1 eruption ages, it turns out, are more variable than previously realized, both within the great apes and within modern humans. Up until recently, chimpanzee M1 eruption ages were obtained primarily from captive individuals, and fell into the range of 3 to 3.5 years (203). Now data are becoming available from individuals who grew up in the wild, and their average age for first molar eruption is close to four years of age (203). Other primate studies have also shown a tendency for dental eruption to occur earlier in captive individuals (237). Possibly this is because in in captivity, greater availability and stability of food resources allow growth rates to accelerate. Meanwhile, there is much variation within great apes. Lowland gorilla first-molar eruption appears to be slightly earlier than that of chimpanzees while orangutans top the great ape M1 eruption chart at 4.6 years of age (203, 207).

As for modern humans, average M1 eruption ages for humans are said to be around 5.8 years (203), yet this average masks much interpopulation variation. In her review of dental eruption data worldwide, dental anthropologist Helen Liversidge (in (238)) found that Africa has great variation in M1 eruption ages. For one Kenyan population, the average age of M1 eruption was 4.74 years in girls and 5.15 years in boys. But also in Kenya, another population exhibited M1 eruption ages of 6.08 years on average for girls and 6.47 years for boys. So how do the recently revised age estimates for M1 eruption in hominins compare?

Kelley and Schwartz reevaluated M1 eruption in six fossil hominins by estimating when gingival emergence would have occurred in these specimens (203). This had the result of shifting M1 eruption to earlier ages than previous estimates, ranging from 2.9 years of age

(LH2, *Australopithecus afarensis*, and STS 24, *Australopithecus africanus*) to 3.8 or 3.9 years of age (SK 62, *Paranthropus robustus*). When they considered the known range of eruption in apes – 3.8 (gorillas) to 4.6 years (orangutans), it seemed to them that dental eruption in hominins occurred even earlier than it does in today's apes!

What might that mean? It might mean that these australopiths also had more accelerated life histories even than apes – except for one small problem. Using newly acquired data, Kelley and Schwartz reanalyzed the relationship Holly Smith showed between M1 emergence and brain size across anthropoid primates. They found that if you plotted brain sizes of hominins on these graphs, you could predict what their M1 emergences ages "should" be for their brain sizes. It turned out that M1 emergence ages predicted in this way were all greater than the new estimates Kelley and Schwartz obtained for M1 emergence ages in the fossil hominins. What could account for the mismatch? Perhaps their fossil hominin M1 gingival emergence estimates were all uniformly too low. Or, perhaps the relationship between brain size and M1 gingival emergence in australopiths differed from that of living hominoids.

And, finally, it is also possible, as Kelley and Schwartz noted, that M1 gingival emergence in australopiths could be out of sync with their pace of life history and rates of somatic growth. There is precedent for such a situation in modern primates. A family of prosimians, the Indriids of Madagascar, have fast rates of dental development and early weaning coupled with slow rates of somatic growth (239). Laurie Godfrey proposes that early dental eruption and weaning together with slow infant growth rates are adaptations to the severe drought conditions Indriids face (239). Essentially, slow infant growth rates reduce the amount of milk mothers need to produce on a daily basis, while the presence of deciduous teeth at birth allows mothers to wean their offspring early. These adaptations lessen the energetic burden of lactation during drought conditions, when resources are scarce. Perhaps in australopiths, like these Indriids, selection pressures associated with energetic stress on lactating mothers account for M1 emergence times that are earlier than expected on the basis of these hominin's brain sizes.

Most recently, anthropologist Tanya Smith and her colleagues shed some light – actually, very high-energy x-rays – on this conundrum (196). They used a technique called x-ray synchrotron microtomography to create "virtual sections" of fossil teeth. The work was done at the European Synchrotron Radiation Facility in Grenoble, France, which is one of only a few such facilities in the world. This technique allowed Tanya Smith and her colleagues to "see inside" teeth without having to cut them up. They were able to image both long- and short-period lines (see Figures 4.3 and 4.4). They were also able to determine actual periodicities and actual time periods for cuspal enamel formation. Finally, they could see the "neonatal" line, an accentuated line in enamel that marks the event of birth. Using that line, and matching the pattern of other accentuated lines like a bar code across other developing teeth, they reassessed age at death in twelve australopiths. As they explained, their method required no estimation by substituting values from great apes or humans for unknown variables. All of the variables estimated in previous studies – periodicity, initiation, and cuspal enamel formation – were directly ascertained from the fossil teeth themselves.

Smith and colleagues then determined what the "dental ages" of the hominins would be based on a chimpanzee-like developmental schedule. In other words, how old would these hominins have been when they died if their teeth developed on a chimpanzee time frame? It turned out that the "chimpanzee" ages didn't match the synchrotron-derived ages at death. But the "dental ages" of the hominins predicted on the basis of human developmental standards also didn't match the synchrotron-derived ages. So, it seems that the autralopiths developed according to their own schedule. Furthermore, some of them appear to have been on the high end of the ape range for M1 emergence – the age at death in one specimen (STS 24) whose first molars had just erupted into occlusion was 4.4 years. One of the robust australopiths (DNH 107) had an age at death of

4.8 years, but with only slight wear (and the right mandibular incisor had not yet erupted), suggesting M1 emergence was not much earlier.

So, not all australopiths, it seems had early ages of M1 eruption. Indeed, the low end of first molar eruption average values in modern humans – 4.74 years in girls and 5.15 years in boys – is close to the M1 eruption age of one of the robust australopiths. Finally, Smith and colleagues also found that australopiths did *not* have uniformly lower periodicities than modern humans. While the averages for each species are small, the fossil australopith periodicities ranged between 6 to 12 days, very similar to those of modern humans. (Chimpanzee periodicities are found in a narrower range of 5–7 days).

CONCLUSIONS

Taking Kelley and Schwartz's and Smith's and colleagues' reassessments together, it now seems that some fossil hominin species had faster dental development than some modern apes, while others were at the slow end of the modern ape developmental range. Based on their M1 eruption ages, australopiths do not seem to have quite reached the slow developmental pace of modern humans, though some individuals may have come close. In a way, this should not come as a huge surprise, as these species had their own evolutionary histories and were neither ape nor human. Their rates of dental development and the paces of their life histories would have been varied, shaped by selection pressures in the diverse environments and time periods in which they lived.

There are still some unresolved questions, however. Recalling the dissociation between dental development and somatic growth in Indriids, it would be interesting to know whether rates of somatic growth in these australopiths matched their rates of dental development. Another unresolved question is how these australopiths' human-like periodicities comport with their generally earlier ages of first molar eruption relative to modern humans. If periodicity is determined by a metabolic rhythm that "sets the pace" of life history as Bromage and colleagues propose (220, 221), then why do these australopiths have generally earlier ages at M1 eruption than do most modern humans? Clearly, more basic research on living primates is required to discover the many factors that may influence periodicity, M1 eruption ages, rates of somatic growth and development and the disjunctions that can occur among them.

This chapter concludes the first part of this book, which to this point has considered how the study of fossil teeth informs us about the biology of our distant australopith ancestors. Different facets of the biology of our ancient ancestors and close relatives were considered: their dietary proclivities and flexibility, the initial causes of and constraints on the evolution of their canine teeth, and their developmental rates. Teeth tell us that these early hominins were diverse – in some ways human-like, in some ways more like great apes, and in some ways, unique. Species of the genus *Homo*, however, demonstrate a clearer trend. With some exceptions (e.g., *Homo floresiensis*), they become more "human-like" over time in their dental morphology, dietary breadth, and developmental rates. Part II traces these changes through teeth.

PART II **Teeth and the Genus** *Homo*

5 March of the Bipeds: The Later Years

> We have come to the conclusion that, apart from *Australopithecus* (*Zinjanthropus*), the specimens we are dealing with from Bed I and the lower part of Bed II at Olduvai represent a single species of the genus *Homo* and not an australopithecine ... But if we are to include the new material in the genus *Homo* (rather than set up a distinct genus for it, which we believe to be unwise), it becomes necessary to revise the diagnosis of this genus.
>
> – Leakey LSB, Tobias PV, and Napier JR
> A new species of the genus *Homo* from Olduvai Gorge. *Nature*.

With these words, Louis Leakey and colleagues named the species *Homo habilis*. In so doing, they widened the definition of the *Homo* genus to include a species with smaller average brain size than that of *Homo erectus*, which was up until then the earliest known species of our genus. To include this species in the genus *Homo*, Leakey and colleagues revised the so-called "cerebral Rubicon" dividing *Australopithecus* from *Homo* down to 600 cubic centimeters from the 750 cubic centimeters used up until that point (240). This is what Leakey et al. meant by revising the "diagnosis of the genus." Indeed, over the history of paleoanthropology, definitions of the genus *Homo* have expanded further, encompassing the varied features of fossils assigned to the genus (177, 241). Thus, how to define the genus *Homo* – and indeed how to define a genus in the first place – are matters of long-standing and vigorous debate (47, 177).

In a 2014 review paper in the journal *Science*, paleoanthropologist Susan Antón and colleagues' employed a broad definition of the genus that included specimens traditionally assigned to the species *Homo habilis* (e.g., KNM-ER 1813). In their view, these specimens shared with later genus members a suite of characteristics that contributed to their evolutionary success. Namely, these are:

"... increases in average body and brain size and changing dental size coupled with increased toolmaking and stone transport" which they contend "suggest dietary expansion, developmental plasticity, cognitive evolution and social investments" (2014: 1236828-8). The present chapter gives an overview of species that have been considered to be members the genus *Homo*, that to varying degrees partake in the package of adaptations Antón and colleagues describe. Key dental features and possible phylogenetic relationships to anatomically modern human are integrated into this overview.

HOMO HABILIS

Discovered at Olduvai Gorge in 1959 were some hominin teeth that were strikingly different from those of Nutcracker man found that same year (13). These teeth, a lower premolar and lower third molar (wisdom tooth), were small and narrow from side to side, quite unlike the enormous and square premolars and molars of Nutcracker man. Yet, the teeth appeared to be of equivalent antiquity. Additional finds, including more teeth, parts of a cranium, and hand, wrist, and foot bones, led Louis Leakey and colleagues in 1964 to coin a new species – *Homo habilis*. This earliest species of the *Homo* lineage dates at least as far back as 2.3 million years ago (242, 243) and possibly as early as 2.8 million years ago (244).

To Leakey and colleagues, this species rather than Nutcracker man was the more likely candidate for the maker of the two-million-year-old stone tools found at Olduvai Gorge. These Oldowan tools (after Olduvai Gorge) were made by hitting one stone against another, removing flakes that were then used as tools. Based on two parietal bones (parts of the cranium), Leakey and colleagues reconstructed the cranium of *Homo habilis*, coming up with a larger cranial volume than for Nutcracker man. So, *Homo habilis* was judged to be the more brainy (i.e., more likely toolmaker) of the two species. Furthermore, their analysis of *Homo habilis* hand bone fossils suggested that this species had could achieve a precision grip: the kind of grip used when grasping an object, like a pencil, between the fingertips and thumb.

Hence, the literal meaning of *Homo habilis*—handyman. Add to this picture the smaller molar teeth and more human-like premolars (although with relatively large incisors), and both mentally and dentally, *Homo habilis* seemed to Leakey, Napier, and Tobias to deserve a place within our own genus.

Later discoveries (of course) greatly complicated the picture. To begin with is a specimen described in 1987 by Donald Johanson and colleagues (245). Its palate and teeth indicated that it was *H. habilis*, but it seems to have had longer arms than Lucy! This is not exactly what was expected for a species within our genus. Finds of *H. habilis* from other sites: Koobi Fora in Kenya and from Malawi (246) suggested that *H. habilis* should be split into two – one species with australopith limb proportions but more *Homo* like teeth and jaws (including the original finds from Olduvai) and a second species called *Homo rudolfensis* with more *Homo*-like limb proportions but with jaws and teeth that were more robust (247). Indeed, one of the *H. rudolfensis* skulls from Koobi Fora has posterior teeth (molars and premolars) greater than the mean for *Paranthropus boisei* (15).

But then, a very *H. rudolfensis*-looking find was recovered from Olduvai, where *Homo habilis* was originally discovered (248). Such variability from a single site suggests that *Homo habilis* may simply be more variable than previously realized, and should not be split into two species (248). In 2012, Meave Leakey and colleagues discovered additional early *Homo* fossils that they argued confirmed the coexistence of two early *Homo* species in Pleistocene East Africa, aside from *Homo erectus* (249). Most recently in their 2014 synthesis on early *Homo*, Antón and colleagues dealt with the diversity of early *Homo* by categorizing them into two different "groups" rather than into two different species, named according to their most well-known representatives. So, they define a KNM-ER 1813 "group" and a KNM-ER 1470 "group" of early *Homo*, differing in brain and body size as well as in several cranial and dental features, but with overlapping ranges of variation (177).[1]

The *H. habilis* vs. *H. rudolfensis* story highlights a perennial problem in taxonomy about how much morphological variation is present within living species and how to use this information to draw species boundaries in the fossil record. It is sometimes difficult to draw species boundaries even among living organisms, and where those boundaries are drawn depends on how species are defined. Ernst Mayr's biological species concept (BSC), defined in various ways (see [250] for a review), rests on the notion that species are interbreeding groups of organisms with no (or negligible) gene exchange with other groups. Such groups evolve independently of one another, maintaining the integrity of the species. Species can also be defined morphologically, in terms of groups of organisms that share distinctive features. But, where one draws the lines among them on this basis may not reflect the species as an interbreeding evolutionary unit, as Mayr's definition does.

In the field of paleoanthropology, fossil species are generally defined on the basis of morphological features. The morphological definition of species is a particular problem in paleoanthropology because, with small and sometimes tiny sample sizes, a fossil species' full range of morphological variation is unknown. A future paleoanthropologist might uncover remains of our highly diverse single interbreeding species of modern humans and erroneously split them into many species. So, when new species are named on the basis of a few new fossils, it may be quite possible that they are in reality simply variants of pre-existing ones (what Tim White argued about *Kenyanthropus platyops* – see Chapter 1).

Furthermore, whether morphologically defined fossil species were interbreeding evolutionary units that would fit Mayr's biological species concept is unknown (although, when possible, analysis of ancient DNA offers insight into gene exchange in ancient populations). Regarding Antón et al.'s (2014) solution to the early *Homo*

---

[1] Their two newly defined "groups" of early *Homo* do not correspond to exactly the same set of fossil specimens formerly divided into *Homo habilis* and *Homo rudolfensis*.

taxonomy problem, naming "groups" of early *Homo* is useful because it reflects our uncertainty about their status as separate species. In this book, simply for ease of reference, these groups will be "lumped" under the *Homo habilis* species name, although the diversity of non-*erectus* early *Homo* will be recognized.

Still, the question of whether certain *Homo habilis* (including *H. rudolfensis* specimens) should be included in the genus *Homo* at all has frequently been raised (251), ever since Louis Leakey and colleagues announced the species and revised the definition of the genus in 1964. That year, the eminent paleoanthropologist Sir Wilfrid Le Gros Clark opined that the differences of *Homo habilis* from *Australopithecus* were trivial (252). A more substantive criticism from Wood and Collard (47) highlights the finding of their cladistic analysis in which *Homo habilis* (and *Homo rudolfensis*) do not form a clade with *Homo sapiens* that is exclusive of australopiths.

On the other hand, Gonzalez-Jose et al. (44) in their modular analysis of hominin crania find the opposite and suggest that the entire *Homo* clade, including *Homo habilis* shares more "flexed cranial bases, more retracted faces and an increase in neurocranial globularity" (2008:776). In a similar vein, Antón and colleagues emphasize that there are greater average brain and body sizes in non-*erectus* early *Homo* (i.e., both 1470 and 1813 groups) than there are in *Australopithecus*. Thus, while *Homo habilis* seems to hover at or just beyond the threshold to the *Homo* genus, the rest of the species discussed in this chapter, have clearly passed beyond it.

HOMO ERECTUS AND HOMO ANTECESSOR

Homo erectus approaches the human condition to a much greater degree than any previous hominin species. In some ways it took a quantum leap in the human direction. It was the first hominin species to leave Africa, expanding into a wide range of habitats in Asia and Europe (13). It was also the first hominin to have long legs and short arms – limb proportions similar to those of modern humans (13). *Homo erectus* possessed a significantly larger brain (on average) than *Homo habilis* (13), had a larger body (253), made more sophisticated stone tools, incorporated more vertebrate meat into its diet (13), and may have been the first hominin to control fire (254–256). But *Homo erectus* was not fully modern: its brain size was on average smaller than that of modern humans and was housed in a distinctive cranium with large brow ridges, receding frontal bones and an angled occipital region.

Dentally, *Homo erectus* comes closer to modern humans than do previous hominins. The largest sample of *Homo erectus* teeth ever recovered from a single location is from Zhoukoudian cave near Beijing, China (15). This is the cave where the first Chinese *Homo erectus* was discovered, at the time named "*Sinanthropus pekininsis*" or "Peking Man." (Unfortunately nearly all of the original fossils were lost just before the outbreak of World War II.) The very first *Homo erectus* fossils were discovered prior to the Peking Man discovery, on the island of Java (hence "Java Man") by anatomist/physician Eugene Dubois in 1891. Dubois assigned these fossils to a species he named "*Pithecanthropus erectus*." It was not until 1950 that that these two species were recognized as having such strong similarity that they were subsumed into the species known today as "*Homo erectus*" (257).

A single well-preserved lower left molar has a special place of honor in the discovery of "Peking Man." It was the human-like morphology of this molar that led anatomist Davidson Black to name a new species of ancient hominin (258). On his lecture tour through America and Europe during 1927–1928, Black reportedly carried this precious molar in a small gold receptacle that hung from his watch chain (13). Christening a new species on the basis of this single tooth was controversial. Yet, subsequent excavations at Zhoukoudian cave revealed a treasure trove of fossils (including several skull caps) representing 40–45 individuals (13) that supported Davidson Black's interpretation: he and his coworkers had indeed discovered an extinct hominin species from China.

In 1933, Davidson Black (259) described the teeth of *Homo erectus* from Zhoukoudian cave in magnificent detail. One of his observations was that, as in modern humans, the first molar is the largest tooth of the molar series and the third is smallest and often much reduced in size. That is generally *not* the case in earlier hominins (15), though molar size relationships are somewhat variable in earlier *Homo*. The complete lack of third molar formation – called "third molar agenesis"– occurs with high frequency in some modern human populations (260). The earliest known case of third molar agenesis in human evolution also appears in Chinese *Homo erectus* – in a 600,000-year-old specimen found near Lantian (261).

Overall, the premolars and molars of Zhoukoudian *Homo erectus* are smaller than those of *Australopithecus* and *Homo habilis* (15). A prominent and distinctive feature of the upper incisors is that they are *shovel-shaped* in having raised ridges along their edges (on the lingual side of the tooth) together with a bulbous "eminence" at their base (Figure 5.1). Shovel-shaped incisors similar to these are found in living indigenous Chinese (262–264). Black further observed that similar to Neanderthals and unlike most living humans, the Zhoukoudian teeth had enlarged pulp cavities with roots that separated at a greater distance from the tooth crown. Such teeth are termed *taurodont*, literally meaning "bull-like teeth" (see Figure 5.2 showing a taurodont Neanderthal molar) (265). Taurodont roots may have had an adaptive function in prolonging the life of teeth subjected to high rates of wear (265). As wear progressed, the exposed pulp would produce additional dentine which would serve as a chewing surface. The division between the roots would not be reached in a taurodont tooth until wear became extreme (265).

Homo erectus spanned a huge geographic range and time period. The earliest appearing *Homo erectus* specimens date to about 1.8 million years ago and are from East Africa, the site of Dmanisi Georgia, and the island of Java (15). The species appears to have persisted in Java to as late as 100,000 years ago and possibly less than 50,000 years ago (266). With such a wide distribution through space and time, *Homo erectus* was quite variable in form, resulting in numerous attempts to divide the genus into different species (reviewed in [253]). Recent interpretations and fossil finds, however,

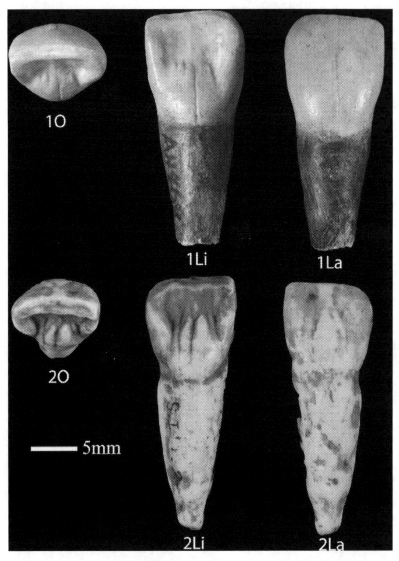

FIGURE 5.1: High fidelity casts of two shovel-shaped incisors of *Homo erectus* from Zhoukoudian Cave, China. There are two specimens shown in different views. Specimen 1 is shown in occlusal view in 1O, in lingual view in 1Li and in labial view in 1La. Specimen 2 is shown in occlusal view in 2O, in lingual view in 2Li and in labial view in 2La. Images courtesy of Song Xing, of the Institute of Vertebrate Paleontology and Paleoanthropology in Beijing.

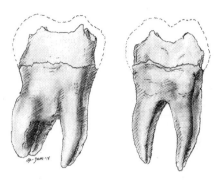

FIGURE 5.2: Neanderthal first molar (left) compared to that of a modern human (right). Drawing by Alyssa Starrett is based on a synchrotron micro CT image of these teeth (Figure 5 in Macchiarelli et al., 2006). The enamel cap has been made transparent to show the shape of the enamel-dentine junction. Note the taurodont roots of the Neanderthal tooth (see text). Adapted by permission from Macmillan Publishers Ltd: *Nature*: Macchiarelli R, Bondioli L, Debenath A, Mazurier A, Tournepiche J-F, Birch W, et al. How Neanderthal molar teeth grew. *Nature*. 2006;444: 748–751.

suggest that these geographic and temporal variants can reasonably be lumped into the single species, *Homo erectus* (267).

The early 1.8 MY *Homo erectus* sample from Dmanisi, Georgia offers a thought-provoking example of variation from a single site. To date, five skulls have been recovered in a great range of shapes and sizes that span the variation present in African *H. erectus*, *H. habilis*, and *H. rudolfensis* (268). Four of these skulls are illustrated in Figure 5.3. Such great variation from one location may suggest that many of the specimens currently allocated to all three of these species could be part of a single variable one, although (of course) not all paleoanthropologists agree with this interpretation (177).

The Dmanisi fossils are also fascinating because they include specimens with small cranial capacities in the range of *Homo habilis*, but with several *Homo erectus*-like features including modern limb proportions, well-developed brow ridges, and progressive reduction in size from the first through third molars (269). Their small cranial

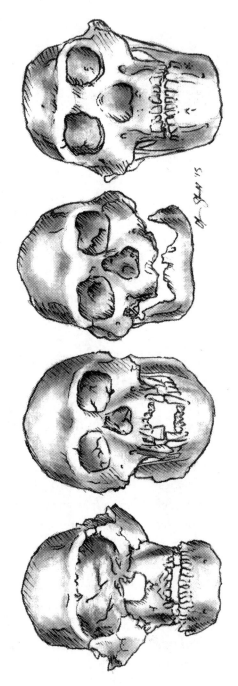

FIGURE 5.3: Four of the skulls from Dmanisi redrawn by Alyssa Starrett from Figure 2 in Lordkipanidze David, Ponce de León Marcia S., Margvelashvili Ann, Rak Yoel, Rightmire G. Philip, Vekua Abesalom, Zollikofer Christoph P.E. A complete skull from Dmanisi, Georgia, and the evolutionary biology of Early Homo. *Science.* 18 OCTOBER 2013;342:328. *Reprinted with permission from AAAS.*

capacities overturned a long-held assumption that brains sizes beyond the *Homo habilis* range, as *Homo erectus* from Java and China possessed, were necessary for hominins to leave Africa and expand into new, less hospitable climes. The Dmanisi hominins' smaller brain sizes link them to earlier African *Homo*. Dentally, they are similar to early East African *Homo erectus* in their molar size and morphology, the more narrow shape of their dental arcades, and their single-rooted upper premolars (269). Modern humans often have two-rooted upper premolars (74).

Whether *Homo erectus* was present in Western Europe is unclear. The earliest occupants there, having a combination of *Homo erectus* and modern human features, have been placed in their own species: *Homo antecessor* (270). They appear for the first time 1.2–1.1 million years ago in Spain (271). The largest sample of this species is from an 800,000 year old site called Gran Dolina, where over a hundred fossils have been recovered (272). These specimens have brow ridges and cranial capacities in the *Homo erectus* range, but faces that are modern in possessing a *canine fossa:* a sunken area above the canine tooth that does not appear in Neanderthals because of the projecting faces of the latter. The teeth retain some primitive morphological features and appear to be more similar in size to those of African early *Homo* than they are to European Middle Pleistocene hominins (273).

Homo antecessor brings us to the Middle and Late Pleistocene, geologic time periods from approximately 781–126,000 years ago and from 126–12,000 years ago, respectively. During this latest stage of human evolution, there was continued regional diversification across the continents of Africa, Asia, and Europe. But, mounting evidence from DNA studies suggests that diverse lineages – Neanderthals, Denisovans, and anatomically modern humans – may have retained enough similarity to have interbred and exchanged genes, as described below.

HOMO HEIDELBERGENSIS

In the fossil-rich Mauer sandpit near Heidelberg, Germany a massive jaw with disproportionately smaller teeth came to light in 1907.

One year later, a new species was named: *Homo heidelbergensis* (274). While not catching on at first, the name has come to refer to comparably aged European, African, and possibly Asian forms (274) that had expanded crania relative to *Homo erectus* with a less-angulated occipital region (among other cranial differences). Along with its bigger brain, *Homo heidelbergensis* exhibited some new behaviors, constructing shelters (on the beaches of the French Riviera no less) and fashioning wooden spears (15). Spears and the remains of large mammals at various sites suggest that *Homo heidelbergensis* was a formidable hunter.

While some authorities include middle Pleistocene Asian hominins in the species *Homo heidelbergensis* (15, 275), others limit the species to middle-Pleistocene African and European forms, and view the Asian forms as later *Homo erectus* (276). Dentally, like *Homo erectus*, *Homo heidelbergensis* had taurodont teeth. But different from earlier species, *Homo heidelbergensis* tended to have smaller posterior teeth (premolars and molars) and larger anterior teeth (incisors and canines) (13, 275, 277). Hypothesized selection pressures, some acting to reduce the size of posterior teeth and others to increase the size of anterior teeth in *Homo heidelbergensis* are discussed in relation to Neanderthals in Chapter 8. In addition to being smaller, *Homo heidelbergensis* molars also tended to be simpler, with a reduced number of cusps (13). There are a number of other distinctive dental traits in *Homo heidelbergensis*, including long anterior tooth roots, asymmetry of the first lower premolar and "swelling" of the buccal face (side facing the cheek) of the molars (275).

Generalizations about *Homo heidelbergensis* belie the diversity of this species, which shows extensive variation in cranial, facial, and dental form (15). Dentally there seems to be a divide between Asian and African *Homo heidelbergensis* on the one hand and European *Homo heidelbergensis* on the other (275). For example, a derived reduction and simplification of the posterior teeth was more apparent in European than Asian and African *Homo heidelbergensis* (275).

European forms also had lower second premolars that were not "molarized," as were those of African and Asian contemporaries (275). In the Jinniu Shan cranium from China, traits such as prominent cheekbones, a broad nasal bridge, a form of incisor shoveling similar to that of the Zhoukoudian teeth (13), seem to be derived in the direction of modern people of Chinese descent.

By contrast, in Europe, especially from a site in the Atapuerca mountains of Spain called "Sima de Los Huesos," (translated "Pit of Bones"), dated to 430,000 years ago (278) *Homo heidelbergensis* has strong cranial, facial, and dental similarities to the Neanderthals that succeed them in the European fossil record. The "pit" is a cave chamber that lies at the bottom of a 43-foot-long natural shaft. From this pit 6,500 hominin fossils from twenty-eight or more individuals have now been recovered (278), along with the remains of cave bears. How so many bones ended up at the bottom of this shaft is a mystery. It's possible these hominins disposed of their dead by dropping them down the shaft, creating a bonanza for future paleoanthropologists (278). This is the largest sample of Middle-Pleistocene hominin remains from a single site ever found (272).

In the summer of 2014, Juan Luis Arsuaga and colleagues published a new analysis of these remains (278). They found that the Sima de Los Huesos remains are different from other European *Homo heidelbergensis* specimens and so derived in the direction of Neanderthals that they should be considered to form the base of the Neanderthal clade as the earliest members of that lineage. The Sima de Los Huesos hominins do not share all the derived traits of later Neanderthals, although they appear to be dentally nearly identical to them (see below for description of Neanderthal dental morphology). The divergence of Neanderthals and modern humans has been estimated at more than 500 KYA based on analysis of Neanderthal DNA (279, 280). Arsuaga and colleagues point out that including these specimens dated to 430,000 years ago as part of a Neanderthal clade is consistent with that evidence.

NEANDERTHALS, ANATOMICALLY MODERN HOMO SAPIENS (AMHS), DENISOVANS, AND HOMO FLORESIENSIS

Although remains now recognized as Neanderthal had been found as early as 1829, Neanderthals are named for the remains of an individual unearthed in 1856 from a quarry in the Neander Valley, Germany (281). "Neanderthal" literally means "Neander Valley," with the alternative spelling, "Neander*tal*," reflecting later revisions to the German language (281). The bones of the skeleton were robust and the skull had a peculiar shape: with heavy browridges, a receding forehead and low cranial vault. In 1856, Charles Darwin's paradigm-changing "Origin of Species by Means of Natural Selection" was still three years away from publication. Thinking outside of an evolutionary framework, the anatomists who initially analyzed the remains thought they might represent a pathological individual, a member of an ancient barbaric tribe, or even a horseback-riding deserter from the invading Cossack army (this last interpretation based on the bowed thigh bones of the remains) (281). Over the next decade, such ideas gave way to the view, bolstered by additional Neanderthal finds, that these remains represented an entirely new species. In 1864, paleontologist William King christened them *Homo neanderthalensis*.[2] But whether Neanderthals are viewed as species separate from modern humans has vacillated throughout the history of paleoanthropology and is a matter of continued debate today.

If one considers the Sima de los Huesos hominins to be Neanderthals, then Neanderthals appear in the fossil record as early as 430,000 years ago. After this time, morphological characteristics typical of Neanderthals accrete gradually, until by 200,000 to 150,000 years ago, fossils are found in Europe with the complete package of Neanderthal features (15). For the crania, these features include such distinctive characteristics as double-arched brow-ridges, long and low cranial vaults, occipital buns (protruding areas at the back of the

---

[2] *Homo neanderthalensis* took priority over the name zoologist Ernst Haeckle proposed for Neanderthals in 1866: *Homo stupidus*. (282). Wolpoff MH, Caspari R. *Race and Human Evolution:* Simon and Schuster; 1997.

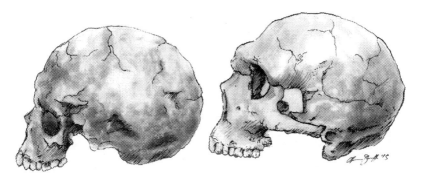

FIGURE 5.4: Artist's rendition of Qafzeh 9 (left) vs. Amud crania (right). Qafzeh 9 is an anatomically modern human dated to approximately 90,000 years ago, from Qafzeh cave in Israel. Amud is a Neanderthal from a cave on the wall of Wadi Amud, Israel, dated to approximately 60,000 years ago. Note the differences in cranial and facial form. Drawn by Alyssa Starrett.

cranium), and projecting midfaces with large nasal apertures (Figure 5.4). With their prognathic faces, Neanderthals lacked canine fossae and had had tooth rows that had shifted forward, creating a *retromolar space*, a space behind the third molar and the mandible's ascending ramus (Figure 5.5). In their post crania, Neanderthals were

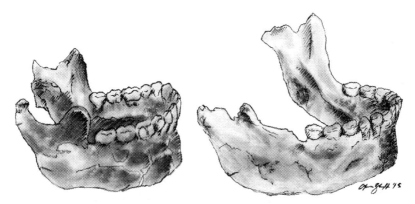

FIGURE 5.5: Artist's rendition of Qafzeh (left) vs. Amud mandibles (right). Retromolar spaces on Amud mandible are noted with arrows. Drawn by Alyssa Starrett.

FIGURE 5.6: Artist's rendition of Neanderthal upper incisors in incisal view. Note strong labial curvature and large tubercle at base of crown. Drawn by Alyssa Starrett.

highly robust, with large and wide rib cages and pelves, and thick-walled limb bones. Given these distinctive features, it is not too hard to see why William King considered Neanderthals to be a species apart from modern humans.

Dentally, Neanderthals were also quite distinctive. Their incisors are generally quite large by modern standards and have long roots (though their incisors reduced in size over time (283). Their incisors also have a distinctive shovel-shape form that differs from that of *Homo erectus* and modern Asian populations. The Neanderthal version of the shovel-shaped incisor involves a very large tubercle at the base of the tooth and strong labial curvature (Figure 5.6) (15, 284, 285).

The size and morphology of the anterior teeth have been seen, by some, as evolutionary adaptations to resist heavy wear on these teeth from their use as "third hands" or from diets high in abrasives (e.g., (286, 287). Many Neanderthal teeth show heavy anterior tooth wear (Figure 5.7).

Anna Clement and colleagues (288) recently argued that the Arctic Inuit, who subject their anterior teeth to high loads, such as in processing animal hides, exhibit even higher rates of wear than do Neanderthals but have smaller and less well-buttressed anterior teeth. On this basis, Clement and colleagues reasoned that these features of Neanderthal anterior teeth are not likely to represent adaptations to excessive wear. Perhaps the size and buttressing of Neanderthal anterior teeth represents an adaptation to tooth *fracture* under high

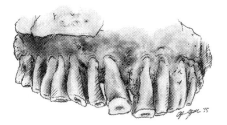

FIGURE 5.7: Artist's rendition of the extremely worn anterior teeth of the La Ferrassie I Neanderthal. Drawn by Alyssa Starrett.

loads. But, this idea has been questioned as well, based upon estimates of the bite force capacity of Neanderthals, which is smaller (289) or comparable to that of recent and living humans (290).

Thus, the idea that the distinctive size and buttressing of Neanderthal anterior teeth are adaptations to either excessive wear or high loads is weakened by these studies. Regardless of the potential adaptive significance of Neanderthal anterior tooth morphology, an interesting behavioral question is what Neanderthals were actually doing with their teeth, a topic taken up in Chapter 8.

Neanderthal lower second premolars are also different from those of modern humans in that they have an asymmetric outline (285). Neanderthal molars, though smaller than those of preceding *Homo* species and within the modern human range of variation, appear to be morphologically distinct from those of modern humans in having cusps that are more closely spaced to one another, different relative sizes of two of their principal upper molar cusps and in having a crest (the mid-trigonid crest) connecting two of their principal lower molar cusps (291). Their lower molars are also taurodont (Figure 5.2) (292). Some of these traits occur in earlier *Homo* as well as in penecontemporary non-Neanderthal hominins from China (e.g., in the early Late Pleistocene Xujiayao hominins of Northern China (293). What makes Neanderthals dentally derived is not the presence of these traits, which are in most cases primitive features of earlier hominins, but the combination of these traits in high frequency (293).

As Neanderthals were the first hominins known to bury their dead (15), they are better represented in the fossil record than any previous hominin. But besides their bones and teeth, Neanderthals left a rich archaeological record that has enabled inferences into their behavior and culture. Neanderthal tools were of the Mousterian variety (named after a site in France called Le Moustier), consisting primarily of stone flakes removed from a prepared core and fashioned into such forms as "sidescrapers," "points," and "flake-blades" (15). Some of these tools have use-wear that indicates their use on animal hides, in turn suggesting the possibility that Neanderthals made clothing (15). Neanderthals left widespread evidence of building hearths, but not much evidence of building shelters, nor of artwork (15). They do appear, however, to have been *capable* of symbolic expression, as evidenced by a more than 39,000-year-old engraving from Gibraltar cave (294).

Toward the end of the Neanderthals' tenure in Europe ending around 33,000 years ago, Neanderthal remains are associated with more sophisticated technology and further artistic expression (15). Neanderthals from 34,000-year-old site of Arcy-sur-Cure in France had a well-developed bone and ivory industry that included grooved animal teeth and ivory rings that appear to have been items of "personal adornment" (295). Finely worked bone and works of artistic expression are common at the sites of anatomically modern humans who inhabited Europe as early as 45,000 years ago (296). Whether late-surviving Neanderthals developed these cultural advances independently or borrowed them from their anatomically modern human contemporaries is not clear (295, 297).

The anatomically modern humans who appeared in Europe at this time had much earlier roots in Africa. Fossils considered to be anatomically modern date back to 195,000 years ago from southern Ethiopia (298). Other early anatomically modern remains are found at diverse locations in Africa, including in South Africa and Morocco (15). So, modern looking forms were present in Africa when Neanderthals occupied Europe.

To be anatomically modern means to have a suite of derived features. In the skull, this includes a cranial vault that is short from front to back but tall, with a high forehead. It also includes a cranium that is rounded at the back, the presence of a canine fossa (associated with a midface that is not projecting), and a chin (15). Post cranially, anatomically modern humans tend to have less robust limb bones than did previous hominins, but these differences are not absolute; they are a matter of degree (15).

But, "What does it mean to be *dentally* modern?" Entitling a book chapter with this very question, Shara Bailey and Jean-Jacques Hublin (299) argued that there is such wide variation in modern human dental morphology that it is not possible to list traits that all modern humans share. On the other hand, it does appear that there are a variety of dental features that are present in *some* modern human populations but are either not present or are much lower in frequency in earlier hominins. These traits include flat (not curved) incisors with no shoveling, lower second premolars that are dentally simplified and more symmetrical in outline, upper second molars with three cusps (rather than four), and lower first and second molars that have four cusps (rather than five). Overall, in some populations, modern human teeth became not only smaller but also morphologically simpler.

The hominin world of the middle-late Pleistocene became a little more crowded in 2010, with the discovery of the Denisovan hominins (300). These hominins were first identified on the basis of DNA extracted from a finger bone and an upper second or third molar (approximately 50–30,000 years old) recovered from Denisova Cave in southern Siberia. Denisovans are the first hominins to be identified on the basis of their DNA rather than on the morphology of their fossil remains, which are meager. But the third molar plays an important supporting role in the Denisovan drama.

DNA analysis suggests that Denisovans were distinct from Neanderthals but shared a more recent common ancestor with them than with modern humans. Neanderthal and Denisovan nuclear DNA sequences, diverged, on average, some 640,000 years ago (300). Neanderthal and Denisovan nuclear genomes on average, diverged approximately 800,000 years ago (300). Here is where the Denisovan upper molar comes in: it supports the distinction of Denisovans from both Neanderthals and modern humans. The molar is huge. It is not clear if it is a second or third molar. If a third molar, it is comparable in size to those of early *Homo* and *Australopithecus* (300). If a second molar, it is nevertheless larger than those of most Neanderthals and early modern humans. Some details of the upper molar's morphology also differ from those of Neanderthals' (300).

Last and also least – only in terms of size – is the tiny hominin species from the Indonesian island of Flores, *Homo floresiensis*, nicknamed the "Hobbit." The hominin remains from this site indicate a species that stood three feet tall with a cranial capacity equivalent to that of *Australopithecus afarensis* but appearing very recently in time – from 100,000 to 17,000 years ago (301, 302). The announcement in 2004 of such a recent primitive species of hominin sent shock waves through the paleoanthropological world and was predictably met with skepticism among experts in the field. Many alternative explanations were offered, some suggesting that the most complete specimen from the site, LB1, simply belonged to a modern human with a pathological condition. One such condition, Laron syndrome, entails a genetic insensitivity to growth hormone and was asserted to have possibly caused the Hobbit's small brain and body size (303).

As paleoanthropologist Leslie Aiello (304) observed, however, none of the pathological explanations accounts for the full set of features exhibited by the Hobbit. These include lower first premolars which were elongated and asymmetric, with large buccal cusps (305). Plotting a shape index of the lower first premolar against that of modern humans, and earlier hominins, Brown and Maeda (305) found that the shape of the *Homo floresiensis* lower first premolar falls outside the range of modern human variation but well within that of early australopiths and early *Homo*. Coupled with these dental finding are those of Debbie Argue's (306) cladistic analysis in which

Homo floresiensis does not form a clade with Asian *Homo erectus*, and branches off just before or after *Homo habilis*.

The teeth and cladistic analysis challenge the view that the diminutive *Homo floresiensis* is a scaled down version of *Homo erectus*. According to that view, *Homo floresiensis* is a product of "insular dwarfism," a reduction in size thought to occur in some island habitats over many generations through natural selection. The lower energy requirements of a small body size are thought to give animals an advantage in survival and reproduction when island food resources periodically dwindle. But, if *Homo floresiensis* is cladistically closer to *Homo habilis*, then it may have been very small to begin with. Instead of being a dwarfed version of Asian *Homo erectus*, it may be a late-surviving descendant of an early migration out of Africa of a small-bodied, smaller-brained hominin (307). Unfortunately, analyses of teeth haven't settled the issue, as a recent study of cranial shape allies *Homo floresiensis* with *Homo erectus* (308). Why the teeth and cranium give different signals is not clear and begs for explanation.

ORIGINS OF MODERN HUMANS AND ISSUES OF PHYLOGENY WITHIN THE GENUS HOMO

Ideas about relationships among fossil species of the genus *Homo* and modern humans have traditionally fallen into three major camps. The "Multiregional Continuity" camp holds that modern humans gradually evolved from more archaic forms (*Homo erectus* in some regions, *Homo heidelbergensis* or Neanderthals in others) that were all in reality part of one global, interbreeding species (309, 310). Proponents of this camp point to local continuity in a variety of regionally anatomical features visible in both archaic and modern humans in particular regions of the world. One of those features is something noted earlier: shovel-shaped incisors occur in high frequency in Chinese *Homo erectus*, Chinese *Homo heidelbergensis* and Chinese modern humans (309), suggesting the continuity of genes from ancient to modern populations within the region. This view does not imply parallel evolution of populations (311), but instead suggests that populations throughout the world that were linked by gene exchange gradually evolved toward modern form.

At the other extreme is the "Recent African Origin" camp, which holds that anatomically modern humans speciated from African *Homo heidelbergensis* in Africa. They then expanded into other parts of the world, and over time completely replaced more archaic forms. A critical piece of evidence in support of this view has to do with DNA variation in modern humans. Both mitochondrial[3] (312, 313) and nuclear DNA analysis (313) suggest that the most genetically diverse peoples today are in Africa. Assuming that mutations in DNA are generally neutral with respect to natural selection and accumulate largely as a function of time, the higher diversity of African peoples than in other regions of the world suggests that AMHS from Africa have a longer history, i.e., they are older, than AMHS in other regions of the world.

Another point going for the Recent African Origins model is that the earliest fossil evidence of anatomically modern humans, comes, as previously noted, from Africa, dating to nearly 200,000 years ago (298). DNA analyses suggest age ranges for the origin of AMHS that include this date (312, 314). Dates and patterns of AMHS dispersal out of Africa are controversial. Some studies suggest expansion out of Africa around 50–60,000 years ago (315, 316) and others (317) find evidence of an initial dispersal of anatomically modern humans into Asia around 130,000 years ago, with a second dispersal into Eurasia around 50,000 years ago.

It is possible that African populations may be more variable genetically simply because they have been larger than other AMHS populations throughout history, not because they are older (318).

---

[3] Mitochondria are tiny structures within cells that break down sugar molecules into small packets of usable energy. The DNA contained in mitchonrdria represents an extremely small portion of our total genome, the vast majority of which is enclosed within the nuclei of our cells. Nevertheless, because there are thousands of mitochondria in each cell and only one nucleus, mtDNA is more easily obtained from ancient bone than is nuclear DNA. Each of us inherits the mtDNA that resided in our mother's egg cells, so these genes are passed down the maternal line.

But, this explanation does not account for the apparent patterning of genetic diversity across the globe: genetic diversity decreases with greater distance from Africa (319). This pattern suggests that as people moved out of Africa they carried only a fraction of the original diversity present in Africa into new areas. As they moved from these new areas into still more distant regions, they then seem to have carried an even smaller fraction of that genetic diversity with them.

The third camp falls in between these two extremes. One view is that there was genetic continuity in some areas outside of Africa, but not all. Another is that anatomically modern humans originated in Africa but interbred successfully to varying degrees with more archaic hominins when they encountered them (320). Alan Templeton's (320) analysis of modern human DNA variation supports this view. Templeton analyzed variation in twelve modern human haplotypes (groups of linked genes) using a statistical method that allowed him to assess the extent and direction of gene flow during human evolution. His results showed that variation in the human genome bears the stamp of three major migrations out of Africa: one at 1.7 Ma, a second around 0.42–0.84 Ma, and third around 0.08–0.15 Ma. The last of these corresponds to the dispersal of anatomically modern *Homo sapiens*. His analysis indicates that AMHS from Africa interbred with, but did not replace more archaic forms.

Some years after Templeton's study, studies of ancient DNA from Neanderthals and Denisovans likewise pointed to interbreeding with AMHS. By 2010, researchers had sequenced much of the Neanderthal nuclear genome (279). Geneticist Richard Green and colleagues estimated that 1–4 per cent of the DNA of some living people (non-Africans) came from Neanderthals (279) (but see [321] for an alternative interpretation of the evidence). Denisovans appear to have contributed a small portion of DNA to modern Melanesians and aboriginal Australians (300) as well as to mainland Asians and Native Americans (322).

Recently, mitochondrial DNA from the Sima de los Huesos *Homo heidelbergensis* fossils has been analyzed (323). Oddly, analysis of their mitochondrial DNA places them closer to Denisovans than to Neanderthals. This is hard to understand because, as noted earlier, the Sima de los Huesos hominins are morphologically very similar to Neanderthals. The Sima de los Huesos molars, in particular are much more similar to those of Neanderthals than to the Denisovan molars. However, mtDNA represents a small portion of the genome that is inherited maternally and so it may not provide as clear a picture of Sima de los Huesos affinities as dental morphology does or autosomal DNA would.

Analysis of variation in modern and ancient DNA is greatly advancing our understanding of modern human origins. Yet, when ancient DNA cannot be recovered, morphological analyses remain the only way to address questions of phylogeny within the genus *Homo*. Teeth, once again, provide a useful tool. As will be explained in Chapter 8, they have been useful in investigating the question of who might be the last common ancestor of Neanderthals and modern humans and as discussed in Chapter 9, they provide insight into modern human origins and dispersal out of Africa.

This chapter marched its way through evolution within the genus *Homo*. Broad trends over time within the genus include expanding brain size, greater reliance on meat in the diet, and growing use and improvement of cultural solutions to problems of survival and reproduction. In this second part of the book, how teeth reflect and respond to these trends begins once again with the fundamental adaptation of diet.

6 Dentally-Derived Dietary Inferences: The Genus *Homo* and Its Diminishing Dentition

> It is not much what is eaten but what is done to it beforehand.
>
> – Brace CL
> *Krapina, "Classic Neanderthals," and the Evolution of the European Face*

Chapter 4 left off on evidence of dietary divergence between *Paranthropus* and early *Homo*, evidence that lends support to Robinson's Dietary Hypothesis. The present chapter considers how dental evidence contributes to our understanding of dietary change within the genus *Homo*, prior to the evolution of Neanderthals and anatomically modern humans (AMHS). During this period of human evolution, archaeological evidence becomes a crucial source of information for dietary reconstruction. Faunal remains with evidence of human alteration (e.g., butchery), stone tools and eventually evidence of controlled use of fire supply crucial pieces of the dietary puzzle in the *Homo* lineage. But teeth, too, yield important clues. This chapter focuses on those clues within their archaeological context.

In addition, this chapter reviews evidence and explores arguments for the possibility that changes in culture – the use of tools and fire – had an effect on dental evolution in *Homo habilis*, *Homo erectus*, and *Homo heidelbergensis*. While a major reduction in the size of the canine apparently occurred at or near the base of the hominin clade (Chapter 3), posterior teeth did not reduce until much later, arguably not until the appearance of *Homo erectus* (251, 324). There were also changes in anterior teeth. Relative to estimated body size, incisor teeth are larger in *Homo habilis* than they are in any australopith, but then decrease in size with *Homo erectus* (325).

The big question is why posterior teeth (and later anterior teeth) reduced in size in the first place. Anthropological legend C. Loring Brace[1] and colleagues found that major reductions in tooth size during the Pleistocene occurred relatively recently, during the last 200,000–300,000 years (commentary in *Current Anthropology* on Wrangham and colleagues' cooking hypothesis [52]). Brace argued that the degree of dental reduction in different regions of the world is proportional to the length of time people have been cooking in these regions (326). Cooking would have had the effect of softening food and thus relaxing the selection pressure on maintaining large teeth to process hard and/or tough foods. Such changes in food preparation are what Brace referred to in the aphorism that heads this chapter. But, what is the nature of the evidence that cooking, as Wrangham and colleagues (52, 57) argue, wrought a decrease in human tooth size much earlier than this, at the time of *Homo erectus*? More generally, what are some of the more plausible ideas for the causes and consequences of dental reduction during this period of human evolution?

Toward the dual goals of this chapter–reviewing the dental evidence for diet in the genus *Homo* as well as delving into hypotheses for and consequences of dental reduction–we first examine the archaeological record with respect to the antiquity of meat-eating and the controlled use of fire.

A BRIEF ARCHAEOLOGICAL CONTEXT

There is ample archaeological evidence of meat-eating in the *Homo* lineage. What is less clear from the archaeological record, however, is the quantity of meat incorporated into the diets of different species and the primary means by which it was procured. The clearest evidence for meat-eating in the early archaeological record comes

---

[1] C. Loring Brace is an American anthropologist whose work showed that physical features could not be used to define racial types and was an outspoken critic of the race concept. His book "'Race' is a Four Letter-Word'" is widely acclaimed and his many influential contributions to physical anthropology, including his ideas on dental reduction, were honored by the American Association of Physical Anthropology in 2006 with its prestigious Charles Darwin Lifetime Achievement Award.

from butchery marks on fossilized animal bones (327). Cut marks made by flake tools leave distinctive marks that can be differentiated microscopically from other markings on bone. It is possible to also see evidence of percussion marks on bones, created when stone tools are used to smash bones to remove their marrow (327).

The earliest widely accepted[2] evidence of cut-marked bone is from the 2.6-million-year-old site of Gona, Ethiopia (328). The first Oldowan tools appear at about this time as well (327). Who made these early tools and butchery marks is not clear (327), as several hominin species existed at this time. Archaeologist Briana Pobiner (327) considers *Australopithecus garhi*, and especially *Homo habilis* to be the most likely culprits.

In the 1980s, archaeologist Pat Shipman (329–331) produced compelling evidence that the majority of the cut marks on animal bones dating to about 2 Ma from Olduvai Gorge were superimposed on marks made by carnivore teeth. Hominins were primarily gaining access to these bones *after* carnivores had had their fill–in other words, hominins were scavenging this meat, not hunting it, as anthropologists previously assumed. The implication was that these hominins had entered a new niche, as scavenging does not occur in modern chimpanzees and presumably did not occur in our last common ancestor.

Scavenging, according to some, may have been hominins' first step into a meat-eating niche (commentary in *Current Anthropology* on Wrangham and colleagues' cooking hypothesis [52]). Recent evidence, however, seems to push the antiquity of hunting as far back as 2 Ma (332). The evidence comes from the site of Kanjera, South Kenya where there are abundant remains of whole small gazelle skeletons with evidence of butchery and disarticulation, and with no evidence of scavenging (332). Larger bovid remains were also found in the form of leg bones and skulls that had been disarticulated and transported to

---

[2] Recent evidence from East Africa may, however, push stone tools back to 3.3 million years ago (the middle Pliocene). (31. Harmand S, Lewis JE, Feibel CS, Lepre CJ, Prat S, Lenoble A, et al. 3.3-million-year-old stone tools from Lomekwi 3, West Turkana, Kenya. *Nature.* 2015;521(7552):310–315.)

the site. Percussion marks on the crania suggest these hominins were eating fatty brains and marrow. Any carnivore tooth marks found on these bones appear to have been made after the bones had been butchered. The authors of this study, Ferraro and colleagues, suggest that this is evidence that hominins were making more than occasional use of meat in their diets, and may well have been hunting small game at this time (332).

In his paleoanthropology blog of 29 April 29, 2013, Anthropologist John Hawks characterized that question of scavenging versus hunting as the "... tiredest chestnut in the anthropologists' Oldowan arsenal." He argues that hominins from Oldowan sites probably did both. At *Homo erectus* Acheuleian sites, stone tools became more varied and animal bones more prevalent (15). The archaeological evidence therefore indicates that meat, however acquired, was increasingly incorporated into the diet of *Homo* species during the Paleolithic. Diets were adaptable, as well, judging from the finding of freshwater shellfish remains beside the bones of *Homo erectus* in Trinil, Java (333). By *Homo heidelbergensis* times archaeological evidence in the form of spears and large mammal remains strongly suggest that the quest for meat had progressed to big-game hunting (15).

Of course, because plant foods decompose quickly, the archaeological record is biased against finding evidence of them. And, it is plant foods, particularly cooked plant foods, that form the basis of the Cooking Hypothesis. When Wrangham and colleagues introduced this hypothesis in Current Anthropology in 1999, they argued that cooking began in earnest in *Homo erectus* (52). Part of their argument rested on the marked reduction in tooth size paired with the increase in brain and body size that occurred with the evolution of *Homo erectus*. These changes, in their view, "signaled" that humans were chewing softer, cooked foods (teeth became smaller) that improved their energy intake (body and brain size were able to increase). The actual archaeological evidence of cooking in *Homo erectus* times, as commentators noted and as Wrangham and colleagues openly acknowledged, was meager.

Wrangham and colleagues relied on evidence of 1.6-million-year-old "reddened patches" at Koobi Fora in east Africa that had been interpreted as hearths. They also cited evidence of burned bones found together with hominin artifacts from Swartrkans from around one million years ago (52). In his commentary, Brace questioned this evidence. As he put it: "Fire happens!" Whether the presence of fire at these sites indicates controlled use of fire rather than a naturally occurring one is not clear. Brace argued that the first "documented appearance of cooking" occurs much later in the archaeological record, around 200–300 KYA. Wrangham and colleagues responded that the kinds of fires that modern hunter-gatherers use to cook underground storage organs (tubers) are "ephemeral" and may not leave an archaeological record. In other words, absence of evidence is not evidence of absence.

Since the publication of Wrangham and colleagues' seminal paper, new evidence pushes the controlled use of fire further back in time–to 1 million years ago. The evidence comes from Wonderwerk Cave, South Africa. A large quantity of burned bone and the ashy remains of plants were recovered from within this cave (256). In total, 675 burned bones or teeth were analyzed with a method called Fourier transform infrared microspectroscopy, enabling these researchers to determine the temperature to which the material had been heated. That temperature is consistent with a fire made with grasses and twigs. It is not likely that wildfire produced the ashes and burnt bone, because they are found a fair distance beyond the entrance of the cave. At another site, Gesher Benot Ya'akov Israel – dated to some 800,000 years ago, clusters of burned bones and charred wood suggest the presence of hearth fire (255). In short, it now seems much more likely than it did in 1999 that *Homo erectus* had the ability to control fire.

With these archaeological points about diet and fire use in mind, it is now time to turn to the dental evidence.

DENTAL EVIDENCE

In his 2012 review of dental evidence for diet in African early *Homo* (325), Peter Ungar states: "The most obvious conclusion we can draw from a review of the fossil evidence for diet in early African *Homo* is that there is not much of it, and what we do have is not very compelling" (2012:S325). As Ungar observes, the number of early *Homo* teeth recovered is far fewer than it is for australopiths, limiting the power of dental investigations into *Homo* diets.

Nevertheless, data on the chemical composition of enamel, microwear, dental morphology, tooth chipping and tooth size (especially in relation to bite force reconstruction) are accumulating and are relatively congruent with one another. Altogether the dental data are also fairly well-aligned with the archaeological record. The dental evidence points to diets within the *Homo* lineage that included meat, diverged from those of *Paranthropus*, were variable, and, as compared to the diets of australopiths, had softer textures. Consistency between microwear and chemical data on the one hand, and certain aspects of tooth size and morphology on the other, seems to denote that changing diets had begun to result in evolutionary changes in teeth.

There is strong trace element support for meat-eating in early *Homo*. Balter and colleagues' (106) study of Sr/Ca and Ba/Ca ratios in the teeth of south African early hominins (Chapter 2) revealed a statistically significant mean difference between *P. robustus* and early *Homo* with respect to both ratios. Means for both ratios were lower in *Homo* than in *P. robustus*, indicating that there was more meat in the diet of the former. The difference in means suggests dietary divergence between these lineages, as Robinson envisioned. There was not, however, complete separation in the ranges of trace element values between the two groups of hominins, raising the possibility of some dietary overlap between them.

Shifting the scene to East Africa, Cerling and coworkers' (88) study of carbon isotopes from the Turkana Basin hominins documents strong divergence in the consumption of C4 resources between early *Homo* and *Paranthropus* by 2 million years ago. Average values for their stable carbon isotope ratios indicate that the proportion of C4 resources in the *Paranthropus boisei* diet was 75% while that of its *Homo* contemporaries was 35%. A strong isotopic divergence aligns with the stark differences in the size of their facial buttressing, muscle attachments, jaws and teeth as well as in the thickness of enamel (334) of these two east African lineages. Antón and colleagues point out that the difference in average carbon isotope values for *Paranthropus boisei* and *Homo erectus* in East Africa at 2.8 ppm is close to the average difference between *Homo erectus* and "non-erectus *Homo*" at 2.9 ppm (177). This is interesting because, as they note, it suggests the possibility of niche divergence *within* the genus *Homo*.

Aspects of tooth size and morphology also hint at increased meat consumption in early *Homo*. Archaeologist Travis Pickering and colleagues note that, when eating ribs, both humans and chimpanzees hold the ribs in their hands while using their incisors to strip meat from them and to "peel" back strips of bone (335). Tooth marks, butchery marks, and evidence of such incisor bone "peeling" occur in fossilized ungulate ribs dated to 1.2 MA from Olduvai Gorge (335). These authors suggest that use of incisor teeth for this purpose may explain why the anterior teeth of early *Homo* are broader (with wider incisal edges) than those of its australopith ancestors (336). Perhaps these broader incisor teeth were adapted to such uses as bone "peeling." Peter Ungar's (337) work showed that in early *Homo*, molar chewing surfaces have greater relief and cusps with steeper slopes than do those of *Au. afarensis*. This finding may point to the ability of early *Homo* molars to shear through tough foods, and one type of tough food is meat.

Microwear texture analysis points strongly to variability in the diet of *Homo erectus*. In particular, the microwear complexity (see Chapter 2) of *Homo erectus* teeth covers a wide range of values, greater than that of any other Plio-Pleistocene hominin yet studied, with the exception of *Paranthropus robustus* (325, 338). Both hard *and* tough foods were likely present in *Homo erectus* diets, given that microwear analysis yields high complexity values (indicative of hard foods) as well as small "adhesion pits" produced by the chewing of tough foods (325, 338).

Ungar and coauthors in their 2006 review article (339) synthesize both dental and archaeological data on early *Homo* (*Homo habilis* and *Homo erectus*) diets, emphasizing their "adaptive versatility." In their view, the mixed nature of the C3/C4 diets of these early *Homo* species, their probable inclusion of both hard and tough food items, and their ability to access high quality meat gave them the dietary flexibility needed to meet the rapidly shifting environmental conditions of the Plio-Pleistocene. These conditions encompassed wide swings in temperature and moisture, as documented in the East African paleoecological record (340). Ungar and colleagues' conclusions support Rick Pott's "Variability Selection Hypothesis" for the evolution of *Homo* (340): the idea that environmental variability itself drove selection for flexibility in diet and behavior.

The size, and especially chewing area of posterior teeth decreases from *Homo habilis* to *Homo erectus*, hinting at the ingestion of softer – or softened– foods. Posterior tooth size in *Homo habilis* appears to be similar to that of *Au. africanus* (247, 341). Yet, in relation to estimated body size the chewing area of the postcanine teeth is smaller than that of any australopith, according to an analysis by anthropologists Henry McHenry and Katie Coffing (342). These researchers used an index of postcanine tooth area relative to body size that paleoanthropologist Henry McHenry had devised in an earlier paper. He called the index the "Megadontia Quotient," or MQ, and it is based on the positive relationship between postcanine tooth area and body size in primates. This ratio compares actual postcanine area to that predicted on the basis of body size. MQs for modern humans and chimps are just below 1 – that is, chimps and humans have slightly smaller postcanine areas that would be predicted on the basis of their body sizes. The values of *H. habilis* and *H. rudolfensis* were 1.9 and 1.5, respectively, which are lower than those of australoptihs, but higher than that of African *Homo erectus*, at 0.9.

Notably, *Homo erectus* has an MQ equivalent to that of modern humans. To some extent these estimates should be taken with a grain of salt because of small sample sizes for some species and because body size estimates are imprecise. Yet, estimated body size *increase*s from australopiths to *Homo erectus* (15) while posterior tooth size *decreases* – opposite to the trend seen across primates.

A more recent analysis suggests that tooth size in *Homo habilis* is *not* less than one would expect on the basis of its estimated body size, but that for *Homo erectus*, tooth size is plainly less than one would expect for its body size (324). Wrangham and colleagues (52) refer to the reduction in tooth size in *Homo erectus* as one of the "signals" that *Homo erectus* had begun to eat food softened by cooking. Consistent with the idea that *Homo erectus* was chewing less mechanically challenging foods is the trend of decreasing enamel thickness in the genus *Homo* (334). From enamel thickness that is quite variable in earlier *Homo* (343), enamel thickness is clearly reduced in *Homo erectus* relative to earlier hominins (334).

Bite force also decreases in *Homo erectus*, but appears to do so in *Homo habilis* as well (344). Using established methods to estimate chewing muscle sizes from attachment areas on the skull, Carolyn Eng and colleagues (344) found that maximum bite force decreased from australopiths to both *Homo habilis* and *Homo erectus*. Maximum bite force in both *Homo* species also decreased in relation to molar area. This means that the amount of stress these two *Homo* species could apply to food between their occluding teeth had declined relative to australopiths.

A reduction in bite force during *Homo habilis* times is consistent with evidence of an inactivating mutation in a myosin gene (MYH16) in humans that appears to have arisen 2.4 million years ago (345). Myosins are a group of proteins in muscle that, together with actin proteins and the energy-yielding molecule ATP (adenosine triphosphate) produce muscle contraction. The MYH16 gene, in particular, is expressed in nonhuman primate head muscles, including the temporalis, a crucial chewing muscle. The inactivation of this particular gene 2.4 million years ago suggests loss of chewing power in *Homo habilis*.

More evidence of a decline in bite force in *Homo erectus* is apparent in Constantino and colleagues' (81) study of tooth chipping. The size of edge chips on the chewing surfaces of teeth is related to the bite force that produced them (see Chapter 2). An equation linking chip size to bite force reveals that *Homo erectus* exerted lower bite forces than did *Paranthropus* species and *Au. anamensis*, *Au. afarensis*, and *Au. africanus*. All of this evidence suggests that at least in *Homo erectus*, and possibly in *Homo habilis* as well, softer (or softened) foods were being eaten and had perhaps had already relaxed the selection pressure for maintaining high bite force.

EXPLORING THE CAUSES AND CONSEQUENCES OF DENTAL REDUCTION IN HOMO

The idea that relaxed selection pressures can explain the reduction, vestigilization, or disappearance of traits dates back to Charles Darwin, who observed many examples of such traits in nature (346). Exactly how trait reduction occurs when selection pressures are relaxed was less clear to Darwin, though he believed that selection favored economy in energy use (347). Indeed the mechanisms and consequences of relaxed selection are still not particularly well understood today (347). What is also unclear is exactly when and why selection pressures were relaxed on tooth size along the *Homo* lineage.

Regarding the mechanism of relaxed selection, Loring Brace (348) believed that in the absence of selection, mutations bringing about "physiological inactivation" would accumulate in the gene pool. Such mutations, in his view, often bring about "structural reduction." He called this phenomenon the "Probable Mutation Effect" (PME). The name refers to the probable effect – trait reduction – of nonfunctional mutations on the size of body structures. Such mutations, it was argued, were likely to disrupt the series of developmental steps that produced a body structure of the size previously maintained by natural selection. Brace (348) attributed molar reduction from australopiths to *Homo erectus* to a shift from a more vegetarian diet to one with more meat, which he felt would require less chewing. (But raw meat can be very tough, which is why the Italian raw beef *carpaccio* is sliced so thinly and pounded!) In any case, in Brace's view, relaxed selection on molar chewing area then brought about molar size reduction through the PME. Brace's views about technology and cooking in relation to dental reduction applied to much later time periods and were based on the archaeological record as then known.

As recounted by Jules Kieser (349), Brace's PME concept was criticized on several fronts. Most problematic was the assumption that nonfunctional mutations would tend to disrupt developmental processes. There was no clear evidence that this was true, and it was argued that most mutations simply have neutral effects and accumulate too slowly for the PME to operate in any case (though see McKee [350]). In sum, it was argued that structural reduction was not a *necessary* consequence of relaxed selection.

Until recently, evolutionary biologists had not given a great deal of attention to the topic of relaxed selection (347). In his and his coworkers' 2009 review, David Lahti and colleagues find that when selection pressures previously maintaining a trait are relaxed, direct selection for trait reduction is often happening simultaneously. For example, many traits require maintenance costs, the most obvious one being the energy it takes to build and/or sustain the trait. Lahti and coauthors offer plant defensive compounds as an example. Production of these compounds decreases under conditions of relaxed selection while allocation of energy to growth and reproduction simultaneously increases. Presumably, then, when these defensive compounds are no longer needed, plants can increase their reproductive success by channeling the energy that was previously used to make them into reproduction instead. In the end, Lahti and colleagues conclude that it is the "... nature of the influences on a trait following the relaxation of a source of selection [that] determines whether the trait will persist, be reduced to a vestige, or lost."

Although selection pressures on maintaining large teeth may have been relaxed during the transition from *Homo habilis* to *Homo erectus* (and perhaps even earlier, depending on which estimates you look at), there may have been concurrent direct selection for reduced tooth size. In the words of Lahti et al. (347) perhaps there were "constitutive" (inherent) costs to maintaining large teeth. Such would be the case if growing large teeth required energy that could be devoted elsewhere. This is the concept that Jules Kieser (349) called the "Energetic Budget Effect." No one knows exactly how much energy it takes to grow teeth of different sizes. Needless to say perhaps, it is also not known whether the energy saved by making smaller teeth could have made a difference for survival and/or reproduction. But, it is worth remembering that with *Homo erectus*, apparent selection for larger body and brain size coupled with fast rates of somatic growth (see Chapter 7) would have put a premium on energy economy.

Even if the energy savings of growing smaller teeth is negligible, Peter Ungar (325) reminds us that it isn't just teeth that reduce with *Homo erectus*, but so too do the bones and muscles of the face and jaw. These, it can be assumed, would add greater energetic costs to the equation. Ungar suggests that there may be a genetic and/or developmental connection between jaws and teeth, citing a study in mice in which some of the same genes affecting tooth size also affected jaw shape (351). In essence then, there is a possibility that tooth size reduction was a genetically correlated consequence of selection for reduced jaw size.

A similar correlational argument has been made (though not involving constituitive energy costs) regarding the relationship between the shape of the face and the size of first molars in modern humans (352). Polychronis and Halazonetis (352) found that that in modern humans, variation in the length of lower first molars is related to variation in cranial shape. They conclude that evolutionary tooth size reduction might be explained, theoretically, as a passive developmental result of changes in cranial shape. Whether the cranial shape variables associated with molar length in this study are the same as those that accompanied molar reduction from *Homo habilis* to *Homo erectus*, however, is what would have to be determined with respect to the problem we are considering here.

Beyond energy economy, a second cost relevant to having large teeth is that of dental crowding and subsequent infection. In this case, the cost can be considered a "contingent" one, as defined by Lahti and colleagues (347), because the cost of large teeth arises from the change in selection pressure. Here, the cost of having large teeth arises from a change in diet to softer foods, leading to a chain of events that ends with dental crowding. Bone growth is stimulated when subjected to mechanical stress (353), as when chewing mechanically challenging foods. Teeth, however, do not grow larger in response to mechanical stress – they attain their final size and shape when they form during childhood. Corruccini and Beecher (354) and Calcagno and Gibson (355) reasoned that softer diets would result in less jaw growth during childhood and adolescence, resulting in insufficient space for later-erupting teeth. The consequences would include dental crowding, displacement, rotation, or impaction of teeth. Indeed, Corruccini and Beecher (354) demonstrated that nonhuman primates who had been fed soft diets (lard) for an atherosclerosis study frequently had crowded or malpositioned teeth (as in Figure 6.1).

Could such dental consequences as these entail costs to reproductive success? Calcagno and Gibson (355) argue that they most certainly could. Plaque containing disease-causing bacteria can become easily trapped between crowded, malpositioned, or partially erupted teeth. Wisdom teeth (or third molars) because they erupt late, are a particular problem if the jaw has not grown large enough to accommodate them. They may become impacted. They may erupt only partially, trapping plaque and bits of food between the tooth and the flap of overlying gum (the "operculum"), leading to infection and inflammation of the soft tissues surrounding the tooth. Unchecked, as

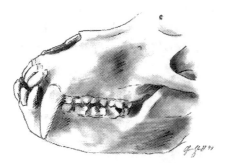

FIGURE 6.1: Malocclusion in a baboon fed a soft diet during development: underjet of the upper incisors. Sketch by Alyssa Starrett based on baboon shown in: How Anthropology Informs the Orthodontic Diagnosis of Malocclusion's Causes by Robert S. Corruccini. *Mellen Studies in Anthropology*, Vol. 1, Lewiston, New York, Queenston, Ontario and Lampeter, Wales: The Edwin Mellen Press, 1999. By permission of Mellen Press and Robert Corruccini.

they would have been before dentistry and antibiotics, such infections could have progressed to life-threatening conditions. These include – among other very unpleasant things – septicemia (blood infection), infections of the cavernous sinus at the base of the skull, and Ludwig's angina– an inflammation and swelling in the mandibular region that can cause asphyxiation.

For the most part, Calcagno and Gibson (355) applied these ideas to the phenomenon of dental reduction in recent modern humans, not in earlier hominins. There are a few cases of dental pathology and tooth loss in *Homo erectus*. The Nariokotome boy has a periodontal lesion on its mandible associated with the retention of deciduous tooth roots (356). Dental pathologies and tooth loss are also present in the Dmanisi hominins (see Figure 5.3) (269, 357). But other than these cases, dental pathologies were not particularly common in *Homo habilis* or *Homo erectus*. The earliest known case of third molar impaction occurs much later in time, in the "Magdalenian Girl" from Cap Blanc rock shelter in France, that is 13,000–15,000 years old (http://sciencelife.uchospitals.edu/2013/

11/25/age-wisdom-teeth/). Thus, it isn't clear that pathology associated with dental crowing was prevalent enough to have acted as a major "contingent cost" during *Homo habilis* or *Homo erectus* times.

To Wrangham and colleagues (52), it was *Homo erectus*'s habit of cooking food that brought about the change to eating softer foods and subsequent reduction of jaws and teeth. On the other hand, there is no evidence of controlled fire use in *Homo habilis*, but bite force reduction was already underway (344) and the human MYH16 gene had mutated to its present nonfunctional form during *Homo habilis* times as well. If eating cooked food doesn't explain bite force reduction in *Homo habilis*, then what might? Eng and colleagues suggest that *Homo habilis* may have softened food with stone tools – by cutting it up into small pieces and/or by pounding it. Still, even if selection pressures on bite force were initially relaxed with *Homo habilis*, dramatic reduction in molar size did not occur until later, with *Homo erectus* (324). A delay in molar reduction in response to eating foods softened with stone tools could simply represent evolutionary lag time. But, it could just as well be that it was not until *Homo erectus* began to cook food that selection pressures on tooth size were sufficiently relaxed. So, the initial causes of bite force and tooth size reduction during this period of human evolution remain obscure, but they are most likely related to the use of stone tools in preparing food, to cooking, or to both.

So far, this entire discussion has been predicated on relaxed selection. There are other possible causes of (or contributors to) dental reduction, as Bermúdez de Castro and Nicolas's analysis of the *Homo heidelbergensis* sample from Sima de los Huesos suggests (358). This 430,000-year-old sample (278) exhibits molar tooth sizes that are smaller than those of later Neanderthals, and are equivalent to those of modern humans. Bermúdez de Castro and Nicolas (358) assert that there are no cultural changes related to food preparation during the Middle Pleistocene nor any increase in dental pathology in this sample that might help explain why molars had reduced to such a degree. Indeed, Pérez-Pérez and Bermúdez de Castro (359) interpret the microwear evidence for this sample as indicative of eating "poorly processed," plant foods. Perhaps, Bermúdez de Castrol and Nicolas (1995) propose, tooth size reduced as a result of genetic drift.

When populations are small and isolated, as they appear to have been for long periods during the Middle Pleisotocene (358) the frequencies of alleles (different forms of genes) can fluctuate dramatically simply by chance. This is what is meant by genetic drift[3] and it may explain why teeth became small in the Sima de los Huesos sample, in the absence of any other evidence that may explain it. So, it is possible – and even likely given the long span of time and diverse environments in which the genus *Homo* has existed – that several different evolutionary forces and selection pressures have been involved in dental reduction.

These questions are difficult to resolve. For now, it seems that relaxed selection coupled with the constituitive energetic costs of maintaining large jaws and teeth when eating food softened by some means (tools and/or fire) is the most viable explanation for the pronounced reduction of postcanine tooth size in *Homo erectus*. Meanwhile, genetic drift may be a more likely cause of the human-sized molars of the Sima de los Huesos sample.

When teeth reduce in size, they may change morphologically as well. Bermúdez de Castro and Nicolas (358) observed that the later forming hypoconulid tooth cusp was often absent from the Sima de los Huesos lower molars, just as it often is it is in human molars. In these teeth and modern human teeth, the number of cusps on molars tends

---

[3] An analogy is flipping a coin – if it is flipped 100 times, the number of heads and tails will likely be very close to 50:50. But if it is flipped 10 times, there will be many occasions, when just by chance, you will get 7 heads and 3 tails, or some other skewed result. If you imagine heads to be one form of a gene and tails to be the other, then it is possible to see how in a small gene pool such skewed results could be common. Furthermore, as soon as such a skewed result occurs in one generation, then because the next generation draws its genes from this skewed pool, it is likely to diverge even further from the 50:50 ratio. In this way, evolutionary trends, such as dental reduction, can occur in small populations simply as a result of genetic drift.

to be reduced relative to earlier hominins. Bermúdez de Castro and Nicolas considered this to be a case of parallel evolution, and given what we now know about how molar cusps form, the case for parallel evolution becomes stronger.

Before teeth begin to mineralize, the pattern of the developing tooth surface is mapped out in soft tissue through a series of transient structures called "enamel knots" (360; Jurnvall and Jung) (Figure 6.2). These structures produce molecules stimulating the folding of dental epithelial tissue (precursor tissue to that which forms enamel) into the shape of dental cusps. But, enamel knots simultaneously emit molecular signals that inhibit the formation of enamel knots nearby and which drop off in concentration with distance from the enamel knot (Figure 6.2). Only at a certain distance with low-enough inhibitor concentration, can a new enamel knot form. This understanding of cusp formation is known as the "Patterning Cascade Model," in reference to the pattern of cusp positions established by the sequential activation of enamel knots (360).

If enamel knots remain the same distance from one another but tooth size reduces, then fewer enamel knots, and hence cusps, can form. With my colleague John Hunter and our students, we showed that distances among the principal cusps of a tooth *relative* to tooth size could predict the formation of accessory (additional) cusps (361, 362). In this case, we were looking at the Carabelli cusp, a small late-forming cusp sometimes present on the lingual (tongue) side of upper first molars (and more rarely upper second molars). If molar size decreased in *Homo heidelbergensis* to a greater extent than the distances among cusps did, then there may have been no space outside of the inhibition zones of previously formed enamel knots for the later developing hypoconulid enamel knot to form. Put simply, as molars in the genus *Homo* reduced in size, it makes sense from the perspective of tooth developmental biology, that they became simpler as well.

It has been suggested (363) that developmental considerations may help explain why hominin species that are more similar to modern humans in their overall rates of development are like modern

154 DENTALLY-DERIVED DIETARY INFERENCES

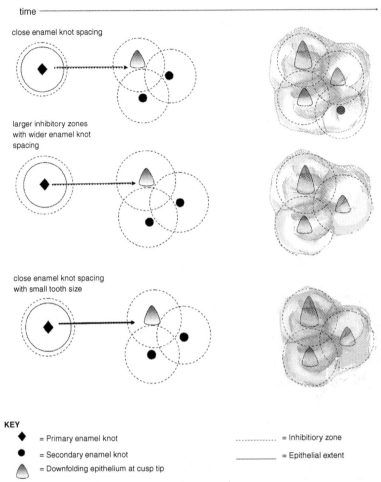

FIGURE 6.2: Patterning Cascade Model for tooth formation for a human upper molar. Top row shows growing dental epithelium with closely spaced enamel knots at three successive points in time. The enamel knots are superimposed over ghosted images of the form that the mineralized cusps will eventually take. After the primary enamel knot forms, secondary enamel knots form only when the dental epithelium grows large enough to exceed the boundaries of the zone of inhibition around the primary knot. As the epithelium grows larger still, exceeding the inhibition zones of secondary enamel knots, additional enamel knots can form. Middle row illustrates the same process, only with larger inhibitory zones around enamel knots. These larger inhibitory zones prevent formation of the fourth enamel knot that was able to form in the tooth

humans in having second and third molars that are especially reduced. The idea is that if there is a delay in the initiation of second and third molars in more slowly developing species but there is no change in the age at which crown formation ceases (or in the rate of crown formation), the period of crown formation in molars would be abbreviated, resulting in smaller crowns. This interesting suggestion could conceivably explain the differential reduction of molars in *Homo heidelbergensis*, Neanderthals and modern humans as a consequence of changing growth patterns in our ancestors (but it remains to be seen if second and third molar initiation and total crown formation times in the second and third molars of these three species are in accord with this hypothesis).

CONCLUSIONS

The present chapter reviewed dental evidence for changes in diet in *Homo*, especially in *Homo habilis* and *Homo erectus*. Departing from their australopith ancestors, these species appear to have consumed diets that were variable, and that incorporated more meat as well as softer (or softened) foods. Variable diets in *Homo erectus* are suggested by this species' variation in microwear complexity, indicating that both hard and soft foods were eaten. Dental evidence of meat-eating from trace elements is compatible with the archaeoglocial context and with evidence of the greater molar occlusal relief and wider incisors of *Homo habilis* in relation to australopiths. The changing morphology of incisors and molars in *Homo habilis* points toward the conclusion that teeth had already begun to adapt to this new diet. Softer (or

---

CAPTION FOR FIGURE 6.2: (cont.)

germ depicted in the top row (in which inhibitory zones were smaller). Bottom row illustrates this process in a tooth of smaller overall size but with enamel knot spacing equivalent to that in the top row. Here, tooth size prevents the formation of the fourth cusp because there is not enough space for the fourth enamel knot to form outside of the inhibitory zones of the other cusps. Drawn by author.

softened) foods are suggested by the reduction of bite force in *Homo habilis* as well as by the marked reduction in molar size in *Homo erectus*. Tool use in processing food as well as fire use may have contributed to this softer diet.

With respect to dental reduction in *Homo erectus*, the case for relaxed selection is plausible, but there may also have been direct selection for dental reduction. Otherwise, if accumulating random mutations do not necessarily lead to reduced trait size as per the Probable Mutation Effect, it is difficult to see why individuals with larger posterior teeth did not continue to pass along their genes for large tooth size. Following relaxed selection for large teeth, one might expect mean tooth size in a population to decrease as smaller-toothed individuals would now be able to survive and pass along their small-tooth genes. However, some factor other than relaxed selection would seem to be necessary to explain why individuals with very large teeth become so scarce, and the entire range of tooth sizes shifts downwards. Here, I have suggested that the most promising place to look for selection against large posterior tooth size in *Homo erectus* may be found in the "constitutive" energetic cost of growing and maintaining large jaws and teeth while simultaneously growing and maintaining large brains and bodies.

Finally, with *Homo heidelbergensis* there is the possibility that genetic drift can explain why this ancient hominin has postcanine tooth sizes equivalent to that of modern humans. One idea reviewed here, about the especially small size of *Homo heidelbergensis* second and third molars, has to do with overall rates of development and hypothesized associated delays in the initial formation of second and third molars. This brings us to the next chapter, which explores the topic of rates of development and the "pace of life history" in the genus *Homo* prior to Neanderthals and anatomically modern humans.

7 Long in the Tooth: Life History Changes in *Homo*

> Last scene of all,
> That ends this strange eventful history,
> Is second childishness and mere oblivion;
> Sans teeth, sans eyes, sans taste, sans every thing.
>
> – Shakespeare
> *As You Like It*

So ends Lord Jacques's soliloquy "All the World's a Stage," summing up human life history from infancy and childhood to toothless old age and death. In Chapter 4, we saw that some australopith species may have had juvenile growth periods shorter than or as long as those of some modern apes, but none were quite equal to modern humans in this regard.

Anthropologist Barry Bogin defined human childhood as the period between weaning and puberty during which offspring continue to depend on others for survival (180). For fossil hominins, the existence of childhood as so defined would be hard to determine. Applying Bogin's definition would require information about ages at weaning, which are difficult to acquire in fossil hominins, though not impossible (see Chapter 10). It would also be necessary to ascertain the length of time over which growing juvenile hominins actually depended on others for survival, and that would be even more difficult to determine. Nevertheless, through the study of teeth, the extension of juvenile growth periods, if not childhood as Bogin defined it, can be traced over the evolutionary history of the genus *Homo*. So too can the evolution of "second childishness" – old age.

In this chapter, we will see that within the genus *Homo*, changes in juvenile growth periods and longevity parallel each other in direction, though it is not clear that these changes in growth periods and longevity occurred in lockstep with each other. A common trajectory toward lengthening both juvenile growth periods and lifespans, but with possible differences in their rates of change, is consistent with the concept of "modular" life history evolution (186). The concept of "modularity" as applied to life history recognizes that different aspects of a species life history can respond to selection independently to some degree. This would be the case if the genes and developmental pathways that affect length of juvenile growth periods, for example, are not the same as those affecting longevity – or at least if not all of those genes and developmental pathways are the same.

Much of the literature on primate life history considers broad patterns across the order, arranging primate species on a continuum of fast to slow life histories (186). Yet, consistent with the concept of modularity, not all aspects of primate live histories can be arranged in this way. For instance, the natural age at weaning is earlier in humans than it is in chimpanzees, but humans reach sexual maturity and die at later ages than chimpanzees do (205). Holly Smith (191) suggests that humans can "afford" their late ages at sexual maturity by weaning early, thereby reducing the time intervals between births and increasing their reproductive rates. This example, and many others like it that can be found among primates (202, 364), highlights the concept of modularity as it applies to life history. Changes in species life history features over evolutionary time scales are not necessarily linked.

Still, with respect to changes in juvenile growth periods and lifespan over the course of human evolution, there is a common direction of change – toward lengthening both. This commonality suggests that these life history features exerted evolutionary influences on each other in some way. One possibility is that a long lifespan compensates for a delay in reproduction caused by an extended growth period. So, selection might have favored extended growth periods that increased learning time only in those individuals who also lived longer. Another possibility is that with reduced extrinsic mortality, natural selection might have favored our investment in physiological mechanisms that helped to extend our natural lifespans. In turn, longer lifespans may have made it possible for extended growth periods, with consequent delays in ages at first reproduction, to evolve. So, whether long growth periods or long lifespans came first is not clear, but one can easily imagine how these life history features might have coevolved.

The Grandmother Hypothesis (365) of human biologist Kristin Hawkes is yet another idea about how life history features coevolved over human evolution. In her work with the Hadza hunter-gatherers of Tanzania, Hawkes observed that postmenopausal women work intensively to provide for their daughters and granddaughters. No longer able to produce their own offspring, they devote their efforts to their existing children and grandchildren. If by so doing our female ancestors improved the reproductive success of their children and grandchildren, then natural selection would favor the lengthening of their natural lifespans beyond menopause.

In Hawkes' view, longer lifespans would enable females to delay reproducing until they built sufficient body capital to sustain the energetic demands of pregnancy, lactation, and offspring care. The extra growing time, in turn, would function as a "preadaptation" for longer periods of brain growth and learning. Finally, with the food and childcare provided by their postmenopausal mothers, ancestral females could wean their offspring earlier, reducing the intervals between births and increasing their reproductive rates.

Whether Hawkes' scenario, or other ideas linking delayed growth to longevity, is correct, the dental evidence suggests that within the genus *Homo*, prolonged juvenile periods coevolved with the lengthening of our natural lifespans. In this chapter, I detail this evidence and consider its potential implications for human social evolution. Specifically, I'll discuss anthropologists' speculations about whether longer juvenile periods and lifespans may have had something to do with the evolution of human "prosocial" behavior – behavior that benefits others (366, 367). As in the previous chapter, this one focuses on the genus *Homo* prior to the advent of Neanderthals and anatomically modern humans, which are discussed in later chapters (Chapters 8 and 9, respectively).

THE NATURE OF THE DENTAL EVIDENCE

As explained in Chapter 4, the primary evidence for gauging juvenile growth periods in fossil hominins relies on associations between dental growth and development and the overall pace of growth, development, and life history in modern primates. The sources of data discussed in that chapter included the dental development of different tooth types relative to one another (a special case being Schultz's Rule). However, also in that chapter, estimates of the actual timing of dental development were argued to provide more reliable indicators of juvenile growth periods.

In terms of dental eruption, the age at which molar teeth erupt most clearly differentiates modern humans from apes (368). Similarly, a new review by dental anthropologists Christopher Dean and Helen Liversidge finds that the age at which teeth begin to form (initiation) and the length of time they take to grow does not differ much for the anterior teeth of modern humans and chimpanzees, but does differ for molar teeth (369). These chimp-human differences in the initiation, tooth formation time, and eruption of molar teeth suggest that their chronological development may provide the most useful yardstick for assessing hominin juvenile growth periods.

Clues to longevity can be gained by estimating ages at death in fossil assemblages. In juveniles, ages at death can be ascertained with a fair degree of precision, using actual or virtual dental histology (see Chapter 4). For adults, estimates of ages at death are unfortunately much fuzzier, as any forensic anthropologist knows. To estimate ages at death in adult fossil hominins, paleoanthropologists Rachel Caspari and Sang-Hee Lee (370) applied the technique of "wear-based seriation" (370), first developed in 1963 by AEW Miles (371). In this method, rates of molar wear are estimated using average ages of eruption.

To illustrate, Figure 7.1 shows two australopith dentitions. In the dentition on the right, the first molar (second from the last in the tooth row) has become worn during the time between its eruption and the eruption of the second molar (last molar in the tooth row).

THE NATURE OF THE DENTAL EVIDENCE 161

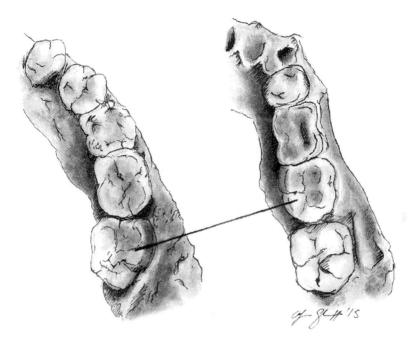

FIGURE 7.1: Wear seriation method of Caspari and Lee (2004; drawing by Alyssa Starrett based on their Figure 1). See text for explanation. Caspari R, Lee S-H. Older age becomes common late in human evolution. *Proceedings of the National Academy of Sciences USA.* 2004;101:10895–10900. Copyright (2004) National Academy of Sciences, USA.

The question is: How much time has occurred between the eruption of these two molars? Caspari and Lee assumed that the first, second, and third molars of hominins (including australopiths) erupted at five, ten, and fifteen years of age, respectively. On that assumption, the individual on the right would have been about ten years of age when he or she died.

Now take a look at the other dentition, on the left. Here, all three molars are in place, but the third molar of this individual is worn to the same degree as the first molar of the individual on the right. Assuming molars wear at the same rate, this would make the individual on the left approximately twenty years of age at death, calculated as so: fifteen years for the eruption of the M3 and five more years for the M3 to reach the degree of wear equal to that of the first molar of the individual on the right.

Similar kinds of estimates can be made with rates of wear for the second molars and matching these to worn third molars of other individuals, yielding age-at-death estimates for older adults. Clearly there is a large margin of error here owing to the assumption of uniform ages at eruption for different hominin species and individuals as well as the assumption of uniform rates of wear within a species. Still, gross distinctions can be made with some confidence between older individuals and younger ones.

Because dental development has been studied in the early members of our genus, as have ages at death, it is possible bring these two sources of evidence together to gain insight into life history changes within the genus *Homo*. There is difficulty in teasing apart these changes at the species level, however. The reasons is that some studies provide evidence for *Homo habilis* (in the broad sense), while others lump *Homo habilis* and *Homo erectus* into "early *Homo*" and others specifically refer to *Homo erectus*. In this chapter, I will follow the classifications used in specific studies, reviewing evidence for *Homo habilis*, "early *Homo*," *Homo erectus*, and *Homo antecessor*.

HOMO HABILIS AND EARLY HOMO: SMART AND FAST

Holly Smith's (1991) analysis of life history variation across living anthropoids suggested a strong relationship between brain size and life history features. Based on these analyses, she suggested that juvenile periods would have begun to lengthen in *Homo habilis*. Using the regression line of brain size on first molar eruption, Holly Smith predicted that first molars would have erupted at around 3 to 3.4 years of age in Australopiths (not so different from chimpanzees) but around four years of age in the larger-brained *Homo habilis*. Larger brain sizes together with later ages at first molar eruption would imply that *Homo habilis* had moved in the direction of a more human-like life history schedule.

The dental data *may* support the view that changes in a human-like direction were beginning in Homo habilis, but overall they suggest relatively fast rates of dental development. To begin with is Holly Smith's analysis of relative dental development (195) in the East African Homo habilis specimen KNM-ER (Kenya National Museum – East Rudolf) 1590. When the developing teeth of this specimen were aged according to chimpanzee dental age charts, they gave relatively consistent ages, suggesting that at least relative to one another, this specimen's teeth were developing in a way that is similar to those of chimpanzees. By contrast, using human charts of dental development, some teeth gave ages that were half of that of other teeth, suggesting that the specimen's relative rates of dental development were not at all similar to those of modern humans.

Absolute rates and periods of tooth formation also appear to be fast in Homo habilis and in some specimens referred to as "early Homo." In their pioneering paper on dental development in hominins suggesting chimpanzee-like first molar eruption times in australopiths, Bromage and Dean (223) estimated an age at death for the East African early Homo specimen KNM-ER 820. Using perikymata counts, along with estimates of root growth based on data from modern great apes, they obtained an age at death of 5.3 years but with a stage of dental development equivalent to that of a seven-year-old child. Bromage and Dean concluded: "Unexpectedly, the age calculated for early Homo, as represented by KNM-ER 820, provides evidence that the trend for prolongation of the growth period had not begun with this group" (1985: 826). Yet, the use of root growth rates of apes to estimate root growth rates in the fossil specimen may go some way toward explaining this result.

Other evidence also suggests rapid rates of dental development in Homo habilis and some early Homo. In Tanya Smith and colleagues' 2015 reassessment of hominin dental development (196), age at death for the south African early Homo specimen DH (Drimolen Hominin) 35 was calculated without recourse to estimates based on modern great ape data, but from growth increments visible using x-ray synchrotron microtomography ("virtual histology": see Chapter 4) from the specimen itself. The resulting age-at-death estimate is 2.18 years, but the specimen has a dental age based on modern human standards of more than 3.5 years. Fast dental development for early *Homo* is also suggested by perikymata numbers on anterior teeth that are generally lower than those of modern humans (225, 226).

Another indication of rapid rates of tooth formation in early *Homo* comes from the analysis of enamel formation rates. Christopher Dean and colleagues (226) counted daily increments at 100 μm intervals along enamel prisms of six early *Homo* specimens. They plotted these counts against enamel thickness measurements at these same intervals to obtain cumulative curves of occlusal enamel formation. Rates of growth, as assessed by the slopes of these lines revealed that none of the early *Homo* specimens formed occlusal enamel as slowly as modern humans do. The fastest rates of all were found in the *Homo habilis* specimen KNM-ER 1590.

There are a few striae of Retzius periodicities determined from the early *Homo* specimens included in the Smith et al. paper (that made use of virtual histology) in which the section plane is controlled: two have a seven-day and one has an eight-day periodicity (196). Meanwhile, a previous study from naturally fractured surfaces estimated periodicities centering around eight days in early *Homo* (372). On current evidence, then, early *Homo* does not appear to differ from modern humans in periodicity. The same appears true of australopiths, as noted in Chapter 4.

These similar periodicities in different hominins species are interesting insofar as there are moderate to strong relationships between Retzius periodicity and life history features across the primate order (Chapter 4). These findings may indicate that in neither australopiths nor early *Homo* are periodicities reliable indicators of developmental rates. Another logical possibility, of course, is that these periodicities *do* indicate overall developmental rates in the human range and/or a human-like life history schedule, but that these hominins had unpredictably fast rates of dental development

(203). In early *Homo*, rapid rates of dental development could be out-of-step with potentially slower rates of somatic growth, as they are in Indriids (Chapter 4).

Finally, Christopher Dean and Helen Liversidge's new comparison of dental development in early *Homo* with a huge and diverse sample of modern humans puts the concept of "rapid" rates of dental development in perspective. These authors estimated ages-at-death in three immature fossil hominins, two *Homo erectus* and one possible *Homo habilis* specimen (STW 151). These hominins died when their second premolars, second molars, and third molars were still forming, so it was possible to put ages to the stages of development these teeth had reached at the time of death.

Dean and Liversidge compared the "ages for stages" of these three hominins to the ages at which 6,540 modern children from across the globe reached these same stages of development. What they found was that *all three* of these specimens fell within the modern human range of ages for these stages, although at the "fast" end of the spectrum. Dean and Liversidge interpret their results to mean that growth prolongation may have already begun in *Homo habilis* (and they suggest also possibly in australopiths). That the two *Homo erectus* specimens fell within the modern human range is much less surprising, though, given previous work on dental development in this species.

HOMO ERECTUS AND HOMO ANTECESSOR: TOWARD A MORE HUMAN-LIKE LIFE HISTORY

There is even stronger evidence that rates of dental growth and development shifted in a human direction in *Homo erectus*. For starters, relative rates of dental development in this species are human-like. Analysis of radiographs reveal that the sequence of tooth development across the dentition is quite similar to that of modern humans (373), although with some advancement of posterior teeth relative to anterior ones (374). Of course, however, this does not mean that the actual length of time for tooth development to take place was the same.

Christopher Dean and colleagues' (2001) *Nature* study on incremental growth in fossil hominins (226) included an estimate of first molar emergence in *Homo erectus*. These authors made histological sections of the *Homo erectus* specimen Sangiran S7-37 from Java and counted dental growth increments. Here is what they did: they assumed that the first molar initiated crown formation shortly before birth, as it does in apes and humans. On that reasonable assumption, they counted growth increments in the histological section to determine the age at which the first molar crown completed formation – approximately 2.5 years of age.

Next, they calculated the rate at which the first molar root grew in length – its "root extension rate" – using growth increments present in root dentine. They noted that first molars erupt into functional occlusion in hominins when about 8 mm of root is formed, suggesting that emergence through the gingiva would have occurred somewhat earlier, when about 7 mm of root had formed. They then applied the root length extension rate they had calculated to 7 mm of root, obtaining the length of time it took to form. Adding root formation time to the age at which the first molar crown completed, they estimated that first molar gingival emergence occurred at about 4.4 years of age. The estimate is consistent with the M1 emergence age of 4.6 years that Holly Smith predicted on the basis of brain size in early *Homo erectus* (200). While this M1 emergence estimate indicates a growth rate shift in a human direction, it does not quite reach average human M1 emergence ages, with means as low as 4.7 years of age (Kenyan girls) to means of six or more years of age in many human groups (Liversidge in [238]).

Performing an analysis similar to this one, Dean and colleagues (226) also estimated gingival emergence of Sangiran S7-37's second premolar. If it erupted as it does in modern humans along with the M2, then M2 eruption would have been around 7.6 years of age. This is higher than the mean of 6.7 years for M2 emergence in captive chimpanzees (375), though it is encompassed within the chimpanzee range in captivity of 5.6–7.8 years of age (375). The Sangiran specimen's M2 emergence estimate is quite low compared to modern humans, whose second molars are often referred to as "12-year-old" molars. The earliest mean M2 emergence ages in modern humans appears to be around ten years of age (girls in Uganda) (Liversidge in [238]), and even this is greater than the 7.6 years estimated for M2 emergence in Sangiran S7-37. So, it seems, the shift toward a more human-like schedule of dental developmental in *Homo erectus* is fairly modest.

Perhaps even more revealing is the analysis Dean and Smith (374) performed of both dental and skeletal growth in WT 15000, the Nariokotome Boy. This nearly complete 1.6 million year old skeleton (Figure 7.2) has provided a wealth of information to paleoanthropologists. Smith and Dean (374) added to that wealth with their analysis. These authors made use of perikymata counts, estimated periodicity (it was not possible to section these teeth), and an estimate of root length extension rates, to propose that the Narikotome Boy was in the range of 7.6 – 8.8 years of age when he died. That estimate is critical to evaluating his rates of dental and skeletal growth and development.

At death, the Nariokotome boy's lower second molars were already in functional occlusion, and based upon this as well as the state of development in his other teeth, he was equivalent to a modern human of 10.2 years of age. He was clearly dentally advanced, then, but it turns out he was even *more* advanced skeletally. This boy, who was at most nine years of age at death, had a state of elbow joint ossification similar to that of a 13.5 year old modern human boy. Furthermore, he had already achieved a stature of 5 feet 3 inches, which in modern terms is extremely tall for such a young boy and in *Homo erectus* terms almost as tall as the average adult, at five feet four inches (based on nine specimens). Smith and Dean point out that even when advanced, modern human adolescent boys do not reach this percentage of adult stature until they are 17–18 years of age, or 16–17 years in the most advanced cases (376).

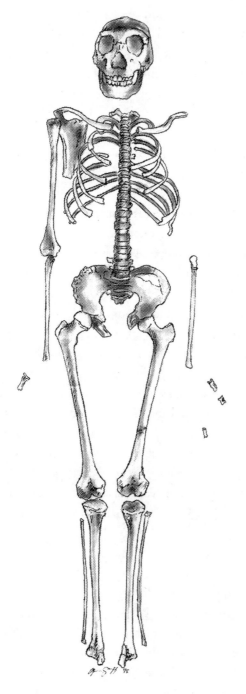

FIGURE 7.2: Artist's rendition of the Nariokotome Boy (WT 15000) skeleton. Drawn by Alyssa Starrett.

In sum, Dean and Smith (374) state "... it is clear that for a child like Nariokotome, with skeletal age advanced by 34+ months over the dentition, a pediatrician would be justified in sending the case to an endocrinologist" (2009). Or, perhaps the pediatrician might send the Narikotome boy to an evolutionary anthropologist, who would helpfully point out that the boy shouldn't worry because species can differ in their "life history modes." Evolutionary anthropologists Steve Leigh and Greg Blomquist (186) define a "life history mode [as] a distinctive pattern or arrangement of ontogeny with respect to the rate and scheduling of growth for various organs, organ systems, or modules" (2007:403). It seems that *Homo erectus* and *Homo sapiens* differ from each other in this respect – with *Homo erectus* having rates of skeletal growth and development that are more rapid in relation to dental development than do modern humans.

Exactly what the selective pressures were that shaped *Homo erectus* life history modes are a matter of speculation. Dean and Lucas (192) suggest that growing to a large size relatively quickly could have been advantageous in an environment where small offspring were at high risk of predation. They also observe that achieving larger body size at a relatively early age would also allow *Homo erectus* juveniles to begin to provide for themselves and for others. What seems most clear from Dean and Smith's (374) analysis is that somatically, *Homo erectus* juveniles grew more like modern apes, lacking the slow growth between weaning and puberty that typifies modern human children.

Filling in more of the picture for *Homo erectus* life histories are Caspari and Lee's (370) longevity estimates in early *Homo*, in which *Homo erectus* specimens were included. Using wear-based seriation estimates as described earlier, they separated individual hominin specimens crudely into groups of young (between 15 and 30 years of age) and old (greater than 30 years of age) adults for each taxonomic group. Australopiths (353 individuals) had an "old to young ratio" or "OY ratio" of 0.12. For early *Homo* (208 individuals), the OY ratio jumps to 0.25, a difference from australopiths that the authors found to be statistically significant. If these OY ratios are taken at face value (though they clearly rely on many assumptions – see earlier discussion) they suggest a strong shift, in which a little more than twice the number of early *Homo* adults were living to ages of thirty or greater as compared to their australopith predecessors. From Caspari and Lee's analysis, it isn't clear if the trend began with *Homo habilis* because *Homo habilis* and *Homo erectus* individuals were grouped together into early *Homo*. At minimum, these data suggest that by the time *Homo erectus* had come on the scene, more individuals were living beyond the age of 30.

Still, given the small number of specimens of *Homo erectus* for which we have information for both dental and somatic growth, the crudity of OY ratio estimates, and the question of whether the fossil assemblages on which OY estimates are calculated are truly representative, it is not possible to determine whether human-trending changes in longevity preceded changes in juveniles growth periods or vice versa. Nor, unfortunately, is it possible to meaningfully compare the *magnitude* of changes in longevity with the magnitude of changes in dental and somatic development in *Homo erectus*. OY ratios only provide two categories into which the remains of fossilized individuals are sorted on the basis of their ages at death – even a small average change in longevity could tip a sizeable number of individuals from the young to old category. On the positive side, these data do suggest that *Homo erectus* took a "small step" toward modern human life histories, both in terms of juvenile growth periods (dentally if not skeletally) as well as lifespan.

It has been suggested, though, that *Homo antecessor* took a "giant leap" toward humanness around 1 million years ago (377). José Bermúdez de Castro and colleagues assessed the pattern of relative dental development in a mandible with mixed dentition (both deciduous and permanent teeth) from the Gran Dolina Lower Pleistocene cave site located in the Sierra de Atapuerca of Northern Spain. They used microcomputed tomography to image portions of the teeth contained within the mandible. Relative dental development was similar to that of modern humans and not to chimpanzees.

In another individual from this site, the upper and lower first molars had only recently erupted, judging from the minimal wear present on the tooth crowns. Unable to apply histological techniques to these fossil remains, the authors applied root length extension rate data from chimpanzees and humans to the length of root formed in the first molars at the time of death (8 millimeters). Doing so allowed the authors to estimate how much time it took for the root to form if it grew at either a chimpanzee or modern human rate.

To the chimpanzee-based root formation time estimate, they added the average crown formation time for an *Australopithecus* first molar to form. For the human-based root formation time estimate, they added the average crown formation time for a human first molar to form. On this basis, they bracketed their estimate between "fast" and "slow" extremes for the time at which the first molars would have emerged through the individual's gingiva: 5.3–6.6 years. While there is a good deal of estimation going on here, even the 5.3 M1 eruption estimate is within the modern human range for M1 eruption, though at the fast end of it. Whether all aspects of dental development fit comfortably within modern human ranges is unclear, as only the developmental pattern and M1 eruption ages were studied here. However, in relation to WT 15000, *Homo antecessor* seems to have moved farther along the path toward extending the period of dental development.

The rest of the life history story in the genus *Homo* concerns Neanderthals and the earliest anatomically modern *Homo sapiens* (AMHS), the subjects of the chapters that follow. Before moving forward to dental insights into Neanderthals and AMHS, I turn to what the dentally-derived insights into life history in *Homo erectus* may imply for the evolution of human prosocial behavior.

TEETH, HELPING HANDS, AND GROWING BRAINS

Anthropologists hypothesize that there are connections between the evolution of slow growth rates, the help of others in rearing offspring, and the human ability to wean their offspring earlier than apes do. Kristin Hawkes' Grandmother Hypothesis considers the special role of grandmothers as helpers. In humans, help in rearing offspring also extends to other members of the group, as well (378). In comparison with many other primates, humans have been said to exhibit "hyper-cooperation" (366). Humans help their relatives and trusted allies, just as chimpanzees do. However, apparently unlike chimpanzees and other great apes, humans also show "proactive prosociality" – they spontaneously act in ways that benefit others, even when assistance is unsolicited (366).

Judith Burkart and colleagues (367) designed an experimental apparatus in which primate and human subjects could help conspecifics reach a food treat they could not reach themselves. Chimpanzees did not behave helpfully, but human children did. The only other primates who spontaneously helped others were those who belonged to species who routinely "allomother."

Allomothers are individuals other than the mother who help raise offspring. Species in which allomothering is habitual and extensive – where siblings, other relatives, and even nonrelatives regularly help parents to raise offspring – are known as "cooperative breeders" (378). Within the primates, only the callitrichids (marmosets and tamarins) and humans satisfy this definition of cooperative breeders (378), though many other primates exhibit allomothering to a lesser degree. In common marmosets, for example, allomothers, which include an infant's siblings as well as the males with whom the mother has previously mated, carry infants and may provide them with food (small prey)(378).

Infant-carrying and provisioning by allomothers is characteristic of humans: it does seem to "take a village" to raise a human child. Furthermore, the help of others may enable mothers move on to their next pregnancy. Human biologist Barbara Piperata showed that in the Brazilian Amazon, women who receive the greatest level of social support – help from others in the community – lose the least amount of weight when they are nursing their babies (379). Energy balance – the relationship between energy taken in and energy expended – is related to the length of time it takes for women to resume ovulatory cycles after they give birth (380). In other words, the amount of energetic stress a mother sustains when she is nursing her offspring affects when she can become pregnant again. So, Piperata hypothesizes that women who receive the most social support may be able to become pregnant sooner than they otherwise wood. Piperata and I (381) argued that that during human evolutionary history, social support may have been a critical adaptation, enabling female hominins to reduce the intervals between births and therefore to have more children. Slowing of juvenile growth rates may have made it possible to support more than one dependent child at a time, because it reduced the total amount of energy needed to support them (382).

Based on an earlier suggestion by evolutionary biologist WD Hamilton (383), Primatologist Sarah Hrdy (378) theorized that cooperative breeding itself *allows* delayed maturation. She pointed out that in birds (in the passerine order, specifically) fledglings of cooperatively breeding species continue to depend on parents for twice as long as they do in those that do not breed cooperatively (citing work by Langen [384]). Essentially, as helpers take over feeding responsibilities, mothers are free to breed again, reducing the pressure on fledglings to become independent. Extending the argument to humans, longer periods of learning may simply be a by-product of prolonged periods of childhood dependency that followed from a system of cooperative breeding. This idea is consistent with Kristin Hawkes' (365) view that extra growing time served as a "pre-adaptation" for longer periods of brain growth and learning.

Differing in emphasis, these explanations all suggest that in some way cooperative breeding, extended growth periods, slow growth rates, and early weaning coevolved. Teeth come into this picture by offering evidence as to when the lengthening of juvenile growth periods began as well as when "grandmothers" could have been around to help. By the time of *Homo erectus*, rates of dental development had begun to slow. Rates of somatic development, however, may still have been quite rapid, judging from the Narikotome boy.

With *Homo erectus*, both body and brain size increased, presumably increasing the energetic demand of growing offspring as well as the energetic demands on pregnant and nursing mothers (385). It would seem, therefore, that during this period of our evolutionary history, there would have been a need for allomothers to help provision offspring (192). Fast rates of somatic growth – if the analysis of the Narikotome boy proves to representative of *Homo erectus* – may have exacerbated the energetic demands of offspring, further increasing this need. According to one recent study, viable population sizes in large-brained *Homo erectus* could not have been sustained *without* a system of cooperative breeding (386). Caspari and Lee's (370) study of dental wear rates suggests that in *Homo erectus*, more than in any previous hominin species, a greater number of grandmothers were available to help.

Children are not the only humans who need a lot of help. On the basis of dental evidence it was suggested that care for older individuals occurred in the 1.8 MA hominins of Dmanisi, Georgia. One of the Dmanisi skulls is missing all but one tooth (see Figure 5.3), with the sockets showing nearly complete bone resorption (357). The resorption indicates that this individual lived for a long period of time without his or her teeth. This specimen represents the earliest such case of such a toothless or "edentulous" individual in the hominin fossil record. How did this individual survive? Lordkipadnze and colleagues think that the individual probably relied on softer foods and possibly the help of other individuals to supply these soft foods (357).

While assistance from others is a plausible explanation, the survival of the toothless does not necessarily imply it. Primatologists Frank Cuozzo and Michelle Sauther (387) studied ring-tailed lemurs in Madagascar who lose plenty of teeth, owing to their feeding-dependence on hard and tough tamarind fruit that they do not appear to be dentally adapted to eat (they have thin enamel, for one thing). Their reliance on tamarind fruit may be a relatively recent phenomenon in their evolutionary history, resulting from human disturbance of their habitat. These lemurs tend to lose the very teeth they use in masticating this fruit. Yet, individuals with extensive tooth loss survive, *without* the active assistance of others. Cuozzo and Sauther attribute their survival to "unintentional" assistance from others in the group.

Being part of a social group allows lemurs to make use of shared knowledge about the location of food resources. Interestingly, Cuozzo and Sauther have seen toothless individuals pick up and eat tamarind fruit that other have that partially chewed and discarded. So, these authors make the excellent point that if toothless lemurs can survive with such "passive" assistance, then toothless hominins may have been able to do the same. And of course, as Cuozzo and Sauther also point out, the Dmanisi individuals had stone tools, so a toothless individual may have been capable of processing his or her own food, making it more chewable.

CONCLUDING THOUGHTS

This chapter brought together dental evidence for the evolution of two defining life history features of modern humans: prolonged growth periods and long lives. Dentally, *Homo erectus* evinces a step toward a longer period of development. First molar eruption was intermediate between that of chimpanzees and humans (226), and the ages at which particular stages of development were reached (second premolars, and second and third molars) were within the modern human range (369).

Still, the advanced state of skeletal development in the Narikotome boy implies somatic growth rates more like that of chimpanzees than like that of modern humans. The Narikotome analysis may signal a life history "mode" in *Homo erectus* quite unlike that of modern humans – with a different combination of developmental rates in the dentition and skeleton. Why that combination differed, i.e., what particular selection pressures may have been involved, is not clear. However, the story of human life history evolution in the genus *Homo* is likely to be more complicated than a series of simple shifts toward a modern human pattern. As emphasized in Chapter 4, different species may have been subject to different sets of selection pressures shaping their own particular life history modes. Expanding the comparative context from living primates – understanding how their life history modes vary in response to diverse selection pressures – will help in interpreting the life history modes of fossil hominins.

By the time of *Homo erectus*, lifespans appear to have lengthened to some degree, taking the OY ratios from dental wear-seriation at face value. If so, then older individuals would have been available to help provision fast-growing, large-brained *Homo erectus* children. The overall picture that studies of teeth have helped to paint is that the beginnings of extended development, longer lives, and cooperative breeding can be traced back to *Homo erectus*. By 1 million years ago, with *Homo antecessor*, first molar eruption seems to have entered the modern human range (377). Whether this was so in Neanderthals and the earliest anatomically modern humans is considered in the next two chapters (respectively) as are other questions about Neanderthal and AMHS biology and into which teeth yield insights.

8 Knowing Neanderthals through Their Teeth

> We cannot avoid recognizing these late Neandertals as the same sort of creatures as ourselves: upright, talking apes with a capacity for technological innovation and symbolic behavior. Questions about interfertility take on a lesser importance in the light of that admission.
>
> – Cartmill M and Smith F
> *The Human Lineage*

Ever since Neanderthals were discovered more than 150 years ago (see Chapter 5), scientists have debated just about every aspect of their biology. Based on the distinctive features of Neanderthals (Chapter 4) is easy to see why King considered Neanderthals to be a different species from humans, christening them *Homo neanderthalensis*. Like other scientists of his time, King also inferred mental capacity from the shape of the cranium, considering Neanderthals to be lowbrows in more than one sense of the word. Between 1911 and 1913, paleontologist-artist Marcelin Boule published illustrations depicting Neanderthals as stooping hairy beasts with grasping toes. This too did not help Neanderthals with their image problem. Boule's conception held sway until 1957, when Straus and Cave showed that Boule had misread the evidence, and that Neanderthals walked upright just as we do (281).

Ideas about Neanderthals began to change in the 1950s, in part because the field of physical anthropology itself was transforming. In the wake of World War II, physical anthropologists repudiated the idea that there are races or types of humans with distinct physical and mental attributes. Instead, the consensus view was, as it is today, that there are no clear physical or mental divisions among human populations along racial lines, that mental attributes are not linked to physical attributes, and that there is no evidence that human populations differ in intelligence. Racist thinking, it was argued, had led to a serious misunderstanding and Neanderthals were welcomed back into our species. Our modern understanding of species rests on evolutionary biologist Ernst Mayr's concept of reproductive isolation – species evolve independently of one another and become distinct if they do not exchange genes. As part of our species, the implication was that when and where Neanderthals and anatomically modern humans coexisted, they could have interbred to produce fertile offspring. By extension, today's humans (though in need of a time machine to do it) could have mated with Neanderthals and had children who themselves were fully capable of reproducing.

This shift in our understanding of Neanderthals did not last. In 1997, we were back to the "two species" place where we started, but this time on what seemed to be firmer, i.e., genetic, grounds. Geneticist Matthias Krings and coworkers successfully extracted mitochondrial DNA (mtDNA) from the original Neanderthal remains, and compared it to the mtDNA of people living today (388). What these researchers found was that the mtDNA differences between Neanderthals and modern humans were three times greater than those between any two groups of modern humans. It now seemed that Neanderthals were only very distantly related to modern humans and that Neanderthals had no direct genetic input into our modern genomes. Still, this was mtDNA, which is such a small part of the genome and represents only maternal genetic input. More definitive evidence would be sought in Neanderthal nuclear DNA.

By 2010, researchers had sequenced much of the Neanderthal nuclear genome. Geneticist Richard Green and colleagues estimated that 1–4% of the DNA of *some* living peoples came from Neanderthals (279). Those living people are Europeans, Asians, and Australasians, but not Africans. This finding suggests that in some region(s) of the world, Neanderthals and our ancient human ancestors interbred to produce viable offspring whose living non-African descendants retain a small percentage of Neanderthal DNA. Yet in 2012, evolutionary biologists Anders Eriksson and Andrea Manica published a paper suggesting that this 1–4% Neanderthal contribution might not be specifically Neanderthal but could have been inherited from a common ancestor of both Neanderthals and modern humans (321). And so debate rages about whether we and Neanderthals are a single species and to what extent we carry Neanderthal genes within us.[1]

The question of just how different Neanderthals were from us, and in what ways, underlies most research on Neanderthal biology and culture. The question is not only integral to defining Neanderthals but also to shedding light on why modern humans survived and Neanderthals did not. Neanderthals inhabited Europe and the Middle East from as early as 430,000 years ago, if the Sima de los Huesos *Homo heidelbergensis* fossil cache represents the base of the Neanderthal clade (see Chapter 5). Their existence spanned cold, glacial conditions to more temperate, interglacial times. Anatomically modern humans, those who look like us, moved into Europe (coming originally from Africa) about 40,000 years ago (296). They appear to have overlapped in time and space with Neanderthals (though see [389] for a different view) but generally had more sophisticated tools and produced copious artistic cultural remains in the form of cave paintings and carvings. These cultural advances associated with modern humans constitute the Upper Paleolithic, the last period of the "old stone age."

This chapter highlights what the evidence from Neanderthal teeth tells us about our similarities and differences from Neanderthals and considers what their evolutionary implications might be. The study of teeth has specifically provided insight into the ancestry of Neanderthals as well as made significant contributions to understanding their diets, behavior, experience of physiological stress, and life history. Neanderthal teeth offer some surprises, some confirmations,

---

[1] Part of the problem in assessing species status based on gene flow is that gene flow *can* occur between species. Interspecific gene flow can occur by the process of introgression, when the hybrid offspring of two different species mate with one (or both) of the parent species.

and some contradictions. But, the contradictions, like the debates about Neanderthal DNA, are ultimately moving us toward a more refined knowledge of Neanderthal nature.

WHAT CAN TEETH TELL US ABOUT NEANDERTHAL PHYLOGENETIC RELATIONSHIPS?

As noted in Chapter 5, Neanderthal teeth have numerous morphological differences from those of modern humans. Among these are their taurodont roots (Figure 5.7) large and labially-convex shovel-shaped incisors, asymmetric lower second premolars, and upper molars with enlarged hypocone cusps (Figure 8.1). Yet, many of these features can be found, although at different frequencies, in earlier hominins. The "bulging" hypocone, once thought to be a derived Neanderthal feature, is present not only in the likely progenitors of Neanderthals – the Sima de los Huesos *Homo heidelbergensis* group – but also in *Homo heidelbergensis* specimens from other regions of Europe (390). Other dental features typical of Neanderthals (e.g., a continuous midtrigonid crest) appear to be present in *Homo antecessor* and even *Homo erectus* (from Zhoukoudian China and in site from Java) (391).

As paleoanthropologist Song Xing and colleagues put it, many typical "Neanderthal-traits" are simply those that Neanderthals exhibit at higher frequencies than previous hominins (293). Elevated frequencies of these traits, some of which have no demonstrated functional significance, suggests the operation of genetic drift.

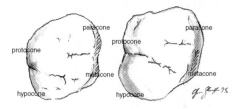

FIGURE 8.1: Anatomically modern human (left) vs. Neanderthal (right) upper first molars. After Gómez-Robles et al. (2007), Figure 7. Note the bulging hypocone of the Neanderthal molar. Drawn by Alyssa Starrett.

If Neanderthals existed at low population densities (392) and were relatively isolated from other contemporary hominins, it follows that their dental trait frequencies would drift in this way. It turns out the genetic drift is the most likely explanation for the distinctive features of Neanderthal cranial morphology (393).

What this patterning of dental trait frequencies might mean for Neanderthal phylogenetic relationships is the more interesting question though. Using the Krapina Neanderthals as an outgroup, Stringer and colleagues (394) performed a cladistics analysis to assess how modern humans from different regions of the world appeared to be related. Their analysis indicated that modern Africans were first to branch off on the modern human line after its divergence from Neanderthals. This result challenged an earlier notion that Neanderthals were the direct ancestors of modern Europeans (395, 396). It may seem difficult to reconcile this result with DNA evidence of Neanderthal gene flow into non-Africans (279). However, the percentage of Neanderthal genes introduced into living non-Africans is small (1–4%). The cladistic analysis of dental traits therefore primarily reflects the accumulation of genetic differences (through genetic drift and possibly natural selection) arising after Neanderthals and these modern human groups diverged.[2]

Rather than focusing on Neanderthal relationships to modern humans, Maria Martinón-Torres and colleagues performed cladistics analysis based on the dental traits of Neanderthals in the context of earlier and contemporary hominins (391). Their analysis revealed two clusters – one with African hominins (including *Homo habilis*, African *Homo erectus*, and Middle-Pleistocene north Africans) and a second with Asian *Homo erectus* (from Zhoukoudian, China and from sites in Java), *Homo antecessor*, Neanderthals and middle Pleistocene *Homo sapiens*. They believe their results show population continuity

---

[2] Shara Bailey found that early anatomically modern humans from Qafzeh cave, Israel (dated to 90,000 years ago) appear to be more similar to sub-Saharan Africans in their dental morphology than to Neanderthals. (284. Bailey SE. Dental morphological affinities among late Pleistocene and recent humans. *Dental Anthropology*. 2000;14:1–8). She suggests that if there was admixture between Neanderthals and anatomically modern humans in Middle East, it did not appear to have influenced Qafzeh dental morphology.

between Europe and Asia during the Pleistocene, with a deep division between Eurasia and Africa. In other words, they attribute the similarity between middle Pleistocene Europeans (including Neanderthals) and Asian *Homo erectus* to extensive gene flow. Of course, more recent common ancestry between Asian *Homo erectus* and middle Pleistocene European hominins – as per a standard reading of a cladogram – could also explain their results.

Whatever the explanation, the Martinón-Torres et al. study presents a challenge to previous notions that Asian *Homo erectus* represents a remote and isolated side branch of the hominin evolutionary tree (276). Furthermore, teeth older than 60 KYA from the site of Xujiayao, Northern China (Xing et al., 2015) exhibit high degrees of incisor shoveling and labial convexity (293), traits that Martinon-Torres and colleagues (391) identified as part of a "Eurasian dental pattern." On the other hand, a recent study of middle Pleistocene *Homo erectus* specimens from another site, that of Hexian in Eastern China, finds no Neanderthal dental traits in these hominins (397). Thus, if there were gene flow during the middle Pleistocene between Europe and Asia, there was at least one pocket of people in Asia into which Neanderthal genes – or, at least those genes coding for dental traits – did not arrive.

Paleoanthropologist Aida Gómez-Robles and her coworkers attempted to reconstruct the dental features of the last common ancestor of Neanderthals and modern humans (398). These researchers then used those features to assess whether any known fossil hominin species fit the dental description of this common ancestor. To do this, they quantified dental morphology using geometric morphometric analysis, a method in which a series of points (landmarks) are placed in homologous positions on either photographs or 3-D scans of similar skeletal elements. In this case the elements were teeth, and 2-D images were used. Various statistical techniques were applied to these data to analyze shape differences. From the "shape variables" obtained in this analysis, the authors used another statistical method (a generalized linear model) to estimate the state of these traits in the last Neanderthal-modern human common ancestor.

Next, the authors compared their reconstructed "dental ancestor" with the dental shape attributes of species that are potential candidates for the Neanderthal-modern human last common ancestor, such as African *Homo erectus, Homo antecessor,* and *Homo heidelbergensis.* The surprising result was that the dental morphology of *none* of the fossil samples matched the reconstructed dental ancestor. The earliest European species, *Homo antecessor* at 1 million years ago, was already dentally derived in the direction of Neanderthals. Gómez-Robles et al. argue that that the last common ancestor between Neanderthals and modern humans must therefore predate *Homo antecessor* and suggest that its remains are most likely to be found in Africa (though, according to their analysis, it is not represented by any currently known *Homo erectus* groups). Their results are seemingly at odds with nuclear DNA analysis that puts the divergence of Neanderthal, Denisovans, and modern human DNA around 800,000 years ago, on average (300). The genetic and dental data could conceivably be reconciled if differences in dental morphology among these groups arose earlier than their average DNA divergence dates.

Altogether then, dental evidence is helping to refine our understanding of Neanderthal evolutionary relationships. Consistent with genetic evidence, the dental evidence controverts the idea that Neanderthals are more closely related to modern Europeans than they are to other modern human groups. The dental evidence from middle Pleistocene hominins raises the possibility that some populations of Asian *Homo erectus* may have had more to do with the evolutionary history of middle Pleistocene Europeans, including Neanderthals, then previously supposed. Finally, the reconstruction of the last common dental ancestor of Neanderthals and modern humans reveals that *Homo antecessor* at 1 million years ago was already derived in the direction of Neanderthals, pushing the initial divergence between Neanderthals and modern humans back in time. While such phylogenetic questions go to the heart of Neanderthal research, a good deal of work on Neanderthal teeth goes more toward the stomach – that is, what and how did Neanderthals eat?

REAL NEANDERTHALS DID NOT EAT QUICHE, BUT DID THEY EAT MUCH BESIDES LARGE MAMMALS?

In July 2012, the scientific journal *Nature* announced that "Neanderthals ate their greens." (http://www.nature.com/news/neanderthals-ate-their-greens-1.11030). The evidence came from teeth. That was breaking news because Neanderthals have traditionally been considered big game hunters, eating such large mammals as woolly mammoths, woolly rhinos, and bison. These are the predominant animal remains found at Neanderthal sites throughout Eurasia and across the timespan of Neanderthal existence. Neanderthals actually hunted (vs. scavenged) these large mammals. They fashioned thrusting spears and javelins, some with stone-tipped points (399). Neanderthal weapons have even been found in the bones of prey animals: a wooden spear amongst the ribs of a straight-tusked elephant (a site in Germany) (400), and a stone point embedded within one of the neck vertebrae of a wild ass (a site in Syria) (401).

Furthermore, studies of stable isotopes suggest that Neanderthals occupied a top carnivore niche (402–404). Of great utility in these studies is N-15 (nitrogen-15), a rare isotope of nitrogen (the much more common form is nitrogen-14). The protein we ingest is rich in nitrogen, which becomes incorporated into the protein of our own tissue. Along the food chain, N-15 (nitrogen-15) becomes more concentrated, increasing by three to five parts per thousand at each step. Plants contain very little N-15, herbivores have more N-15, and carnivores have the most. Thus, the hair of vegans tends to be depleted in N-15 compared to those who include meat in their diets (405).

Whereas hair does not preserve well in the fossil record, bones and teeth do, and their main protein component, collagen, contains a lot of nitrogen. Collagen in a tooth (specifically its primary dentin) reflects diet at the time a tooth was forming, while collagen in bone reflects the average protein portion of the diet over the course of several years before death. For this reason, unless a researcher is specifically interested in childhood diets, most studies of N-15 focus on bone collagen. We'll return to the starring role of teeth later, but for entirely different reasons.

Neanderthals appear to have had levels of N-15 high enough to suggest that almost all of their dietary protein was obtained from animals and not plants (402–404). Paleoanthropologist Hervé Bocherens is an author of several of these studies, and in 2009 he synthesized data from the most reliable studies to date (406). For six Neanderthals from northern Europe (France and Belgium), he reported N-15 values that were one to two parts per thousand higher than those found in contemporaneous fossil carnivores, such as hyenas, wolves, and cave lions. The high N-15 levels can be explained if Neanderthals were primarily eating herbivores such as woolly rhinoceros, large bovids, and woolly mammoth, which themselves had higher N-15 levels than other animals around at the time. Furthermore, these six Neanderthals spanned a 65,000 year time frame, suggesting stability, if not rigidity, in Neanderthal diets.

Aquatic species tend to have even higher levels of N-15, and a while a few freshwater fish might have elevated these Neanderthal's N-15 levels, they are not as high as would be expected if fish were a major component of Neanderthal diets. Sources of marine protein can also be ruled out because levels of Carbon-13 make it possible to differentiate between marine and terrestrial sources of protein. By contrast, stable isotope studies suggest that anatomically modern humans with whom Neanderthals shared Europe (between 40,000 and 28,000 years ago) had wider ranges of isotope values suggesting a more varied diet, and one that included both freshwater and marine animals (403). Archaeological data support the idea that anatomically modern humans during this time period had broad diets that included fish and fleet prey such as birds and small mammals (407). The tool kits of anatomically modern humans of the European

Upper Paleolithic have long been known to have been quite diverse, contributing to the ability to make use of varied resources.

The archaeological and isotopic data clearly tell us that Neanderthals were eating large terrestrial mammals, but do they necessarily imply that Neanderthal diets were limited to these food sources? The answer to this question is critical because our understanding of Neanderthal behavioral complexity, extinction, and social organization may hang in the balance. If Neanderthals rarely ate plants or small, hard-to-capture prey, is this because they lacked the ability and or technology to do so? Did their narrow diets lead to their extinction in competition with more adaptable anatomically modern humans? And, if they relied nearly exclusively on large game for subsistence, did this mean that Neanderthal women were not spending their time gathering plant foods or hunting small animals, as they do in modern foraging societies?

These questions have been discussed at length. Neanderthals appear to lack such implements as crushing and grinding stones (408) that are necessary to obtain maximum nutritional benefit from seeds and nuts. Large mammals, although rich in energy, are unpredictable food sources. Without other sources of foods to fall back on, such as small animals and plants, Neanderthals would have been likely to experience periodic famine. Anatomically modern humans would have had a more uniform supply of food, perhaps contributing to lower mortality and higher fertility. Anthropologists Steven Kuhn and Mary Stiner, in their creatively entitled "What's a Mother to Do?," suggested that Neanderthal women may have helped in the pursuit of large game, but that they did not provide the plant foods and small mammals that allowed anatomically modern humans to buffer and enrich their food supply, and thus gain a competitive edge (408).

Clearly depending on just how limited Neanderthals diets were relative to those of modern humans, these ideas about Neanderthal behavioral inflexibility, extinction and the division of labor by sex may require rethinking. To be fair, plant remains do not preserve well in the archaeological record. Also, a significant plant component of the diet may be hidden by isotopic studies. The high values of N-15 in the diets of Neanderthals are produced by their reliance of large herbivores. Yet, according to paleobiologist Hervé Bocherens (the author of many of these stable isotope studies), if low-nitrogen plants had contributed *up to 50 percent* of the dry weight of Neanderthal diets, they would not have altered these values (406). Thus, the archaeological as well as the isotopic evidence are biased against plant foods. In recent years, evidence is beginning to mount suggesting that Neanderthal diets were more diverse than previously thought. The archaeological record is filling in, and with it, evidence of Neanderthal consumption of fish, birds, and a variety of plant foods at different times and places is accumulating (409).

Into the Mouths of Neanderthals

Although archaeological evidence places such diverse food sources at Neanderthal living sites, the dental evidence puts these foods right into Neanderthal mouths. At Bolomor Cave in Spain, archaeologists Ruth Blasco and Josep Peris found 202 bird remains dated to about 150,000 years ago, a time when only Neanderthals were in Europe (410). The remains belong to diving ducks, from the genus *Aythya*. Besides the stone tool cut marks and burnt areas on these bones, there are human tooth marks. The authors identified these tooth marks as human by comparing them to human tooth marks made by modern foragers as well as to tooth marks made by other animals. Like human tooth marks, those on the *Aythya* bones are small. They are concentrated around the broken edges of bones, and in some cases are associated with the kinds of longitudinal fractures produced by human gnawing. None of the tooth marks appear similar to those made by carnivores or to the kinds of marks made by large birds of prey.

However persuasive these results may be, even more substantial evidence of diverse foods in Neanderthal mouths comes from plant microfossils trapped in Neanderthal dental calculus. In 2011, anthropologist Amanda Henry and colleagues found phytoliths and starch grains in the dental calculus of a 44,000-year-old Neanderthal from

Shanidar cave in Iraq and two 36,000-year-old Neanderthals from Spy Cave in Belgium (411). As explained in Chapter 2, different plants have differently shaped phytoliths, so it is possible to identify the plants that produced them. Starch grains are the tiny granules some plants use to store starch, and like phytoliths, they have diagnostic features. In the Shanidar teeth, Henry and her coworkers found starch grains from a tribe of plants that includes the wild relatives of wheat and barley. Some of these had changes consistent with having been cooked. Other starches appear to have come from legumes, while the phytoliths were a match to those of date palms. As for the Belgian teeth, they contained starch grains which appear to have come from the tubers of water lilies.

But even more surprises came from the Neanderthal dental calculus that formed the basis of *Nature's* 2012 "Neanderthals ate their greens" story. In their study of teeth from five 47,000–50,000-year-old Neanderthals from El Sidron Spain, anthropologist Karen Hardy and colleagues not only found starch granules, but they also chemically identified organic compounds suggesting the consumption of nuts, grasses, and even green vegetables (412). Furthermore, they discovered the presence of compounds found in bitter-tasting plants, such as yarrow and chamomile, which have little nutritional value. It is known that Neanderthals had a gene allowing them to taste such compounds, and Hardy's team thinks that Neanderthals may have used these plants as medicines. That's not such a stretch of the imagination because herbalists today used them as antiseptics and anti-inflammatories. Even chimpanzees seem to have learned to self-medicate. Tanzanian chimpanzees swallow whole bitter-tasting leaves of the genus *Aspilla* that contain thiarubine A, a compound that kills bacteria, fungi, and parasitic worms (413).

These two studies of dental calculus have clearly demonstrated that diverse plant species were present in the mouths of Neanderthals from different times and places. Yet, they represent only a handful of individuals, and the presence of plant microfossils embedded in calculus does not attest to what degree Neanderthals relied on plant foods.

New evidence from the study of dental wear, however, suggests that plant use was neither restricted to a few individuals nor that plants were eaten only occasionally.

Dental macrowear on permanent teeth (wear observable on teeth without the use of microscopes) reflects the cumulative effect of chewing different types of foods over an adult's lifetime. In 2011, anthropologist Luca Fiorenza and colleagues analyzed macrowear patterns on nineteen Neanderthal teeth from as many individuals and compared it to that of twelve early modern humans (414). They did not find macrowear pattern differences between Neanderthals and modern humans from similar environments, implying that where Neanderthals and early modern humans had similar foods available, they ate similar things. Where they both occupied deciduous woodland environments, their macrowear patterns matched those of today's humans who include abrasive plants in their diets. And where they both inhabited steppe and coniferous forests, their macrowear patterns matched those of today's humans who are predominantly meat-eaters. Similarly, studying microscopic wear[3] on Neanderthal teeth, anthropologist Sireen El Zaatari's team in 2011 concluded that Neanderthals from wooded habitats included more plant material in their diets than did those from steppe environments (415).

These dental findings, from tooth marks on bird bones to cooked plant remains in Neanderthal dental calculus and geographic variability in Neanderthal dental wear all weaken the assumption that Neanderthal diets were narrow and inflexible. They suggest instead that in some places, Neanderthals made use of a wide variety of food types. If this is the case, then ideas discussed earlier about what Neanderthal diets reveal about Neanderthal behavioral complexity, extinction, and the sexual division of labor will, at the least, require modification. Perhaps some of these ideas are more applicable in steppe rather than in woodland or temperate environments. Yet, the similarity in Neanderthal and Upper Paleolithic modern human macrowear

---

[3] Microwear texture analysis, used in this study, is described in Chapter 2.

from similar habitats suggests that habitat, rather than differences in behavior and technology, was the primary determinant of both of these hominins' diets. To paraphrase archaeologist Omar Bar-Yosef, both types of hominins appear to have been "eating what was there" (416).

INSIGHTS INTO BEHAVIOR: ANTERIOR TEETH AS "THIRD-HANDS," NEANDERTHAL TABLE MANNERS AND RIGHT-HAND DOMINANCE

Analysis of tooth wear enlightens us not only about what Neanderthals ate but also aspects of their behavior, specifically about how they used their anterior teeth. Today, some of us use our front teeth as "third-hands" in such tasks as popping caps off of aspirin bottles. More talented (and thirsty) individuals use them to open beer bottles. (There are detailed instructions on www.wikihow.com about how to do this – with a warning about broken teeth.)

We know that Neanderthals used their anterior teeth in ways that caused them to exhibit massive wear (Figure 5.6). The biting surfaces of Neanderthal anterior teeth show "beveled" wear (417), rounded wear, and are in general more worn than the biting surfaces of their posterior teeth (418). In Neanderthals from such disparate regions as Iraq (Shanidar I) and France (La Ferrassie), some anterior tooth crowns were worn away completely (419, 420). Neanderthal anterior teeth are also often chipped or fractured (421). Assuming Neanderthals weren't opening beer bottles with their front teeth, what were they doing with them?

Considering this question (among others relating to tooth wear) Steven Molnar noted that "nondietary" functions of anterior teeth are often associated with heavy wear in several cultures (418). Such functions include cracking or splitting bones, opening mollusk shells, softening animal hides, using front teeth to clamp an object while twisting the free ends with one's hands, or using them to tear and cut seal meat. Eskimos, who have extensive anterior tooth wear and chipping, are noted to use their teeth in some of these ways and more, such as tightening a harness by clamping the end between the anterior teeth and pulling backwards. Perhaps Neanderthals, too, were using their anterior teeth to do more than just eat.

Kristin Kreuger and colleagues' (422–424) comparative studies of dental microwear have helped to answer this question. These researchers used microwear texture analysis to determine associations between microwear texture variables and the diets and behavior of well-studied archaeological groups. Krueger found that two microwear texture variables – *anisotropy* and *texture fill volume* – were able to differentiate among the anterior tooth microwear patterns of these groups (423). As explained earlier (Chapter 2) anisotropy refers to the orientation of features – high anisotropy means high directionality, while low anisotropy is the reverse. High anisotropy reflects dietary uses, as abrasive particles are dragged along the surface of incisors in the same direction when biting into an object. Texture fill volume (Tfv) measures feature depth. High Tfv is associated with high applied force or with repeated use (loading) of anterior teeth, while low Tfv indicates the opposite – low applied force or infrequent loading.

Ipiutak Eskimos of Point Hope Alaska have low anisotropy and high Tfv, consistent with the customary of their use of their anterior teeth as a "third hand" for softening hide. Sixty-five Neanderthals from diverse regions were studied in Krueger and colleagues newest work (424). Neanderthals from cold-steppe regions had microwear textures similar to the Ipiutak, strongly suggesting they were employing their teeth as "third hands," as the Ipiutak did. Perhaps these Neanderthals too were using their anterior teeth to process animal hides to survive frigid, ice-age, conditions. By contrast, those Neanderthals from warm/woodland regions had high anisotropy and lower Tfv, suggesting that nondietary uses of teeth were far less frequent. As with the evident environmental influences of Neanderthal diets, here, environmental influences are associated with differences in Neanderthals' use of anterior teeth as "third hands."

One of the other wear-related attributes of Neanderthal anterior teeth are prominent long scratch marks visible with the naked eye (Figure 8.2). Marie-Antoinette De Lumley first noted these striations

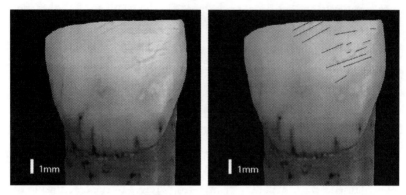

FIGURE 8.2: Left: Oblique striations on the upper left central incisor of Hortus 8. Right: Lines showing the approximate angles and length of these striations on the same tooth. Illustration by author.

in the Hortus Neanderthal teeth in 1973, attributing them to a habit seen in some Eskimos and Inuit, whereby a piece of meat is put into the mouth, and then cut close to the mouth, frequently causing scratches on the enamel surfaces of incisors and canines (425). Loring Brace dubbed this eating tradition the "stuff and cut school of etiquette" (426).

The Sima de los Heusos hominins (427, 428) and Neanderthals over a 100,000-year span seem to have had table manners similar to those of Eskimos and Inuit. The long scratches on their anterior teeth have the same appearance under a scanning electron microscope (SEM) viz. parallel margins with an internal groove marked by tiny longitudinal microstriations (427). Most convincingly, Lozano-Ruiz and colleagues (429) were able to generate these same markings experimentally. They glued incisor teeth to buccal protectors (like those worn by athletes) and had subjects wear these while they made cuts on them with flint flake tools. Like the cuts on the fossil teeth, these cuts had a similar appearance under the SEM – with the same diagnostic features.

Most intriguing about these scratches, though, is that they are often oblique, in most cases coursing from the top left of the tooth to the bottom right (here right and left refer to the perspective of the person whose mouth the teeth are in). In their experiment, Lozano-Ruiz and colleagues had left-handed and right-handed people make cut marks, and as you would expect, the right-handers predominantly made scratches traversing the tooth surface from top left to bottom right, while left-handers predominantly made scratches that went from top right to bottom left (429). Taken together, of twenty-nine Sima de los Huesos and Neanderthal individuals with anterior tooth scratch marks, twenty-seven of the twenty-nine exhibit the "right-oblique" marks made in high frequency by right-handers. Only two exhibit the predominant "left-oblique" marks of left-handers (430). Like modern humans today, most Neanderthal individuals were right-handed. Although archaeological analysis of stone tools also suggests a right-hand bias (perhaps as far back as the lower Pleistocene), Frayer and colleagues point out that these analysis do not reflect the population frequency of right-handedness, as stone tools obviously don't count as individuals (430).

A species-wide tendency toward right-hand preference is unique to humans among primates. Although some great apes do show hand preference, Frayer and coauthors (430) comment that population frequencies of right handedness do not come close to approaching the 90% frequency present in modern humans worldwide. Right-hand dominance is a decidedly human trait that we shared with Neanderthals, and one that goes back nearly 500,000 years. Whether right-hand dominance indicates brain lateralization and language ability is debatable (431), but David Frayer thinks it might be. The argument is based on the fact that language ability is left-lateralized in humans and the left side of the brain controls the right-side of the body. Hence, humans are mostly right-handed, presumably because their brains have "left-cerebral dominance" (430). By extension, Frayer and colleagues argue that this is one more piece of evidence (including others, such as the Kebara 2 hyoid bone ([432]) that Neanderthals were language-competent (430).

When David Frayer came to give a talk at Ohio State, he asked me if I had noticed these oblique striations in any Neanderthals he had not studied. When I looked back at my notes, I saw that had noticed them in the Regourdou 1 Neanderthal, from southwestern France. I showed him the dental replicas from this specimen and he was intrigued because our colleagues Virgine Volpato, Roberto Macchiarelli, Ivana Fiore, and Luca Bondioli had documented differences in the cross-sectional area of cortical bone in the skeleton of Regourdou 1. The right upper limb of Regourdou 1 had a greater cross-sectional area, indicating that it had been subject to higher biomechanical loads, strongly indicating exactly what the oblique striations did: Regourdou 1 was right-handed. In 2012 we published these results, adding one more individual to the preponderance of right-handed Neanderthals (433). Since then, still more have been added to the list: 11 of 11 of the El Sidrón Neanderthals from Spain also appear to have been right-handed (434).

STRESSED-OUT NEANDERTHALS?

Although the gap between the diets of Neanderthals and their early modern human contemporaries is closing, this of course does not mean that these two kinds of hominins were equally able to meet their energy needs. For one thing, Neanderthals (as inferred from their bones) were far more muscular than early modern humans. Greater muscle mass may have been an adaptation to cold climates, giving Neanderthals an ability to generate more internal body heat and providing them with better insulation. But, greater muscle mass also takes more energy to maintain. Evolutionary anthropologists Andrew Froehle and Steven Churchill estimated that primarily as a result of their larger muscle masses, Neanderthals would have required 100–350 kcal per day more than modern humans inhabiting similar climates (435). (This begs the question of whether early modern humans were as capable as Neanderthals of resisting cold stress, but some archaeological evidence suggests they might have done so by making better-insulating clothing than Neanderthals did.) Froehle and Churchill argue that the higher energy needs of Neanderthals could have put them at an evolutionary disadvantage, as it takes energy both to survive and to reproduce.

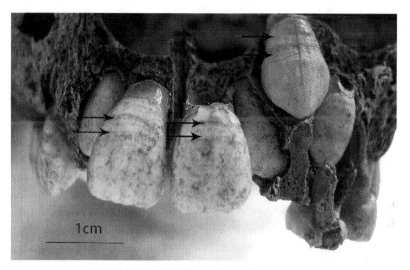

FIGURE 8.3: Linear enamel hypoplasias (denoted by arrows) on the upper incisors and upper left canine of a juvenile specimen from Point Hope, Alaska. (American Museum of Natural History Specimen 385.) Photograph by author.

Unambiguous evidence of energetic stress does not exist in skeletons and teeth, but two irregularities of teeth – linear enamel hypoplasia and fluctuating asymmetry – are broadly indicative of physiological stress. Physical anthropologists use the term "physiological stress" to refer to external demands on the body that tax its ability to maintain its normal state. Such stress include, but are not limited to, nutritional stress. Linear enamel hypoplasias (LEHs) manifest as grooves, of varying width and depth, in the hard enamel covering of teeth (Figure 8.3) (436). When physiological stress is severe enough, it will disrupt enamel formation, leaving behind these linear deficiencies in enamel thickness. Enamel does not repair itself after it is formed, so these grooves become a permanent fixture of a tooth. The other irregularity, fluctuating asymmetry, manifests as random departures from symmetry in paired biological structures, such as right- and left teeth. Normally, development proceeds equally on both sides of the body, but physiological stress can disrupt symmetrical development. Teeth do not grow in size after they have formed, so differences in size between right- and left teeth represent the cumulative result of such stresses during the tooth formation period (437).

Personal Dental Impressions

I have studied both of these irregularities in Neanderthal teeth, but began with linear enamel hypoplasia because in living humans, LEH is most often associated with caloric deficiency, illness, or the combination of the two (436). In one prospective study, Mexican children who received nutritional supplements were found to have half the frequency of LEH of those who were not given supplements (438). Some years ago, my colleague Zeynep Benderlioglu and I found elevated levels of LEH in rhesus monkeys that grew up in a medical colony before a consistent feeding program was established (439). This is the colony on Cayo Santiago, a small island off of the cost of Puerto Rico, where regular provisioning of monkeys was not established until 1956.

Given the links between LEH and malnutrition, I traveled to Israel and throughout Europe one summer, courtesy of the Leakey Foundation, in part to study LEH in Neanderthals and early modern humans, but also to collect data on Neanderthal fluctuating asymmetry and enamel growth. This was a lot of fun because Neanderthal remains are spread out across museums from various countries. So, with my husband Dan Steinberg coming along for the ride (or actually providing the ride, since, as he said, "Somebody had to drive the car,"), I went from Tel Aviv to London, and from Berlin to Rome. Dan also served as a French-English translator. With his two years of high school French, Dan pled my case with Madame Marie-Antoinette de Lumley (of the Institut de Paléontologie Humaine) to allow me to study the Hortus fossils in Marseilles.

Previous studies suggested that Neanderthals had frequencies of LEH that were at the top of the range found in archaeological and living modern human populations. However, I wanted to get a more accurate read on Neanderthal LEH by applying some methods previous studies had not. For one, I wanted to be sure that when I counted an individual as being affected by LEH, the individual had defects appearing on more than just one tooth. When LEH appears on a single tooth it could be because of local causes (trauma, infection) acting on that single tooth during development. When LEH appears on two or more teeth at approximately the same time during tooth development, it is more likely that the defects were caused by a systemic stressor, such as malnutrition or illness.

I also wanted to get an estimate of the duration of the stress episodes these LEH defects represented. Some grooves are wide, and some are quite narrow, and to some extent their width is related to the period of time enamel growth was disrupted. To get an even better estimate of the length of stress events, it is possible to count enamel growth increments within LEH defects. As described in Chapter 4, microscopically observable enamel growth increments, *perikymata*, cover the sides of teeth. Dental anthropologist Tanya Smith and colleagues determined that in Neanderthals, perikymata generally represent seven to eight days of growth (440). In modern humans, research by dental anthropologists Donald Reid and Christopher Dean indicates that the length of time represented by a *perikyma* (singular) centers around eight to nine days (217). Through microscopic investigation, dental anthropologist Simon Hillson and microscopist Sandra Bond determined that LEH grooves usually take the form of V-shaped furrows (441). Perikymata are more widely spaced than normal in the top half of the furrow, reflecting the period of disrupted growth. To count these growth increments, I made high-resolution impressions of these teeth, followed by making high-resolution replicas, and examined them under an SEM.[4]

---

[4] I also used replicas of the Krapina Neanderthals, kindly provided by Clark Spencer Larsen and Dale Hutchinson, who were included as coauthors in this study. (442. Guatelli-Steinberg D, Larsen CS, Hutchinson DL. Prevalence and the duration of linear enamel hypoplasia: a comparative study of Neanderthals and Inuit foragers. *Journal of Human Evolution*. 2004;47(1–2):65–84.)

I compared the Neanderthals to a recent human foraging group that inhabited a cold environment and that, like Neanderthals included large mammals as an important component of their diets. These were the coastal whale-hunting people known as the Tigara of Point Hope Alaska, who occupied this region between AD 1300 and 1700. Of 18 Neanderthal individuals (from Krapina and southern France), 7 were affected by LEH, which was quite similar in frequency to the 8 of 21 Tigara individuals who exhibited LEH. Neanderthals showed a range of defect durations, including defects with just 2 perikymata to a defect that had 12 perikymata in the top half of the V-shaped furrow. Assuming that each perikyma represented 7 to 8 days of growth, the latter defect represents a growth disruption that lasted from 84 to 96 days. But when I compared the average number of perikymata in the top half of the "V" between my Neanderthal and Tigara samples, these didn't differ much.

To summarize, both Neanderthals and Tigara appeared to have experienced a fairly high level of physiological stress, each with more than a third of the individuals in their respective samples exhibiting one or more enamel growth disruptions (442). Some of these disruptions were of short duration and some were quite long, but the average durations were not that different between the two groups. On the one hand, this means that my research supports previous findings showing high stress load in Neanderthals. On the other hand, it also suggests that Neanderthals may not have been all that exceptional, as these Tigara foragers inhabiting a cold climate were similarly stressed.

Of course, it would have been interesting to compare Neanderthal LEH to that of their Upper Paleolithic modern human contemporaries. That was something I had wanted to do, but I had too few Upper Paleolithic teeth to work with. As the fossil record fills in, it may be possible to eventually perform this comparison.

In a later study, my collaborators Chris Barrett, Paul Sciulli, and I compared fluctuating asymmetry in the teeth of Neanderthals and several archaeological groups, some of which were agricultural and others of which were foragers, and once again we included the

Tigara (437). Although previous studies had suggested high levels of fluctuating asymmetry in Neanderthal teeth, we felt that certain methodological issues detracted from these studies, and we wanted to correct them in our own. Yet, we confirmed these previous findings. Neanderthals had higher levels of fluctuating asymmetry than our comparative samples, and they were, not surprisingly, most similar to the Tigara. Neanderthals do seem to have been sustaining high levels of physiological stress during development, and this might have had something to do with their high energetic demands. Whether it has anything do with Neanderthal extinction is extremely unclear. It may, however, have had an effect on the pace of Neanderthal life histories.[5]

NEANDERTHAL DEVELOPMENT, GROWTH, AND DEATH

Teeth have made a major contribution in recent years to the area of Neanderthal life history, but the road to understanding has been full of twists and turns. Along that road, Neanderthals at some points seemed to have grown up more quickly than modern humans do; at others, not so differently at all. Of all primates, humans take the longest to grow up and reproduce, and they have the longest natural lifespans. As discussed in the previous chapter, signs of protracted dental development within the genus *Homo* are most clear for *Homo erectus*, although this species rates of somatic growth may been quite rapid, if analysis of the Nariokotome boy is an indication (374). By the time of *Homo antecessor*, about 1 million years ago, dental development seems to have shifted more toward the human direction (377). But what about Neanderthals? In this book, I have stressed the modular nature of development as well as the point that one shouldn't necessarily expect gradual shifts toward a modern human life history over the course of human evolution. The complex combination of selection pressures influencing a hominin species' life

---

[5] "Life history," as discussed in Chapter 4, refers to the key benchmarks and stages in the lifetime of an organism. For mammals, this includes gestation length, age at weaning, age sexual maturity, age at first birth, the intervals between births, and finally death.

history can theoretically result in unique life history modes, and *has* resulted in unique life history modes in living primates (186).

Viewed through the lens of life history "theory," it isn't clear what to expect *a priori* for Neanderthals. Consider what one major theoretical perspective, introduced by evolutionary biologists Eric Charnov and David Berrigan (182), might mean for Neanderthal life histories. According to these theorists, there are two countervailing selection pressures affecting the optimal age of primate sexual maturity. The first of these is adult mortality due to "extrinsic factors," meaning the risk of death by such causes as predation, disease, or accidents. If that risk is high, the earlier a primate can start reproducing, the better for leaving lots of offspring. However, there is a limit to how young a primate (especially a female) can be when she becomes sexually mature and ready to have babies. Primate females, to varying degrees, make use of fat stores as body "capital" to supply the energy needed to gestate and nurse offspring. They cannot stint too much on the time it takes to grow their bodies to a size large enough to sustain pregnancy and lactation.

By this reasoning, if Neanderthals had a higher risk of dying during adulthood than do modern humans, as some studies have suggested, they would have been expected to grow up faster than we do. Yet, if they were energetically challenged compared to modern humans, they might have required a *longer* time to reach a reproductively-competent adult body size.

Maybe we can gain more insight into what to expect by considering Neanderthal brain size and brain growth rates. In Chapter 4, much was made of the relationship between brain size and the pace of life history in primates. Whatever the connection, large-brained primate species take a long time to grow, and with brain sizes as great as those of their anatomically modern human contemporaries and greater than those of today's humans, Neanderthals could be expected to have taken just as long to grow up as we do.

Furthermore, rates of Neanderthal brain growth during the first two years of life are estimated to have been quite rapid (443). Based on

Steve Leigh and Greg Blomquist's maternal energetics hypothesis (see Chapter 4), Neanderthal females could be expected to have had long growth periods during which they achieved body sizes capable of sustaining the energetic demands of nursing infants with fast growing brains. And of course, if Neanderthal biology was characterized by all of these factors: high adult mortality, high energetic stress and fast brain growth rates, the predicted "life history outcome" would depend on the magnitude of these factors, which are difficult to estimate with precision.

What Do Teeth Have to Tell Us?

As previously explained (Chapter 4 and Chapter 7), the chronology of tooth growth is preserved in incremental growth markings within the enamel – the microscopic daily increments (*cross-striations*) and the longer-period increments, *striae of Retzius*, that emerge onto the enamel surface as perikymata. This chronological record has been the subject of multiple studies on Neanderthal teeth over the last twelve years.

Personal Dental Impressions

When I made high resolution dental impressions of Neanderthal teeth, part of my plan was to count the total number of perikymata on each tooth. I used anterior teeth – incisors and canines – because 85–90% of their crown formation time is accounted for by perikymata on the enamel surface. The remainder of their crown formation time is hidden at the tip of the crown – the cuspal region – where the internal striae of Retzius do not emerge onto the tooth's surface as perikymata. Posterior teeth – premolars and molars – have a much greater portion of hidden growth, and so I did not study these initially. By counting perikymata in anterior teeth, and by using estimates of the number of days perikymata take to form, I could obtain estimates for the time it took for Neanderthals to form their anterior tooth crowns (actually for 85 to 90% of that time). Figure 8.4 shows perikymata on the surface of a Neanderthal incisor.

202 KNOWING NEANDERTHALS THROUGH THEIR TEETH

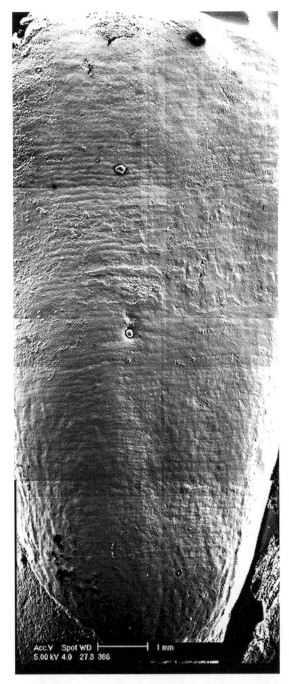

FIGURE 8.4: Montage made by author from scanning electron micrograph (SEM) images taken at 20x magnification of a Neanderthal lower I2 replica (Krapina 90).

When reading previous studies, I had been surprised that a large-scale study of Neanderthal perikymata had not yet been undertaken. After all, dental anthropologist Christopher Dean and others had pioneered these methods in early hominins like *Australopithecus* (223, 226). But, it turned out that a similar project was indeed underway by anthropologists Fernando Ramirez-Rozzi and Jose Maria Bermúdez de Castro. In 2004, these researchers published a paper in *Nature* on 146 Neanderthal teeth from 55 individuals, concluding that Neanderthals formed their anterior teeth more rapidly than did anatomically modern humans who lived during and just after the Upper Paleolithic (444). The basis of their conclusion was that the number of perikymata in comparable divisions of Neanderthal and anatomically modern human teeth was lower in Neanderthals. Their conclusion assumed that perikymata in Neanderthals did not take any longer, on average, to form than those of modern humans, which later research by Tanya Smith and colleagues would substantiate (440). Ramirez-Rozzi and Bermúdez de Castro interpreted the difference in anterior tooth formation times between Neanderthals and these anatomically modern humans as a species-level difference in growth rates. Neanderthals grew their teeth quickly and must have grown up fast.

One year later, my colleagues and I published our results (445). We compared fifty-five teeth from thirty Neanderthal individuals to my Tigara samples from Alaska, and to my colleague Don Reid's samples from England and southern Africa. When compared to teeth of these geographically dispersed modern humans, the numbers of perikymata on Neanderthal teeth were not exceptional. The average number was less than that of the Tigara teeth, variable by tooth type when compared to that of the sample from England, and generally greater than that of the sample from southern Africa. We considered a range of possible estimates, based on modern humans, for the number of days it took Neanderthal perikymata to form, concluding that Neanderthals could not be definitively shown to have formed their anterior teeth any faster than did some of these modern humans.

Lower incisor teeth, again based on a range of periodicity estimates, even seemed likely to have formed more slowly in Neanderthals than they did in the southern Africans. Clearly our findings weakened the conclusion of a species-level difference between Neanderthals and modern humans. Our study did not exactly endear us to the authors of the *Nature* paper, who engaged us in a vigorous exchange in the *Journal of Human Evolution* a few years later. But studies of perikymata on the surfaces of anterior teeth were about to be eclipsed.

Going beneath the Surface

Just one year after our study was published, dental anthropologist Roberto Macchiarelli and coworkers published a study on how Neanderthal teeth grew that involved sectioning a Neanderthal tooth to actually determine the number of days it took to form the internal striae of Retzius in enamel (446). They could also make use of similar incremental growth lines that are present in the tooth root. The tooth was an adult first molar, which is known to begin forming right around birth. Given these pieces of information, it was possible to determine the age at which the entire tooth (crown plus root) had completed formation in this individual, which was close to the average age of nine years when this happens in modern humans. Based on how much of the root is usually formed when teeth erupt into the oral cavity, these authors estimated that this Neanderthal individual's first molar would have erupted at around 6.7 years of age, which is no different from modern humans.

Although only based on a single Neanderthal individual, this was stronger evidence of similar timing in dental development between Neanderthals and modern humans than our study because (1) the number of days it took to form growth increments was actually determined by cutting into the tooth, and (2) the tooth was an adult first molar. First molars have a special place in studies of primate life history because of the foundational studies (discussed in Chapter 4) establishing a strong association between adult first molar eruption ages and the pace of primate life histories. That relationship is perhaps a functional one, as adult first molars generally erupt around the time primates are weaned, giving them more chewing power (but see Chapter 4). No one has ever bothered to see if anterior tooth development has such a strong relationship with primate life histories across the order. As noted in previous chapters, anterior tooth crown formation times in chimpanzees are greater than those of modern humans (196), suggesting that at least within the great and hominin clade, anterior teeth may not be particularly reliable indicators of life history.

Yet Macchiarelli and colleagues did not have the final word. Tanya Smith and colleagues published three papers in succession that seemed to settle the question once again in favor of rapid Neanderthal dental development (440, 447, 448). Using x-ray synchrotron microtomography (see Chapter 4) these researchers could peer inside Neanderthal teeth to determine how long it took for growth increments to form without having to slice into precious fossils. That allowed them to look at more than just one tooth. For six immature Neanderthal individuals who had not yet finished forming all of their teeth, Tanya Smith and colleagues were able to count dental growth increments to determine how old each individual was at the time of death (449). This was possible by counting growth increments from the neonatal line (an accentuated marking within the enamel that forms at birth) to the last increment of growth that formed when the individual died. They then scored the Neanderthal individuals for how far along they were in their state of dental development when they died. It turned out that Neanderthals had completed more of their dental development than do modern humans at comparable ages. The Neanderthals' entire dentitions were developing at an accelerated pace.

End of story? Not quite. Two years later, Laura Shackelford and colleagues published a paper asserting that there are several sources of variation that need to be taken into account when using modern human dental charts. Smith and coworkers had used modern human dental aging charts to convert the stage of each Neanderthal's dental development into a "dental age" based on modern human standards.

These "dental ages" – i.e., the ages at which modern humans achieve certain stages of crown and root development – were compared to the actual ages of death as determined from the growth increment data. Since their modern human dental ages were older than their actual ages, Neanderthals were growing faster than modern humans do. When Shackelford and colleagues incorporated the uncertainty involved in converting stages of dental development into dental ages, the dental ages of the Neanderthals spanned age ranges that in four of six cases included their actual ages at death (451). The two Neanderthals which are not encompassed by the 95% confidence intervals were the older individuals: Scladina and Le Moustier. Shackelford et al. note that for Le Moustier, estimated dental age rests on the third molar (with half the root formed), as all the other teeth are complete. That Le Moustier is advanced in M3 development, is consistent with previous evidence suggesting that third molars are advanced in both Neanderthals and early modern humans (450).

All of this leads to uncertainty about whether the Neanderthals were as dentally advanced compared to modern humans as it first seemed in the Smith et al. 2010 study. And, it is important to point out that the ages at first molar eruption in the Smith et al. study, as well as that of the Macchiarelli et al. study, were estimated to be within modern human ranges (446, 449). My own view is that Neanderthals were not categorically different from modern humans in their dental development, but were simply at the fast end of the human developmental spectrum.

Finally, we have to remember that not all body systems may develop at the same rate. It's possible that this might be happening in Neanderthals.[6] Anthropologist Jesús Martín-González and colleagues' in 2012 constructed height vs. age growth curves for Neanderthals during infancy and early childhood for ten individuals (453). They plotted the estimated heights (based on the skeleton)

---

[6] In fact, this was first suggested by anthropologists Jennifer Thompson and Andrew Nelson (452. Thompson JL, Nelson AJ. The place of Neanderthals in the evolution of hominid patterns of growth and development. Journal of Human Evolution. 2000;38 (4):475–495.)

of these individuals against their chronological ages at death as determined from modern human dental standards (and in a few cases, based on more accelerated estimates of rates of dental development in Neanderthals). Their result: Neanderthals were growing in height much more slowly than modern humans. This difference would make sense if Neanderthals were energetically stressed and could not support rates of brain and body growth equivalent to those of modern humans. It's not clear whether their slow growth was an evolutionary adaptation or an individual-level response to energetic stress. Furthermore, the extent to which these ten individuals represent Neanderthals in general is not clear, particularly because they all died at young ages. That is to say, did they die at young ages in part *because* they were particularly nutritionally stressed? In any case, children eventually do grow up, reproduce and die, and it's that last life history event where teeth again emerge into the limelight.

Dying Young

As explained in Chapter 7, Rachel Caspari and Sang-Hee Lee compared the number of young versus old individuals in fossil assemblages from *Australopithecus* to modern humans using wear-based seriation (370). They defined "old" adults (thirty years of age) as those that were twice the age at which sexual maturity is reached (assumed to be fifteen years of age) because they were interested in how many potential grandparents might have been around. The existence of overlapping generations is thought to give modern humans the benefit of learning from their wise and experienced elders. Furthermore, grandmothers, according to Hawkes' Grandmother Hypothesis provide much needed assistance as allomothers (366). In addition, with long lifespans, modern humans have many years over which to produce children, which is an evolutionary plus. Caspari and Lee found that 30,000 years ago, during the Upper Paleolithic, the number of older versus younger individuals in modern human fossil assemblages took a quantum leap. Neanderthals, by contrast appeared to have died young (though not as young as did earlier hominins).

A few years later, Anthropologist Erik Trinkaus confirmed that there is a high ratio of young to old individuals in Neanderthal fossil assemblages, but contrary to Caspari and Lee, he found similar ratios in Upper Paleolithic modern humans (454). About 75 % of both types of hominins died before reaching the age of forty. The reason for the discrepancy in these two studies isn't clear, though it may have to do with subtle differences in their methods and samples. But if Neanderthals and Upper Paleolithic modern humans both died young, then the Neanderthals' anatomically modern human contemporaries did not have the evolutionary advantages of a long lifespan associated with people today. Surely, modern medicine has lengthened human lifespans, but the question is whether even prior to medical advances, our modern human ancestors were living longer than their Neanderthal cousins.

Still, all of this discussion must be tempered by the fact that no one really knows the extent to which the ratio of old to young individuals in fossil assemblages resembles that of the once- living populations they came from. As Trinkaus points out, these could differ for a variety of reasons, including biases produced by burial practices favoring a particular age class or by the preservation potential of older versus younger skeletons. There are problems then, but at present, it seems that Neanderthals, and maybe also modern humans of the Upper Paleolithic, died young relative to the generally longer-lived (366) hunter-gatherers of today.

CHEWING ON NEANDERTHAL DEBATES

Science is in a never-ending process of revision, so we will probably never know the whole truth about Neanderthals. But we can consider where the different lines of dental evidence lead us. In terms of Neanderthal origins, analysis of dental morphology suggests even greater time depth (more than 1 million years ago) than do genetic studies regarding the initial divergence between Neanderthals and modern human. Yet, as revealed by dental studies, several aspects of Neanderthal biology do not appear so different from those of modern humans. In terms of right-hand dominance, Neanderthals were like modern humans. Evidence from tooth marks, dental calculus and tooth wear of Neanderthals suggests that their diets were not radically different from those of their anatomically modern human contemporaries. Their experience of physiological stress during childhood appears to have been high relative to other modern humans prehistoric groups, but it is not clear that Neanderthals were completely outside the range of "stress levels" these groups experienced (see also [455]). Neanderthals were on the fast end of the human range in their dental development, but they may have had slower rates of skeletal growth during infancy and childhood. They probably did not often live to see their grandchildren, but that also may have been true of the anatomically modern humans with whom they coexisted.

The differences seem subtle, but even seemingly subtle differences can influence evolutionary outcomes. One might speculate that with extensive dietary overlap, Neanderthals would have competed for resources with their modern human contemporaries. Resource competition might have put energetically challenged Neanderthals at a disadvantage. With less energy available for growth, their skeletal and somatic growth rates during childhood would have been slow, and they may have reached sexual maturity at later ages than do modern humans. Coupled with young ages at death, delays in sexual maturity might have meant that Neanderthals produced fewer offspring during their lifetimes than did their modern human competitors. That's one scenario. But speculative scenarios like these, which abound in the Neanderthal literature, are only useful for pointing out that subtle differences in life history *could* have had evolutionary ramifications, not whether they actually did.

Speculation about the Neanderthal extinction question will probably continue for as long as humans are around to think about it. To me, what is more interesting is that through dental studies we have gained some surprising insights into what life was like for Neanderthals. Neanderthals now seem to have been smart enough to have captured and eaten elusive prey, to have eaten a variety of plant foods, and to have used plants as medicines. They experienced elevated levels of physiological stress, had somewhat faster rates of dental development and somewhat slower rates of skeletal growth, and probably died young. This vision of Neanderthal lives comes into focus through the unique attributes of teeth: unlike other parts of the skeleton, they interact directly with food and they chronicle their own growth in real time. Here, as is evident throughout this book, teeth have given us an exclusive source for understanding the lives of our ancient predecessors. While the present chapter highlighted multiple insights into Neanderthal nature that teeth provide, the next chapter focuses on dental insights into modern humans.

9 Insights into the Origins of Modern Humans and Their Dental Diseases

> They [wisdom teeth] do not cut through the gums till about the seventeenth year, and I am assured by dentists that they are much more liable to decay, and are earlier lost, than the other teeth.
>
> – Darwin CR
> *The Descent of Man and Selection in Relation to Sex,* Vol.1

In 1871, in the "Descent of Man," Charles Darwin speculated that human third molars, or "wisdom teeth," were evolving into rudimentary structures (115). Such structures, he explained, tend to be highly variable and reduced in size or even "wholly suppressed." Wisdom teeth fit this definition well in that they show great variability in size, shape, and development. Furthermore, although the congenital absence of third molars is extremely rare in great apes (456), it is quite common in humans, with a worldwide frequency (at least one missing third molar) of 22.63% according to a new meta-analysis (260).

The reduction or absence of third molars can be viewed as part of the larger trend of dental reduction in recent human evolution, one of several aspects of modern human biology that the study of ancient teeth illuminates. Dental studies also give us insight into the phylogenetic origins and patterns of dispersal of anatomically modern humans (AMHS) out of Africa, our long developmental periods, and the evolutionary history of our dental diseases. In detailing these insights, I develop two main themes. The first is that some of these aspects of modern human biology are interrelated. As one example, our present long lifespans may give us a reproductive payoff in offspring number and/or offspring survival, but longer lifespans require teeth to function for longer periods of time, increasing the risk of dental disease.

The second theme is the dynamic relationship between culture and biology in the evolution of modern human dental reduction and dental disease, both of which have been influenced by changes in diet, food processing, and eating habits. Nevertheless, much remains to be understood about the extent to which differences among cultures over time and space can be linked to population patterns of dental reduction and dental pathology. In Chapter 7, I discussed the case of dental reduction in the Sima de los Huesos *Homo heidelbergensis* hominins, which José Bermúdez de Castro's analysis suggests has more to do with genetic drift than with culturally-induced relaxed selection on tooth size. Cultural variation over time and space has surely had a great impact on patterns of modern human dental reduction and pathology, but as with the case of the Sima de los Huesos hominins, there are limits to how much culture can explain.

But before exploring these topics, we first address dental insights into two other aspects of modern human biology: (1) What do teeth tell us about modern human origins and dispersal out of Africa? and (2) Can teeth tell us whether the first anatomically modern humans were like people today with respect to the length of their childhoods?

TEETH AND MODERN HUMAN ORIGINS

In Chapter 6, different models of human origins were reviewed. These range from the Recent African Origins model, which at one extreme posits a replacement of archaic hominins by anatomically modern humans from Africa, to the Multiregional Evolution model at the other, which hypothesizes evolution from earlier hominins into modern form in multiple regions of the world. In their review of these models, Weaver and Roseman (457) explain that the genetic evidence for the importance of sub-Saharan Africa in the origin of modern humans is now widely accepted, but that there is dispute about how much admixture with earlier hominins occurred as anatomically modern humans from Africa dispersed into new regions.

The number of dispersals of anatomically modern humans out of Africa is also disputed. Some genetic analyses suggest a single dispersal (315, 319). Other genetic and craniometric analyses find evidence of multiple dispersals (317, 458, 459). The recent genetic and craniometric study of Reyes-Centeno and colleagues suggests an early dispersal out of Africa, via a southern route across the Arabian peninsula, into Asia around 130,000 years ago (317). Based on analyses of both their DNA and crania, indigenous Australians appear to be directly descended from these initial migrants (317, 460). A second dispersal of out of Africa, through the Levant region, and into northern Eurasia appears to have occurred around 50,000 years ago (317).

I have repeatedly asserted that comparisons of dental morphology among species provide insight into their phylogenetic relationships. Biological anthropologist Amelia Hubbard (together with dental anthropologist Joel Irish and me) recently confirmed that DNA and dental morphology data produce similar answers about population relationships within a single species – humans. Specifically, we found that for living people in Kenya, both genetic and dental data taken from the same individuals clearly differentiated populations of "Swahili" origin from populations of "Taita" origin (461). So, what does the evidence from dental morphology say about modern human origins and dispersal out of Africa and is it consistent with genetic and craniometric lines of evidence?

Based on his comprehensive analyses of teeth from thousands of modern people, the late dental anthropologist Christy G. Turner (462) concluded that of all people in the world, Southeast Asians are the "least specialized" dentally. Essentially what this means is that Southeast Asians exhibit crown and root traits at frequencies that are intermediate between those of other peoples of the world. Turner referred to their "generalized" dental pattern as "Sundadonty," after the Sunda shelf, an extension of the continental shelf of Southeast Asia that was exposed during the last ice age when sea levels receded. Mainland Southeast Asia would have been connected to the islands of Java, Borneo, and Sumatra, facilitating gene flow, and presumably

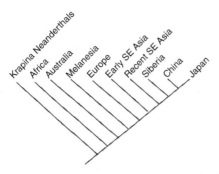

FIGURE 9.1: Cladogram redrawn by author based on Figure 1a from Stringer et al. (1997). See text for explanation.

resulting in the common dental morphology of people in this region. Turner argued that because Sundadonty is generalized, it is the closest to the ancestral dental pattern of anatomically modern humans. Southeast Asia, rather than Africa, he then concluded, would be the most likely place of origin for modern humans. Based on phenetic analyses, Turner additionally found a close connection between sub-Saharan Africa and Australia (463), a connection which he seemed unable to explain.

Stringer and colleague's cladistic analysis of modern human dental morphology (introduced in the previous chapter) made it possible to separate primitive (ancestral) and derived traits and so to provide much needed clarification about biological relationships among modern human populations. Using the Krapina Neanderthals as an outgroup, these researchers found that sub-Saharan Africans branched off from our common ancestor with Neanderthals earlier than did other modern human groups. Next to branch off – i.e., the second "least-derived" group – were Australians. Europeans and people from Northeast Asia (China, Japan, and Siberia) were more derived in their morphology, branching off later (Figure 9.1). The analysis suggested that the modern human "dental ancestor" had, among other characteristics, low frequencies of upper incisor shoveling, low frequencies of third molar reduction, and a high frequency of upper first molar fifth cusp.

Different from Turner's phenetic analysis, Stinger et al.'s cladistic one suggested that Southeast Asians did *not* have the greatest frequency of ancestral dental features – instead, Africans and Australians did. Furthermore, the affinity between sub-Saharan Africans and Australians that Turner noted was now shown to be simply the result of shared ancestral features.

Dental anthropologist Joel Irish and I performed a follow-up study to that of Stringer and colleagues, building on Irish's previous work on sub-Saharan dental morphology. Irish had previously concluded that sub-Saharan Africans retained a greater number of ancestral features than other peoples of the world (464). Using Irish's data on dental morphology from modern peoples, together with my data on dental morphology from australopiths and early *Homo*, we found that sub-Saharan Africans were least far removed from "gracile" hominins (*Australopithecus* combined with early *Homo*) in their dental morphology. Australians and Melanesians, likewise, retained many ancestral features and were therefore also relatively close to early hominins (Figure 9.2).

Our analysis reinforced Stringer and colleagues' conclusion of an African origin for anatomically modern human dental morphology. Our analysis also showed that as distance from Africa increases, dental morphology becomes more derived, with East Asian and European populations diverging in different ways. This result is evident in Figure 9.2, where Europeans and East Asians are most distant from the combined "gracile hominins" and are also widely separated from each other. These results – from Stringer et al. and Joel Irish and me – are consistent with the now overwhelming genetic evidence of African origins for modern humans. They are also consistent with the great antiquity and retention of ancestral features in Australian populations that the multiple-dispersal model posits. Australians therefore appear to retain genetic, cranial, *and* dental signals of an early dispersal out of Africa.

Although the idea of an early migration of anatomically modern humans from Africa via a southern route across the Arabian Peninsula

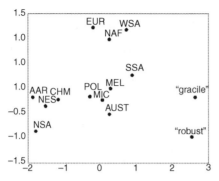

FIGURE 9.2: Multidimensional scaling graph (redrawn by author) based on biodistance measures in Irish and Guatelli-Steinberg (2004). Abbreviations are as follows: EUR = Europe, NAF = North Africa, WSA = West South Asia, SSA = sub-Saharan Africa, POL = Polynesia, MEL = Melanesia, MIC = Micronesia, AUST = Australia, AAR = American Arctic, CHM = China-Mongolia, NES = Northeast Siberia, NSA = North and South America. "Robust" = robust australopiths and "Gracile" = sample of nonrobust australopiths and early *Homo*. Details regarding these samples and methods used to generate the graph are in Irish and Guatelli-Steinberg (2004).

into Asia and Australia is supported genetically, cranially, and dentally, it is less well-supported by direct fossil evidence. As Reyes Centeno et al. note, there is, as yet, no fossil evidence of modern human presence in the Arabian Peninsula around 130,000 years ago that would support this idea (317). On the other hand, in China, a fossilized mandible with a chin, a distinctive modern human feature, was recovered from the site of Zhiren Cave (465) dated to more than 100,000 years ago. Furthermore, 70,000–127,000 year old teeth from the sites of Luna Cave (Guangxi) (466) and 81,000–101,000-year-old teeth from Huanglong Cave (Hubei) (467) have size and shape affinities to recent modern human teeth. Evidence of an early dispersal from Africa into Asia is therefore accumulating.

It may be recalled from Chapter 6 that the high frequency of shovel-shaped incisors in East Asian *Homo erectus* and later East Asian hominins, including anatomically modern East Asians, has been cited as support for the "Multiregional Continuity" hypothesis. In particular, it was argued that high frequencies of "marked" shoveling are specific to East Asian fossil hominins and are also prevalent in peoples of East Asian descent today(468).[1] Incisor shoveling is not the only dental trait to show apparent continuity in East Asia. Wu Liu, of the Institute of Vertebrate Paleontology and Paleoanthropology (IVPP) in Beijing, identified seven dental traits typically present in modern East Asians that were also present to varying degrees in fossil hominins from East Asia (468). These include marked incisor shoveling, third molar agenesis (or reduction), and three-rooted lower molars, all of which are less common in other areas of the world. But these observations do not lend exclusive support to the "Multiregional Continuity" hypothesis. Interbreeding between archaic East Asian hominins and anatomically modern people dispersing from Africa can also explain the persistence of these dental traits over time.

The analysis of dental morphology is therefore entirely consistent with an African origin for anatomically modern humans, coupled, at least in East Asia, with genetic input from archaic hominins. As we turn to next, the analysis of growth increments in teeth shows that dentally, these early African anatomically modern humans had achieved modern human developmental rates.

DENTAL DEVELOPMENT AND GROWTH IN EARLY ANATOMICALLY MODERN HUMANS

Dated to approximately 160,000 years ago (470), the Jebel Irhoud hominin remains from Morocco share several derived features with anatomically modern humans (471) but also retain some primitive features. Paleoanthropologist Jean-Jacques Hublin suggests that the combination of primitive and derived traits in these fossils remains reflects the gradual

---

[1] Shovel-shaped incisors were critical to elucidating the East Asian origins of Native Americans. Aleš Hrdlička, founder of the *American Journal of Physical Anthropology*, was the first to note the high frequency of shovel-shaped incisors in both East Asians and Native Americans and grasp their importance as indicators of ancestry. (469. Hrdlička A. Shovel-shaped teeth. *American Journal of Physical Anthropology*. 1920;3(4):429–465.)

evolution of anatomically modern form in Africa (472). Paleoanthropologists Matt Cartmill and Fred Smith (15) consider the Jebel Ihroud hominins to be part of an "African Transitional Group," that is "... considerably more like modern humans than Neanderthals, though they retain some archaic features" (2009:422).

The Jebel Irhoud fossil remains include a complete cranium (Jebel Ihroud I), but from the standpoint of development, the more exciting remains from this site are the teeth and jaws of the juvenile, Jebel Irhoud 3. In 2007, Tanya Smith and colleagues used synchrotron x-ray micro CT to image incremental markings in the juvenile's teeth establishing its stria of Retzius periodicity (ten days), crown and root formation times, state of dental development and age at death (470). With large crowns that the authors term "macrodont," Jebel Ihroud's crown formation times are at the long end of the modern human spectrum. Jebel Irhoud 3 was estimated to have died at 7.78 years age. Its state of dental development is just what would be expected of a modern human child of equivalent age in that its premolars and second permanent molar had begun to form their roots. Modern Europeans in this stage of development are between 7.2 and 7.6 years of age. The lateral incisor is nearly fully erupted, an event that usually occurs between seven to eight years of age in European children (470).

Despite the modernity of its state of dental development, Jebel Ihroud 3 appears to have had extremely accelerated rates of root formation relative to that of living humans. The authors estimate root formation rates in this specimen to be twice what they are today (470). Smith and coworkers suggest that the juvenile's longer periods of crown formation coupled with its fast rates of root formation result in eruption timing comparable to that of living humans. If this is so, then Jebel Ihroud 3's dental eruption schedule is like that of living Europeans but is not achieved in quite the same way. The modern scheduling of Jebel Irhoud 3's dental development indicates that prolonged juvenile growth periods were present in anatomically modern humans 160,000 years ago, but that not all aspects of human dental growth and development had reached their current state.

Other early anatomically modern humans also retain some dental growth differences from modern humans. Overall, the 90,000–100,000 year old hominins from Qafzeh in Southwest Asia have been said to exhibit an anatomical pattern of "derived modern human features with a minority of retained archaic features" (473). These hominins are thought (by some) to represent an early migration out of Africa that did not give rise to living humans today (317, 459). Smith et al. found that Qafzeh 10 did not differ from living humans in the scheduling of its dental development (449). However, my colleague Donald J. Reid and I found that the distribution of perikymata on the enamel surface of Qafzeh anterior teeth tends to differ from that of living people today from diverse regions of the world – South Africa, Europe, and Alaska (474). Thus, with both Jebel Ihroud 3 and the Qafzeh anterior teeth, there are some aspects of dental growth that are not quite modern even though the scheduling of dental development does seem to be.

As has emerged in previous discussions in this book, skeletal growth and development also require consideration in assessments of developmental periods. We have seen that it is possible for the pace of skeletal and dental growth to differ, and if they do, then interpreting what they mean for the overall length of juvenile growth periods becomes unclear. Recall that the "life history mode concept" characterizes a species' life history strategy in terms of its particular combination of developmental rates and scheduling in different systems – dental, somatic, and reproductive – in recognition that natural selection can act independently on these different systems (186). Characterized in this way, a fossil species unique combination of developmental rates becomes the subject of further inquiry. The life history mode concept therefore provides a more productive approach to understanding fossil species life histories, and we currently do not have the evidence to reconstruct rates of skeletal growth in these early hominins to help fill in the picture

Though moving in a modern direction developmentally, the teeth of Jebel Irhoud 3 are nevertheless quite large by modern standards (470) as are those from Qafzeh (326). Dental reduction in anatomically modern humans happened later in time, as we turn to next.

DENTAL REDUCTION REDUX

When we last encountered paleoanthropologist C. Loring Brace it was in the context of dental reduction at an earlier stage in the genus *Homo*. Brace and colleagues devoted even greater effort to understanding patterns of dental reduction in more recent times. In 1987, Brace, Rosenberg, and Hunt published a major paper in the journal *Evolution* in which they calculated rates of tooth size reduction in multiple areas of the world since the onset of the last glaciation, 100,000 years ago (326). Before this time, throughout the Middle Pleistocene, tooth size remained relatively stable. In their analyses, Brace et al. used a summary measure of the cross-sectional area of all teeth of the dentition. From 100,000 to 10,000 years ago (the end of the Pleistocene), the mean of this summary measure reduced gradually at a rate of 1% per 2,000 years. Since the end of the Pleistocene, though, and coincident with the beginnings of agriculture, the rate of dental reduction doubled to 1% per 1,000 years in diverse regions of the world. The exception was Australia, where tooth size remained relatively stable up until the end of the Pleistocene, only undergoing reduction more recently.

Brace and his coauthors explained these trends in relation to cultural changes that relaxed selection on tooth size. In their view, during glacial times, survival in northern regions required the ability to cook frozen food "... if for no other reason than simply to thaw it to the point where it can be eaten" (1995: 715). Such "obligatory cooking," as Brace called it, had the effect of softening food. In Brace's view, dental reduction then followed as a consequence of relaxed selection on tooth size and the Probable Mutation Effect (see Chapter 6). In support of this explanation, Brace and colleagues (1987) observed that dental reduction has been greatest in the areas of the world where cooking has been routine for the longest periods of time – in the northern regions of Europe and Asia. As Brace put it "... the fossil record shows a degree of dental reduction strictly proportional to the length of time that the ancestors of the sample had been dependent upon cooked food for their survival" (1995:715).

The accelerated rate of dental reduction over the last 10,000 years was attributed to the development and use of pottery and "pounding, grinding and milling" tools (326). Such tools softened plant foods that were otherwise to hard or tough to eat. Pottery made it possible for foods to be processed to "drinkable consistency." Brace et al. point out that for the first time in human history, sizeable numbers of people were surviving to old age with few remaining teeth in their jaws. Teeth were becoming almost nonessential. In the view of Brace and colleagues, these changes further relaxed selection pressures, quickening the pace of dental reduction via the Probable Mutation Effect (PME).

These are fascinating observations because they imply that cultural evolution has strongly influenced dental evolution. On the other hand, not all changes in dental reduction can be clearly chalked up to culture. In his review of Brace's studies, the late Jules Kieser pointed out that "technological sophistication" and tooth size are not inversely related. As an example, he offers the hunting and gathering southern African San, who employ a hunting and gathering set of tools but who nevertheless have incisor teeth smaller in size than those of most other peoples (349). In a similar vein, commenting on one of Brace's papers in *Current Anthropology*, dental anthropologist Patricia Smith asked, "Do Brace and Hinton seriously consider that the presence of Middle-Pleistocene teeth in recent populations as diverse as Amazonian Indians and Australian Aborigines means that they have Middle Pleistocene technologies?" (1981:561).

Peter White of the University of Sydney in Australia notes that food processing tools such as seed grinders go back 17,000 years in Australia, but that the greater part of dental reduction in Australian aborigines occurred much later, around 6,000 years ago. There seems to be a mismatch between technological change and dental reduction that is difficult to explain based on the cause-effect relationship between the two that Brace and colleagues hypothesized. Some evolutionary lag time is to be expected but it is not clear how much to allow before rejecting their hypothesis.

These criticisms do not negate the importance of culture in relaxing selection pressures on teeth. They, do, however, suggest that patterns of tooth size variation across the modern world must also reflect other influences, such as genetic drift, gene flow, and/or currently unidentified selection pressures. Roberto Macchiarelli and Luca Bondioli suggested that tooth size could have reduced simply as a consequence of body size reduction (475). Their evidence came from the rapid reduction in both stature and tooth size across the transition from Pleistocene hunting and gathering to sedentary agriculture 10,000 years ago. The problem with this view, as many have noted, is that other studies find very low correlations between body size and tooth size in humans (349).

While Brace saw the PME as the mechanism underlying dental reduction in modern humans, others have made a compelling case for tooth-jaw size mismatch as a strong selection pressure (355). The idea (see Chapter 6) is that softened foods do not stimulate jaw bones do to grow to a size large enough to accommodate big teeth. Consequences include crowded, malpositioned, and impacted teeth, all of which increase the risk of dental disease and in some cases, can lead to death.

A skeletal series from the Iron Gates site of Vlasac, Serbia spanning the years from 6300 to 5300 BC offers correlational evidence of this mechanism in action. In this study, archaeologist Gloria Y'Edynak found that diet did not change over the thousand year period, but technology did: flint "microliths" with sharper edges were becoming used more frequently over time (476). Concurrently, jaw dimensions decreased. In the earlier period of this 1,000 year span, anterior teeth exhibited high frequencies of crowding and rotation. In the later period, tooth size decreased. Y'Edynak's data are consistent with a cause-effect relationship: decreased jaw size with dental crowding precedes the reduction in tooth size.

The selective mechanism, in Y'Edynak's view was periodontitis – a severe gum infection. Tooth crowding can create pockets around teeth in which the bacteria causing periodontitis proliferate. The infection triggers the immune system's inflammatory response in which blood plasma and white blood cells seep into the infected area. As a result, the tissues that anchor a tooth in its socket – the periodontium – become loose. Bone is resorbed and the tooth can be lost (74). Y'Edynak maintained that tooth loss itself could have affected survival, but the extent to which this was true isn't clear. There are no data in this study on the numbers of individuals surviving to old age with missing teeth that would give some indication of the effects of tooth loss on survival.

Still, there are other reasons besides tooth loss to think that periodontal disease might affect reproductive success. Recent studies suggest that periodontitis is associated with heart disease (477) and premature birth (478). Severe dental infections can lead to life-threatening sequelae, such as septicemia (blood infection) or cavernous sinus thrombosis (a blood clot in the cavernous sinus, at the base of the brain). Y'Edynak's study provides a circumstantial case that changes in culture (here changes in stone tool technology) can preclude jaws from growing large enough to accommodate large teeth, resulting in dental infections that decrease the reproductive success of large-toothed individuals. In this situation, genes for smaller teeth are preferentially passed down to subsequent generations.

Third molar agenesis would seem to be related to the overall trend of dental reduction. The third molar is particularly vulnerable to impaction, as it is the last tooth to erupt into the oral cavity. Wisdom teeth that have trouble erupting can trap food and plaque, resulting in severe infection (see Chapter 6). According to one study, there is evidence that selection acted specifically on a gene mutation associated with third molar agenesis in humans – the Ala240Pro mutation of the PAX 9 gene (479). The authors of the study suggest that natural selection would have favored individuals who harbored this mutation. While that is certainly possible, the worldwide distribution of this mutation does *not* coincide with worldwide patterns of third molar agenesis. The Ala240Pro mutation is more common in Europeans than it is in Asians (479), but Asians have a greater frequency of third molar agenesis than Europeans do (260).

It is possible that third molar agenesis in modern humans is, in part, a genetic or developmental correlate of overall dental reduction. There is a connection between reduced tooth size and third molar agenesis (480) – individuals with smaller teeth are more likely to have congenitally absent third molars. Why might the size of other teeth have anything to do with third molar agenesis? An answer might be found in the "Inhibitory Cascade Model" of tooth formation. The model relies on the elegant experimental work of Kavanagh and coworkers (481). These researchers grew mouse tooth germs in vitro, finding that molecular inhibitors made by the first molar tooth germ caused a delay in the initiation of the second molar tooth germ. The delay reduced the time available for the second molar tooth to form, producing a second molar of smaller size than the first or even a completely missing second molar. When Kavanagh and colleagues cut the connection between the first and second molar tooth germs, the second molar was "rescued" from this inhibition.

From first to second to third molars, there is a "cascade" of inhibition, whereby first molars inhibit second molars, and second molars inhibit third molars. The magnitude of inhibition depends on the strength of activating and inhibiting molecular signals emanating from tooth germs. Kavanagh et al. developed a mathematical model for predicting the size of molars based on the strength of activation and inhibition and the position of molars along the tooth row. The model predicts that greater inhibition relative to activation causes a progressive decrease in molar size from first to second to third molars. The model further predicts that when the second molar falls below one-half the size of the first, the third molar does not form at all.

While the inhibitory cascade model offers a proximate explanation for how third molar agenesis occurs and relates it to the relative size of other molars, it is not currently known whether the model can explain variation in third molar agenesis among modern human populations. The model is *not* able to explain third molar agenesis in the Callitrichine subfamily of New World monkeys (482). This subfamily always lacks third molars, but the second molar is not less than one-half the size of the first. In other words, the Inhibitory Cascade Model would predict that the third molar *should* form in this subfamily, but it does not. Mutations in the PAX 9 gene do not explain third molar agenesis in Callitrichines either, because both Callitrichines and squirrel monkeys have identical mutations, and squirrel monkeys have third molars.

Another factor to consider in third molar reduction and agenesis was first alluded to in Chapter 6 – this is the idea, proposed by Bermúdez de Castro (483) that prolonged developmental periods in modern humans may have resulted in a delay in the initiation of the M3. All other aspects of tooth growth held constant, delayed initiation of the M3 would result in less time for tooth formation, with smaller tooth size or simply absence of the M3 as a consequence. While this explanation might work for the high frequency of third molar agenesis in humans in general, it is not clear if variation in M3 initiation timing can explain patterns of variation in third molar agenesis among living human populations. Moreover, all of the factors discussed here may interact in complex ways, influencing the high frequency of third molar agenesis in modern humans and its variable expression among modern human populations. We are still far from understanding the relative importance of these factors in producing patterns of human third molar agenesis.

Dental reduction, including third molar agenesis, is an important trend in recent human evolution, the causes for which, at both proximate and ultimate levels are still being worked out. Changes in diet and food-processing not only influenced this trend but also had a dramatic impact on the evolution of bacteria causing dental disease.

THE RELATIVELY RECENT RISE OF DENTAL DISEASE

A few cases of dental pathology pepper the hominin fossil record. Malocclusions – when upper and lower teeth do not come together correctly – were present in the Nariokotome boy and the Dmanisi hominins (see Chapter 6). Cavities in fossil hominin teeth have been found in *Paranthropus robustus* (484)– but only in about 3% of over 100 teeth. There are a handful of Neanderthal teeth with cavities (485). Bone loss associated with periodontal disease occurs in a few *Australopithecus africanus* individuals, but is somewhat more common in the Dmanisi hominins and in Neanderthals (485, 486).

The loss of teeth before death, antemortem tooth loss (AMTL), has been reported in just eleven hominins (487). AMTL can occur through different pathways. One way AMTL can occur was described earlier, through periodontal infections that destroy the periodontal tissues tethering teeth to their sockets. Another way AMTL can occur is through exposure and subsequent bacterial infection of the dental pulp (pulpitis). Pulp exposure can occur when cavities are very deep or when teeth are heavily worn. Whatever the pathways leading to it, AMTL in earlier hominins was rare.

A 2014 FDI World Dental Federation report [http://www.worldoralhealthday.com/wp-content/uploads/2014/03/FDIWhitePaper_OralHealthWorldwide.pdf] estimates that worldwide, between 60–90% of children are afflicted with dental caries – the disease process resulting in cavities. Up to 5 to 20% of the world's populations are afflicted by periodontitis, which the FDA states is the leading cause of tooth loss. How did we go through so much of our evolutionary history with so little dental pain, only to experience so much of it today?

In 1984, anthropologists Mark Cohen and George Armelagos published a collection of studies from around the world documenting increases in pathology – including dental pathology – during the transition from a hunting and gathering to an agricultural way of life (488). As that transition took place, and people began to eat large quantities of carbohydrate-rich cereals, caries rates increased. Caries is a disease caused by a group of oral bacteria called mutans streptococci. These bacteria live in the plaque that bathes our teeth, and live off of the fermentable carbohydrates (starches and sugars) that we ingest. In the process of fermenting sugars, caries-causing bacteria produce lactic acid, which demineralizes teeth causing cavities in them (74). In North America, caries rates increased in multiple regions as people became reliant on maize agriculture (488). Increases in caries during the transition to agriculture have also been noted in South Asia (489), South America (490) and Nubia (491), among other places.

Thanks to the work of Christina Adler and colleagues (492), we now know there was a shift in the composition of oral bacteria during the transition to agriculture. These researchers sequenced bacterial DNA from the dental plaque of hunter-gatherer- and early agricultural European dental remains. Hunter-gatherers had few disease-causing bacteria but the agricultural Europeans, who ingested large quantities of wheat and barley, were hosts to disease-causing bacteria that lived off of bits of these cereals in their mouths. Otzi the Neolithic iceman, who died in the Italian alps around 3300 BC, suffered from rampant caries and periodontitis (493).

I am slightly overstating the case though, making it seem as if there were near identity between agriculture and dental disease. Even the diets of foragers, if they contain high quantities of fermentable carbohydrates, can be associated with high caries rates. Louise Humphrey and colleagues (494) recently published evidence of high caries rates – 51% of teeth affected – in the adult teeth of 15,000-year old foraging North Africans who included a high proportion of wild acorns and pine nuts in their diets. Meanwhile, archaeologists Marc Oxenham and Nancy Tayles (495) found little evidence for an increase in oral disease (including caries) with intensifying rice agriculture in Southeast Asia. By themselves starch rich foods are actually much less cariogenic than sugary foods, or foods that combine both starch and sugar (74).

Where agriculture and high caries rates are linked, females seem to bear the brunt of the burden (496). Dental anthropologist John

Lukacs (who happens to have been my dissertation adviser) performed a meta-analysis of caries in both prehistoric and modern societies. Females were found to often have higher rates of caries than males do (496). Bioarchaeologist Clark Spencer Larsen (who happens to be my Department Chair) reported high rates of caries associated with Native American maize agriculture in Georgia, with females being more often afflicted than males (497). He suggested that higher rates of caries in females had to do with sex differences in food preparation and consumption, with females consuming larger quantities of carbohydrates.

John Lukacs (496), together with Leah Largaespada (498) countered that the higher rates of caries in females might have more to do with their biology than with culturally constructed gender roles. For example, experimental studies in rats associate high concentrations of estrogens (but not testosterone) with increased caries formation (499). Estrogens reach their highest concentrations in women when they are pregnant (496). Moreover, there is evidence that saliva biochemistry changes during pregnancy, so that it is less able to buffer increases in acidity (500, 501) On the basis of these findings (and others), Lukacs suggested that increases in fertility associated with agriculture "accentuated" the difference in caries rates between males and females. Lukacs maintains that in agricultural societies, where multiple pregnancies occur over the life course, caries rates increase with age at a faster rate in females than they do in males. Females are also more susceptible to periodontal disease and tooth loss than males (502). There seems to be truth in the adage "A child, a tooth" common to many cultures (502).

While dental disease began to rise during the transition to agriculture, it soared with the introduction of refined sugar into our diets during the Industrial Revolution. The Adler et al. study of bacterial DNA in dental calculus found that caries-causing bacteria became the dominant species of oral bacteria only after the medieval era (492). They suggest that the industrial production of refined sugar and flour changed oral environments, providing caries-causing bacteria with ample simple sugars to ferment. In the process, these bacteria produced lactic acid that demineralized enamel and caused cavities. Simple sugars are the primary molecules on which cariogenic bacteria act. In England, the greatest increase in caries rates occurred from 1800 to 1850, when sugar began to be imported from the West Indies in large quantities (503).

Today, when Western diets replace traditional ones, caries rates rise dramatically. Researchers Andrea Cucina and Elma Vega Lizama studied young adults living in an area of the Yucatan peninsula. Those who lived in the town area, where sodas and other sugary foods were available had three times the number of cavities as those living in a nearby village, who did not have access to these items (503). Western diets not only bring about higher caries rates but also higher rates of malocclusion. Soft diets do not stimulate jaw growth, and teeth, especially third molars, become impacted. Precontact Australian aborigines, for example, had fewer malocclusions than postcontact groups (504). Third molar impaction became ten times more common after the Industrial Revolution than it was previously (503).

It might seem strange that natural selection, acting over millennia, has not selected for individuals who are more resistant to dental disease. The reason this has not happened has to do with evolutionary mismatch – our current diets, with soft, processed, and sugary foods are nothing like the hunting and gathering diets to which we are adapted. It is estimated that 99% of our evolutionary history was spent eating wild foods that were gathered or hunted. Agriculture and the Industrial Revolution are recent phenomena in our long evolutionary history. Essentially, natural selection has not prepared us well for the kinds of foods we eat today.

A less often appreciated contributor to our current dental malaise is our long lifespans. Caries is an "age-progressive" disease – the longer you live the more caries you can accumulate. Cassandra Gilmore recently compared human hunter-gathers and apes in their frequencies of antemortem tooth loss (487). She found that AMTL is higher in human hunter-gatherers than it is in chimpanzees, but that this difference is not related to differences in rates of wear or caries between them.

What explained the difference in human hunter-gatherer versus chimpanzee rates of AMTL was simply age. The odds of losing a tooth tripled for every ten years of age. Living longer than chimpanzees, hunter-gatherers simply have greater opportunity to lose teeth. Still, Gilmore found that even when age was accounted for statistically, hunter-gatherers had somewhat elevated frequencies of AMTL as compared to chimpanzees. She therefore suggests that some aspect of human behavior – the ability to use tools to soften foods or the help of others – must contribute to the human ability to survive with few teeth. (Divine intervention is probably out as an explanation, because, according to cartoonist Matt Groening, "God often gives nuts to toothless people.")

OUR TEETH, OURSELVES

In sum, the study of ancient teeth provides multiple insights into modern human biology. Analysis of dental morphology is consistent with a two-wave dispersal of anatomically modern humans from Africa. The retention of ancestral dental traits in sub-Saharan Africans and in Australians can be explained by the two-wave dispersal model. Similarly, the continuity of dental features in East Asia from *Homo erectus* to early anatomically modern humans in this region around 100,000 years ago, suggests admixture between more archaic hominins in Asia with the first dispersers out of Africa. Early anatomically modern humans, such as Jebel Ihroud 3 from Morocco and the Qafzeh 10 from Israel, appear to have modern human schedules of dental development, but are not quite modern in some of the details of their root (Jebel Ihroud 3) and enamel (Qafzeh hominins) growth. Their modern developmental schedules suggest that their overall pace of growth during childhood was similar to that of living people today, but we lack information about their rates skeletal development to complete the picture.

Modern humans have much smaller teeth than their anatomically human ancestors, such as Jebel Ihroud and Qafzeh. Calculating rates of dental reduction through time, Loring Brace and colleagues highlighted the roles of cooking, tool use, and eventually pottery in relaxing selection pressures on maintaining large teeth. Brace explained the decrease in tooth size as a result of the Probable Mutation Effect. Calcagno and Gibson's (355) tooth-jaw size mismatch hypothesis may be a more promising explanation for dental reduction at this stage in human evolution. Both explanations attribute changes in tooth size to changes in culture, although as noted, not all cases of dental reduction can be clearly linked to culture change. It is hard to imagine that cooking, tools, and pottery did not have a tremendous influence on the overall modern human trend toward dental reduction – yet, more careful studies such as Y'Edynak's study of the Iron Gates site are needed to test hypothesized correlations and the mechanisms that underlie them.

Finally, from the study of ancient teeth, it is clear that only in our very recent history has dental disease become so widespread. Caries and malocclusions were very rare in earlier hominins. Bacterial DNA recovered from dental calculus testifies to shifts in the composition of oral bacteria coincident with the transition to agriculture and the Industrial Revolution. Our long lifespans also contribute to our dental plight. Perhaps there are lessons to be learned here for how dental practitioners treat teeth today. A 2013 meeting of dental anthropologists and dental practitioners at the National Evolutionary Synthesis Center pondered this question. Conclusions from that meeting as well as other ways that an evolutionary perspective can inform the dental present are considered in the final chapter.

10 Every Tooth a Diamond

> "... for I tell thee Sancho, a mouth without teeth is like a mill without a millstone, and a tooth is much more to be prized than a diamond.
>
> – Cervantes
> *Don Quixote*

So lamented Don Quixote when shepherds bearing slingshots took out several of his "grinders." He had attacked their flock of sheep, which he mistook for an army (easy mistake). However misguided, the noble knight-errant clearly understood the value of teeth.

To paleoanthropologists, the value of teeth lies in the wealth of information they preserve about our past. Morphological analyses of fossil teeth elucidate biological relationships among species and populations within them. Studies of the chemical composition of enamel and of dental wear inform us about the diets of our ancestors and close relatives. And, investigations of dental growth and development enlighten us about their life history modes. These are some of the more vital contributions of teeth to understanding our evolutionary history. Here, I will synthesize dental insights into human evolution discussed throughout this book and consider what's next for what can be called "dental paleoanthropology," the subfield of paleoanthropology that makes use of fossil teeth to understand hominin biology. Finally, I will reflect on how an evolutionary perspective on our dental past helps us understand how we view and treat teeth today.

PUTTING IN ALL TOGETHER: THE WHOLE TOOTH

If we were to draw up a list of differences between humans and our chimpanzees relatives, that list would include – among other things – our differences in brain size, language ability, ability to adapt to new environments, our reliance on cultural solutions to problems of survival and reproduction, the length of our periods of juvenile growth and dependency, and the length of our lifespans. Fossil teeth give us a record of the origins and evolution of several of these and other unique human attributes.

The origins of human adaptability can be traced back to the teeth of our australopith ancestors. Stable carbon isotope analysis of their dental enamel (Chapter 2) reveals that, unlike modern chimpanzees whose diets even in savanna environments are limited to C3 plants, australopith species were in most cases incorporating both C3 and C4 resources into their diets (83). As dietary "generalists" australopiths would have had the ability to survive a wide range of environmental conditions, as resources waxed and waned. Australopiths had to contend with rapid oscillations from wet to dry environments over time. They had to be able to adjust to the patchwork of local habitats that characterized the African Plio-Pleistocene. According to Rick Potts' "Variability Selection Hypothesis," these unstable and diverse environments selected for our ancestors' dietary and behavioral flexibility (505).

Data gleaned from marine cores and ancient soils tells us about the varied environments in which australopiths evolved. Chemical signatures in their teeth reveal that they survived within these environments by diversifying their diets. This is not to say, of course, that australopiths were perfectly adapted to these conditions. There is a fair amount of linear enamel hypoplasia in australopith teeth, signifying physiological stresses that were severe enough to disrupt enamel formation (506, 507). We descended from those able to survive these stresses and pass along the genes that made them successful. In Darwinian terms, we therefore owe some part of our hallmark human adaptability to the "struggle for existence" of our australopith ancestors.

Evidence from teeth further suggests how two very different hominin lineages – *Paranthropus* and *Homo* were able to coexist. Chemical and microwear analyses bolster John Robinson's "Dietary

Hypothesis," which postulates that the two lineages occupied different niches. In East Africa, *Paranthropus boisei* consumed much greater quantities of C4 plants that did its *Homo erectus* contemporary (88). The featureless microwear on *Paranthropus boisei* teeth is consistent with a diet of tough C4 plant parts that required repetitive chewing to break down into digestible pieces (338). Meanwhile, in South Africa, trace element analysis of Sr/Ca and Ba/Ca ratios in tooth enamel point to the incorporation of significant quantities of meat in the diet of *Homo habilis*, with *Paranthropus robustus* remaining primarily vegetarian (106).

We can also trace the origins of our small canine teeth back to australopith times. Our diminutive canines are unique among our living great ape cousins, and multiple hypotheses have been proffered to explain them (Chapter 3). Here, I argued that the small degree of canine sexual dimorphism at in *Ardipithecus ramidus* at 4.4 Ma (19) is hard to explain on the basis of current dietary hypotheses for canine reduction. That is because *Ar. ramidus* was primarily a C3 resource feeder, like chimpanzees, and lacked the craniodental adaptations to eating the mechanically challenging foods consumed by later australopiths. For *Ar. ramidus*, it is most plausible that minimal canine sexual dimorphism signifies either decreased male-male competition for mates or that competition among males had ceased to involve canine teeth. Peter Lucas' (123) and William Hylanders' (124) biomechanical analyses indicate that dietary-associated reduction in jaw gape in later hominins would have constrained the evolution of large canines.

If the origins of our dietary flexibility and our small canine teeth can be found in our australopith ancestors, do our prolonged periods of juvenile growth, so intimately tied to our large brains and flexible behavior, also originate with them (Chapter 4)? The answer to this question has changed over time, as our understanding of the range of variation in human and ape dental development has broadened and as x-ray synchrotron microtomography has provided a clearer picture of hominin dental development than ever before. It now seems that in some australopiths, periods of dental development were longer than those of chimpanzees. This is even true of some individuals of *Paranthropus robustus* (196), a species generally considered to represent a side branch of our evolutionary tree. Perhaps the first steps toward lengthening growth periods were taken in the common ancestors of *Paranthropus* and *Homo*, as brain sizes and dietary breadth began to expand. Perhaps these lineages were also evolving larger brains and longer developmental periods in parallel.

In their recent synthesis of research on early *Homo*, Susan Antón and colleagues (177), argued (as had Peter Ungar and coauthors earlier [339]), that variability selection drove the further evolution of dietary and behavioral flexibility in the genus *Homo*. A broad range of complexity values characterizes *Homo erectus* dental microwear, indicating a diet that spanned soft as well as hard foods (338). The decreasing size of premolar and molar teeth reflects increasing reliance on cultural solutions for survival. We know from the archaeological record that stone tools became more sophisticated during *Homo erectus* times, and that there is a good possibility that *Homo erectus* controlled and used fire. Foods softened with stone tools and/or with fire would have significantly relaxed selection for growing and maintaining large posterior teeth and jaws at this time in our evolutionary history. It is possible that the steep reduction in the size of posterior teeth and jaws in *Homo erectus* was a result of selection for energy efficiency in this large-brained, large-bodied hominin (Chapter 6).

Periods of dental development lengthen in *Homo erectus* (Chapter 7), possibly signifying a further step along the way to prolonging juvenile dependency and time available for learning. Greater opportunity for learning would be consistent with the large brains and flexible behavior of *Homo erectus*. Unexpectedly though, skeletal growth rates, as assessed by using teeth to age the Narikotome boy, may have been quite rapid. If that is so, then perhaps our protracted periods of dental and skeletal development evolved in a mosaic fashion, with dental development slowing down first. Why this dissociation between dental and skeletal development would have occurred is unclear, but such dissociations characterize the life history modes of some living primates (186). Filling in the life history picture for *Homo erectus* is Caspari and Lee's wear seriation analysis indicating that *Homo erectus* also enjoyed longer lifespans than any hominin species that came before it. That evidence is consistent with the view that cultural adaptations in *Homo erectus* reduced the risk of extrinsic mortality in adults (177). Under this condition, biological investment in prolonged juvenile growth periods and extended natural lifespans would have been possible.

The human trends that teeth reveal continue to be traceable through later stages of human evolution (Chapters 8 and 9). Although for many years Neanderthals had been viewed as meat specialists, new work on Neanderthal dental calculus, microwear, and macrowear clearly shows that Neanderthals were including plant foods in their diets (411, 412, 414, 415), perhaps in some cases for medicinal purposes (412). They also tended to eat foods similar to that of their anatomically modern counterparts where they occupied similar habitats (414). These dental data are consistent with recent archaeological evidence, all of which suggests that Neanderthals were flexible foragers.

Evidence from the study of linear enamel hypoplasia and fluctuating dental asymmetry indicates that Neanderthals experienced relatively high levels of physiological stress, but not necessarily greater than that of recent anatomically modern human foragers (Tigara) who occupied marginal habitats (437, 442). Elevated levels of physiological stress are consistent with the notion that maintaining large and muscular bodies in cold environments was energetically costly (435), and may have led to slow rates of skeletal growth (453) in Neanderthals, either as an evolutionary adaptation or as a plastic (flexible physiological) response.

In contrast to rates of skeletal growth, rates of dental development and age at first molar eruption in Neanderthals are at the "rapid end" of modern human variation, but are both generally encompassed within the modern human range. Laura Shackelford and colleagues showed this for Neanderthal dental development (451), while M1 eruption estimates from two studies placed Neanderthals among modern humans (446, 449). Third molar development and eruption may have been accelerated in Neanderthals (449), but what this may mean, if anything, for other aspects of Neanderthal life history is obscure (508). All of these findings add up to that conclusion that Neanderthals were more like us than the earliest paleoanthropologists imagined. Analysis of oblique striations on Neanderthal anterior teeth suggests that like us, most Neanderthals were also right-handed.

Study of dental morphology puts the initial divergence between Neanderthals and anatomically modern humans around 1 million years ago, earlier than the 800,000-year estimate from genetic studies (Chapter 9). Evidence from dental morphology is consistent with that from DNA indicating a two-wave migration of AMHS out of Africa: an earlier migration into Asia around at around 130,000 (as estimated from genetic studies) and a later one into northern Eurasia around 50,000 years ago (again estimated from genetic studies). As I write this chapter in late 2015, new evidence has come to light from a cave in Daoxian (Hunan Province) China, where forty-seven teeth with modern human morphology dated to at least 80,000 years ago were recovered (509). The presence of such old modern-looking human teeth in Daoxian (and from other sites in China, as reviewed in Chapter 9) is consistent with genetic evidence of an early migration of AMHS from Africa into Asia.

Finally, with early anatomically modern humans, such as Jebel Ihroud (approximately 160,000 years old) and Qafzeh (about 90,000 years old), overall rates of dental development are not distinguishable from those of living people (449, 470). Interestingly, however, not all aspects of their dental growth and development are modern, with Jebel Ihroud evincing fast rates of root growth (470) and some of the Qafzeh teeth showing a more archaic perikymata distribution pattern (474). These early anatomically modern humans still had rather large teeth.

It is only with the origins of agriculture that the rate of dental reduction accelerated, and with it rates of dental pathology. Of all our human characteristics that can be traced back in time through fossil teeth, our myriad dental problems are the most recent.

A TASTE OF WHAT'S NEXT FOR DENTAL PALEOANTHROPOLOGY

The future of dental paleoanthropology holds new questions, further research into the genetics and development of dental morphology, diverse applications of new technologies, and expansion of the comparative primate and human database for dental morphology, diet, and development.

New fossils raise new questions. *Homo naledi*, a South African hominin species announced by paleoanthropologist Lee Berger and colleagues in late 2015 raises many (510). This species, of currently unknown antiquity, combines a tiny brain (similar to that of australopiths) with the cranial morphology of *Homo erectus* and an estimated stature that falls among smaller modern human values. The molars of *Homo naledi* are smaller in size than those of *Homo habilis* and fall at the smaller end of *Homo erectus* values. Why this species had such small molars, smaller than most other hominins of comparable brain size (Figure 10.1), is one question this species raises. The molars have a simplified occlusal morphology, and this makes sense for molars of such small size molars under the Patterning Cascade Model for tooth formation (see Chapter 6 for discussion). All kinds of questions will undoubtedly be asked of the *Homo naledi* teeth – especially because there are 140 or so of them – aiming to understand the morphological affinities of this new species, its dietary proclivities and its rates of dental growth and development.

The use of dental morphology to assess biological relationships requires a refined understanding of the genetics and developmental processes that underlie them. Morphological dental features are routinely treated as independent in phylogenetic analyses, even though some of these features may share common genetic and developmental

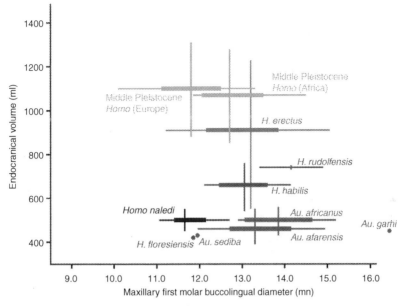

FIGURE 10.1: Breadth of upper first molar (buccal-lingual dimension) related to endocranial volume for a variety of hominins, including the recently discovered *Homo naledi*. The image is from Berger et al., 2015 in *eLife*, reprinted here under the terms of the *Creative Commons Attribution License*, https://creativecommons.org/licenses/by/4.0/

underpinnings (360, 361, 511). For example, my colleagues Stephanie Moormann and John Hunter and I (362) found that there were statistically significant low-level correlations between the presence of the Carabelli cusp and other accessory cusps on upper molar teeth, suggesting that these cusps do not develop independently, just as the Patterning Cascade Model of tooth development predicts. It may eventually be possible to reconstruct the developmental events that lead to patterns of dental trait covariation (361) and to use these events, rather than the traits themselves, in phylogenetic analyses. If that proves too difficult, then as paleoanthropologist Leslea Hlusko pointed out more than a decade ago, efforts can be made to identify suites of correlated traits, and use these rather than "atomized characters," in phylogenetic analyses (511).

With respect to new technologies, there are exciting avenues to further explore. One of the most fascinating of these is laser-ablation inductively-coupled-plasma mass spectrometry analysis of Strontium-Calcium (Sr/Ca) and Barium-Calcium (Ba/Ca) ratios in tooth enamel, which offers a way to reconstruct weaning timelines in fossil teeth (512, 513). Louise Humphrey and colleagues demonstrated that the Sr/Ca ratios along enamel prisms in children's deciduous teeth reflected known dietary shifts from mother's milk to infant formula or complementary foods (512). There is greater discrimination in the transfer of Sr relative to Ca across the mammary gland, such that during the period of exclusive breastfeeding, the Sr/Ca ratio in infant tissues, including enamel, is low. When complementary foods are introduced into the infant's diet or when the infant transitions to formula, the Sr/Ca ratio of the infant's tissues increases. Humphrey et al. used incremental growth markings in enamel, starting from the neonatal line that marks birth, to pinpoint when the weaning process began. She and her colleagues then compared weaning timelines reconstructed from these children's deciduous tooth enamel with their actual feeding histories. In three of the four children, Sr/Ca ratio increases coincided with the ages at which formula or complementary foods were introduced.

A similar analysis is possible with Ba/Ca ratios, only in this case values of Ba/Ca are higher during the period of exclusive breastfeeding and decrease as weaning foods are added to an infant's diet. Christine Austin and colleagues (513) showed that the rate of decrease in the Ba/Ca ratio during weaning closely paralleled the rate at which breast milk was withdrawn from the infant's diet. This was true for both human children and captive macaques. Furthermore, these researchers reconstructed dietary transitions in a Neanderthal juvenile. Ba/Ca ratios in this juvenile's enamel revealed a seven-month period of exclusive breastfeeding. This was followed by a seven-month period of supplementation, after which the Ba/Ca ratio rapidly fell to prenatal levels. The authors interpreted the rapid fall as an "abrupt" termination of breastfeeding at around 1.2 years of age in this Neanderthal individual. It is not clear to what extent (if at all) this juvenile reflects the weaning habits of Neanderthals, but the possibility of similar analyses in other fossil teeth may eventually make it possible to understand at what ages and in what manner Neanderthals and other fossil hominins weaned their children.

Inferences made from fossil teeth rest on understanding how the teeth of nonhuman primates and living humans relate to their diets and life histories. This is the essence of the comparative method. Many advances in understanding these relationships have been made by studying extant species and populations, and many more are sure to follow. Examples from nonhuman primates include the findings, based on multiple years of feeding data, that very thick enamel can be an adaptation to eating hard foods either as fallbacks or as dietary staples (62, 66). They include the finding that in the wild, ring-tailed lemurs with significant tooth loss can survive to advanced ages without the active care of others (387), challenging the notion that one can infer caregiving directly from the presence of individuals with severe antemortem tooth loss in the fossil record.

The effort to understand relationships between teeth and the environment is clearly crucial to our ability to understand the signals of adaptation, diet, behavior, growth, development, and life history that are present in fossil teeth. To coalesce research on this topic, anthropologists Frank Cuozzo, Peter Ungar, and Michelle Sauther organized a symposium entitled "Primate Dental Ecology: How Teeth Respond to the Environment." In their introduction to the symposium papers published in the *American Journal of Physical Anthropology* in 2012, Cuozzo and co-organizers expressed the hope that this newly defined research field will gain momentum in coming years (514).

With respect to the comparative database from living humans, there is much more that can be learned about ranges of variation in modern humans as well as how modern human teeth respond to *their* environments. Christopher Dean and Helen Liversidge's comparative sample of over 6,000 children of diverse ancestry made it possible to situate the ages at which dental stages were reached in early *Homo* among modern children with advanced dental development (369). Histological data on modern human variation has been greatly advanced by the work of Donald Reid (515) and is necessary for direct comparison to histological data from fossil teeth. Much histological study of developmental variation remains to be done, with respect to the ages of initiation of teeth, rates of hard tissue formation, and ages at crown and root completion in diverse populations. Moreover, greater understanding of relationships between population variation in human dental development and the environmental influences that may have shaped that variation is much needed for interpreting what, for example, different rates of dental development might mean when we see them in fossil anatomically modern humans or in Neanderthals (508).

TEETH TODAY

We need to understand teeth today in order to better interpret teeth in the past. But, it is also true that our understanding of ancient teeth can inform us about our dental present.

A key lesson emerging from the recent National Evolutionary Synthesis Center (NESCent) meeting on "Evolutionary Dentistry" was that dental caries, periodontal diseases and orthodontic conditions are maladies of modernity (Chapter 9). Kevin Boyd, a pediatric dentist participating in the meeting, suggests in an interview with "Dentistry iQ" (www.dentistryiq.com) that this evolutionary perspective is instructive – it tells us that these dental problems are entirely preventable. It was suggested at the NESCent meeting that chewing tougher foods during childhood like our ancestors did might help to stimulate jaw growth and prevent malocclusions (think beef jerky) (503). One of the co-organizers of the meeting, John Sorrentino, came away from the meeting with several evolutionary-inspired recommendations https://www.jackkruse.com/evolutionary-biology-meets-dentistry), which include eliminating processed sugar from our diets and reducing our consumption of natural sugars. He also points out that brushing and flossing your teeth "is not going to hurt you."

An evolutionary perspective may also be instructive from the standpoint of dental esthetics. Evolutionary psychologists view our facial preferences in terms of sexual selection. The idea is that over the millenia we have evolved mental preferences for facial cues of an individuals' "mate value" (516). As the authors of one review article put it, "... preferences guide us to choose mates who will provide the best chance of our genes surviving" (516). On the most basic level, lesions or sores on a person's face are not generally considered attractive. Symmetrical faces with average features tend to be perceived as more attractive, phenomena evolutionary psychologists ascribe to genetic quality and disease resistance.

In the framework of evolutionary psychology, a recent study found that human teeth also "signal" mate quality. In their study, Hendrie and Brewer manipulated the color and spacing of teeth in both young male and female digital images (517). These authors hypothesized that because smiling is an overture of sexual interest in humans, teeth would be particularly visible as cues. Tooth loss could signal a dental problem, such as caries or periodontitis, and dental crowing, of course is also related to dental disease (Chapter 9). Psychological preferences for having a full set of straight teeth would have evolved because these were reliable cues of a mate's ability to help us get our genes into the next generation.

The authors also hypothesize that white teeth are also a cue to mate quality. As we age, additional deposition in our teeth of underlying (yellow) dentine and the thinning of the whitish outer enamel layer contribute to progressive darkening and yellowing of teeth. Yellower teeth, in the authors' view are therefore age indicators. The more limited reproductive lifespans of women relative to men suggest that age indicators would have been particularly salient cues of female "mate value." The authors found what they expected to find:

nonnormal spacing of teeth and teeth that were more yellow in color were rated as less attractive, and for yellowing, this was particularly true for the female models.

The Hendrie and Brewers results are not so surprising given that their sample population was from the UK and given that Western cultures are increasingly influenced by Hollywood ideals of straight and white teeth. The question is whether such preferences for straight, white teeth are "cultural universals" that would reflect an underlying evolved psychology for our species. And the answer to this question is unclear. Charles Darwin remarked that standards of beauty vary so greatly among different cultures that such universal standards must not exist (115).

On the face of it, tooth modification practices, some of which are done for aesthetic reasons, are so variable across cultures as to make one question the universal appeal of a full set of white teeth. In Southeast Asian cultures tooth "blackening" with plant products to enhance attractiveness can be traced back 4,500 years (518), but the custom is beginning to wane as people are exposed to the Western ideal of white teeth. The reasons offered by those who blacken their teeth include reducing the prominence of canine teeth, which is also accomplished by filing the canine teeth. Perhaps we have an evolved preference for small canine teeth that in this society supersedes a preference for white teeth?

That's possible but then how does one explain why Mentawi people of Sumatra, some groups in Kalimantan, and the Kamorans of Papua New Guinea file their incisors to *make* them pointy (519)? And, then there are also many cultures – in Indonesia and especially in sub-Saharan African peoples – in which the anterior teeth are extracted and this is considered to be beautiful (520). Thus, while there might be something to an evolutionary psychology approach to understanding how we view teeth today, it will be challenging to come up with testable hypotheses for such diverse cultural practices associated with dental "beauty" under an evolutionary psychology paradigm.

Future dental paleoanthropologists will likely have field day with modern human teeth, especially with the various ways that cultures modify them, which include notching teeth, inlaying them with jewels or gold, lengthening them, filing them down, and removing them altogether. One thing these future paleoanthropologists may safely conclude is that these modifications reflect the human ability to think flexibly, creatively, and not always adaptively.

References

1. Switek B. *Written in Stone: The Hidden Secrets of Fossils and the Story of Life on Earth.* London: Icon Books; 2011.
2. Hsu K-T. The path to Steno's synthesis on the animal origin of glossopetrae. *Geological Society of America Memoirs.* 2009;**203**:93–106.
3. Steno, Morello N. The fossils, the rocks, and the calendar of the Earth. *Special Papers Geological Society of America.* 2006;**411**:81.
4. Freller T. "Lingue di seripi", "serpents' tongues" and "glossopetrae." Highlights from the history of popular "cult" medicine in early modern times. *Sudhoffs Archiv.* 1997;**81**:62–83.
5. Rudwick MJS. *The Meaning of Fossils: Episodes in the History of Paleontology.* Chicago: University of Chicago Press; 1985.
6. Scott GR, Turner CGI. *The Anthropology of Modern Human Teeth: Dental Morphology and Its Variation in Recent Human Populations.* Cambridge: Cambridge University Press; 1997.
7. Ayala FJ, Valentine JW. *The Theory and Process of Organic Evolution.* Menlo Park: Benjamin Cummings; 1979.
8. Dawkins R, Wong Y. *The Ancestor's Tale: A Pilgrimage to the Dawn of Evolution.* Boston: Houghton Mifflin; 2005.
9. Tobin A, Dusheck J. *Asking about Life*: Florence, KY: Cengage Learning; 2004.
10. Langergraber KE, Prüfer K, Rowney C, Boesch C, Crockford C, Fawcett K, et al. Generation times in wild chimpanzees and gorillas suggest earlier divergence times in great ape and human evolution. *Proceedings of the National Academy of Sciences.* 2012;**109**:15716–15721.
11. Dart RA. The Taungs skull. *Nature.* 1925;**116**:462.
12. McKee JK, McGraw WS, Poirier FE. *Understanding Human Evolution.* Upper Saddle River, NJ: Pearson Prentice Hall; 2005.
13. Conroy GC, Pontzer H. *Reconstructing Human Origins: A Modern Synthesis*: New York: WW Norton; 2012.
14. Gibbons A. *The First Human: The Race to Discover Our Earliest Ancestors*: New York: Anchor Books; 2007.

15. Cartmill M, Smith FH. *The Human Lineage*: Hoboken, NJ: John Wiley & Sons; 2009.
16. Wolpoff MH, Hawks J, Senut B, Pickford M, Ahern J. An ape or *the* ape: is the Toumaï cranium TM 266 a hominid? *PaleoAnthropology*. 2006;**2006**:36–50.
17. Brunet M, Guy F, Pilbeam D, Mackaye HT, Likius A, Ahounta D, et al. A new hominid from the Upper Miocene of Chad, Central Africa. *Nature*. 2002;**418**:145–151.
18. Wood B, Harrison T. The evolutionary context of the first hominins. *Nature*. 2011;**470**:347–352.
19. White TD, Asfaw B, Beyene Y, Haile-Selassie Y, Lovejoy CO, Suwa G, et al. Ardipithecus ramidus and the paleobiology of early hominids. *Science*. 2009;**326**:64–86.
20. Leakey MG, Feibel CS, McDougall I, Walker A. New four-million-year-old hominid species from Kanapoi and Allia Bay, Kenya. *Nature*. 1995;**376**:565–571.
21. Leakey MG, Feibel CS, McDougall I, Ward C, Walker A. New specimens and confirmation of an early age for *Australopithecus anamensis*. *Nature*. 1998;**393**:62–66.
22. Kimbel WH, Delezene LK. "Lucy" redux: a review of research on *Australopithecus afarensis*. *American Journal of Physical Anthropology*. 2009;**140(S49)**:2–48.
23. Kimbel WH, Lockwood CA, Ward CV, Leakey MG, Rak Y, Johanson DC. Was *Australopithecus anamensis* ancestral to *A. afarensis*? A case of anagenesis in the hominin fossil record. *Journal of Human Evolution*. 2006;**51**:134–152.
24. Ward CV, Leakey MG, Walker A. Morphology of *Australopithecus anamensis* from Kanapoi and Allia Bay, Kenya. *Journal of Human Evolution*. 2001;**41**:255–368.
25. Beynon AD, Wood BA. Variations in enamel thickness and structure in East African hominids. *American Journal of Physical Anthropology*. 1986;**70**:177–193.
26. Leakey MG, Spoor F, Brown FH, Gathogo PN, Kiarie C, Leakey LN, et al. New hominin genus from eastern Africa shows diverse middle Pliocene lineages. *Nature*. 2001;**410**:433–440.
27. White T. Early hominids – diversity or distortion? *Science*. 2003;**299**:1994.
28. Brunet M, Beauvilain A, Coppens Y, Heintz E, Moutaye AHE, Pilbeam D. The first australopithecine 2,500 kilometres west of the Rift Valley (Chad). *Nature*. 1995;**378**:273–275.
29. Haile-Selassie Y, Gibert L, Melillo SM, Ryan TM, Alene M, Deino A, et al. New species from Ethiopia further expands Middle Pliocene hominin diversity. *Nature*. 2015;**521**:483–488.

30. Spoor F. Palaeoanthropology: The middle Pliocene gets crowded. *Nature.* 2015;**521**:432–433.
31. Harmand S, Lewis JE, Feibel CS, Lepre CJ, Prat S, Lenoble A, et al. 3.3-million-year-old stone tools from Lomekwi 3, West Turkana, Kenya. *Nature.* 2015;**521**:310–315.
32. Asfaw B, White T, Lovejoy O, Latimer B, Simpson S, Suwa G. *Australopithecus garhi*: a new species of early hominid from Ethiopia. *Science.* 1999;**284**:629–635.
33. Aiello L, Dean C. *An Introduction to Human Evolutionary Anatomy.* New York: Academic Press; 1990.
34. Johanson D, White T. A systematic assessment of early African hominids. *Science.* 1979;**203**:321–330.
35. Delezene LK, Zolnierz MS, Teaford MF, Kimbel WH, Grine FE, Ungar PS. Premolar microwear and tooth use in *Australopithecus afarensis*. *Journal of Human Evolution.* 2013;**65**:282–293.
36. Berger LR, de Ruiter DJ, Churchill SE, Schmid P, Carlson KJ, Dirks PH, et al. *Australopithecus sediba*: a new species of *Homo*-like australopith from South Africa. *Science.* 2010;**328**:195–204.
37. Kivell TL, Kibii JM, Churchill SE, Schmid P, Berger LR. *Australopithecus sediba* hand demonstrates mosaic evolution of locomotor and manipulative abilities. *Science.* 2011;**333**:1411–1417.
38. Kibii JM, Churchill SE, Schmid P, Carlson KJ, Reed ND, De Ruiter DJ, et al. A partial pelvis of *Australopithecus sediba*. *Science.* 2011;**333**:1407–1411.
39. Broom R. The Pleistocene anthropoid apes of South Africa. *Nature.* 1938;**142**:377–379.
40. Morell V. *Ancestral Passions: The Leakey Family and the Quest for Humankind's Beginnings.* New York: Simon and Schuster; 1995.
41. Wood B, Wood C, Konigsberg L. *Paranthropus boisei*: an example of evolutionary stasis? *American Journal of Physical Anthropology.* 1994;**95**:117–136.
42. Constantino PJ, Lucas PW, Lee JJW, Lawn BR. The influence of fallback foods on great ape tooth enamel. *American Journal of Physical Anthropology.* 2009;**140**:653–660.
43. Strait DS, Grine FE. Inferring hominoid and early hominid phylogeny using craniodental characters: the role of fossil taxa. *Journal of Human Evolution.* 2004;**47**:399–452.
44. González-José R, Escapa I, Neves WA, Cúneo R, Pucciarelli HM. Cladistic analysis of continuous modularized traits provides phylogenetic signals in *Homo* evolution. *Nature.* 2008;**453**:775–778.

45. Irish JD, Guatelli-Steinberg D, Legge SS, de Ruiter DJ, Berger LR. News and views: Response to "Non-metric dental traits and hominin phylogeny" by Carter et al., with additional information on the Arizona State University Dental Anthropology System and phylogenetic "place" of *Australopithecus sediba*. *Journal of Human Evolution*. 2014;**69**:129–134.
46. Irish JD, Guatelli-Steinberg D, Legge SS, de Ruiter DJ, Berger LR. Dental morphology and the phylogenetic "place" of *Australopithecus sediba*. *Science*. 2013;**340**(6129).
47. Wood B, Collard M. The human genus. *Science*. 1999;**284**:65–71.
48. Robinson JT. Prehominid dentition and hominid evolution. *Evolution*. 1954: 324–334.
49. Robinson JT. Adaptive radiation in the australopithecines and the origin of man. *African Ecology and Human Evolution*. 1963;**36**:385–416.
50. Dart RA. The first australopithecine fragment from the Makapansgat pebble culture stratum. *Nature*. 1955;**176**:170.
51. Brain CK. *The Hunters or the Hunted?* Chicago: University of Chicago Press; 1981.
52. Wrangham RW, Jones JH, Laden G, Pilbeam D, Conklin-Brittain N. The raw and the stolen. *Current Anthropology*. 1999;**40**:567–594.
53. Aiello LC, Wheeler P. The expensive-tissue hypothesis: the brain and the digestive system in human and primate evolution. *Current Anthropology*. 1995;**36**: 199–221.
54. Navarrete A, van Schaik CP, Isler K. Energetics and the evolution of human brain size. *Nature*. 2011;**480**:91–93.
55. Tanner N, Zihlman A. Women in evolution. Part I: Innovation and selection in human origins. *Signs*. 1976;**1**:585–608.
56. O'Connell JF, Hawkes K, Lupo KD, Jones NB. Male strategies and Plio-Pleistocene archaeology. *Journal of Human Evolution*. 2002;**43**:831–872.
57. Wrangham RW. The cooking enigma. In Ungar PS, editor. *Evolution of the Human Diet: The Known, the Unknown, and the Unknowable*. Oxford: Oxford University Press. 2006; 308–323.
58. Strait DS, Constantino P, Lucas PW, Richmond BG, Spencer MA, Dechow PC, et al. Viewpoints: diet and dietary adaptations in early hominins: the hard food perspective. *American Journal of Physical Anthropology*. 2013;**151**:339–355.
59. Daegling DJ, Judex S, Ozcivici E, Ravosa MJ, Taylor AB, Grine FE, et al. Viewpoints: feeding mechanics, diet, and dietary adaptations in early hominins. *American Journal of Physical Anthropology*. 2013;**151**:356–371.

60. Mittermeier R, Louis Jr E, Richardson M, Schwitzer C, Langrand O, Rylands A, et al. *Lemurs of Madagascar*, 3rd ed., Tropical Field Guide Series. Conservation International, Arlington, VA. 2010.
61. Kay RF. The nut-crackers – a new theory of the adaptations of the Ramapithecinae. *American Journal of Physical Anthropology*. 1981;**55**:141–151.
62. Lambert JE, Chapman CA, Wrangham RW, Conklin-Brittain NL. Hardness of cercopithecine foods: implications for the critical function of enamel thickness in exploiting fallback foods. *American Journal of Physical Anthropology*. 2004;**125**:363–368.
63. Dumont ER. Enamel thickness and dietary adaptation among extant primates and chiropterans. *Journal of Mammalogy*. 1995, **76**:1127–1136.
64. Martin LB, Olejniczak AJ, Maas MC. Enamel thickness and microstructure in pitheciin primates, with comments on dietary adaptations of the middle Miocene hominoid Kenyapithecus. *Journal of Human Evolution*. 2003;**45**:351–367.
65. Liem KF. Adaptive significance of intra-and interspecific differences in the feeding repertoires of cichlid fishes. *American Zoologist*. 1980;**20**:295–314.
66. McGraw WS, Vick AE, Daegling DJ. Dietary variation and food hardness in sooty mangabeys (*Cercocebus atys*): implications for fallback foods and dental adaptation. *American Journal of Physical Anthropology*. 2014;**154**:413–423.
67. Pampush JD, Duque AC, Burrows BR, Daegling DJ, Kenney WF, McGraw WS. Homoplasy and thick enamel in primates. *Journal of Human Evolution*. 2013;**64**:216–224.
68. Lucas PW, Omar R, Al-Fadhalah K, Almusallam AS, Henry AG, Michael S, et al. Mechanisms and causes of wear in tooth enamel: implications for hominin diets. *Journal of the Royal Society Interface*. 2013;**10**:2012.0923.
69. Xia J, Zheng J, Huang D, Tian ZR, Chen L, Zhou Z, et al. New model to explain tooth wear with implications for microwear formation and diet reconstruction. *Proceedings of the National Academy of Sciences*. 2015;**112**:10669–10672.
70. Ungar PS. *Mammal Teeth: Origin, Evolution, and Diversity*: Baltimore: Johns Hopkins University Press; 2010.
71. Teaford MF. What do we know and not know about diet and enamel structure. In Ungar PS, editor. *Evolution of the Human Diet: The Known, the Unknown and the Unknowable*. 2007;56–76.
72. Bibi F, Souron A, Bocherens H, Uno K, Boisserie J-R. Ecological change in the lower Omo Valley around 2.8 Ma. *Biology Letters*. 2013;**9**:2012.0890.

73. Teaford M. Scanning electron microscope diagnosis of wear patterns versus artifacts on fossil teeth. *Scanning Microscroscopy.* 1988;2:1167–1175.
74. Hillson S. *Dental Anthropology.* Cambridge: Cambridge University Press; 1996.
75. Ungar PS, Brown CA, Bergstrom TS, Walker A. Quantification of dental microwear by tandem scanning confocal microscopy and scale-sensitive fractal analyses. *Scanning.* 2003;25:185–193.
76. Scott RS, Ungar PS, Bergstrom TS, Brown CA, Grine FE, Teaford MF, et al. Dental microwear texture analysis shows within-species diet variability in fossil hominins. *Nature.* 2005;436:693–695.
77. Scott RS, Teaford MF, Ungar PS. Dental microwear texture and anthropoid diets. *American Journal of Physical Anthropology.* 2012;147:551–579.
78. Teaford MF, Oyen OJ. In vivo and in vitro turnover in dental microwear. *American Journal of Physical Anthropology.* 1989;80:447–460.
79. Grine FE. Dental evidence for dietary differences in *Australopithecus* and *Paranthropus*: a quantitative analysis of permanent molar microwear. *Journal of Human Evolution.* 1986;15:783–822.
80. Daegling DJ, Grine FE. Terrestrial foraging and dental microwear in *Papio ursinus*. *Primates.* 1999;40:559–572.
81. Constantino PJ, Lee JJ-W, Chai H, Zipfel B, Ziscovici C, Lawn BR, et al. Tooth chipping can reveal the diet and bite forces of fossil hominins. *Biology Letters.* 2010;6:826–829.
82. Constantino PJ, Lee JJW, Gerbig Y, Hartstone-Rose A, Talebi M, Lawn BR, et al. The role of tooth enamel mechanical properties in primate dietary adaptation. *American Journal of Physical Anthropology.* 2012;148:171–177.
83. Sponheimer M, Alemseged Z, Cerling TE, Grine FE, Kimbel WH, Leakey MG, et al. Isotopic evidence of early hominin diets. *Proceedings of the National Academy of Sciences.* 2013;110:10513–10518.
84. Grine FE, Sponheimer M, Ungar PS, Lee-Thorp J, Teaford MF. Dental microwear and stable isotopes inform the paleoecology of extinct hominins. *American Journal of Physical Anthropology.* 2012;148:285–317.
85. Sponheimer M, Loudon J, Codron D, Howells M, Pruetz JD, Codron J, et al. Do "savanna" chimpanzees consume C_4 resources? *Journal of Human Evolution.* 2006;51:128–133.
86. Sponheimer M, Lee-Thorp J, de Ruiter D, Codron D, Codron J, Baugh AT, et al. Hominins, sedges, and termites: new carbon isotope data from the Sterkfontein valley and Kruger National Park. *Journal of Human Evolution.* 2005;48:301–312.

87. Cerling TE, Levin NE, Quade J, Wynn JG, Fox DL, Kingston JD, et al. Comment on the paleoenvironment of Ardipithecus ramidus. *Science.* 2010;**328**:1105.
88. Cerling TE, Manthi FK, Mbua EN, Leakey LN, Leakey MG, Leakey RE, et al. Stable isotope-based diet reconstructions of Turkana Basin hominins. *Proceedings of the National Academy of Sciences.* 2013;**110**:10501–10506.
89. Suwa G, Kono RT, Simpson SW, Asfaw B, Lovejoy CO, White TD. Paleobiological implications of the Ardipithecus ramidus dentition. *Science.* 2009;**326**:69–99.
90. Ungar PS, Scott RS, Grine FE, Teaford MF. Molar microwear textures and the diets of *Australopithecus anamensis* and *Australopithecus afarensis*. *Philosophical Transactions of the Royal Society B: Biological Sciences.* 2010;**365**:3345–3354.
91. Maas MC, Dumont ER. Built to last: the structure, function, and evolution of primate dental enamel. *Evolutionary Anthropology.* 1999;**8**:133–152.
92. Lee-Thorp J, Likius A, Mackaye HT, Vignaud P, Sponheimer M, Brunet M. Isotopic evidence for an early shift to C4 resources by Pliocene hominins in Chad. *Proceedings of the National Academy of Sciences.* 2012;**109**:20369–20372.
93. Dominy NJ. Hominins living on the sedge. *Proceedings of the National Academy of Sciences.* 2012;**109**:20171–20172.
94. Wynn JG, Sponheimer M, Kimbel WH, Alemseged Z, Reed K, Bedaso ZK, et al. Diet of *Australopithecus afarensis* from the Pliocene Hadar formation, Ethiopia. *Proceedings of the National Academy of Sciences.* 2013;**110**:10495–10500.
95. Cerling TE, Mbua E, Kirera FM, Manthi FK, Grine FE, Leakey MG, et al. Diet of Paranthropus boisei in the early Pleistocene of East Africa. *Proceedings of the National Academy of Sciences.* 2011;**108**:9337–9341.
96. McKee JK, Thackeray JF, Berger LR. Faunal assemblage seriation of southern African Pliocene and Pleistocene fossil deposits. *American Journal of Physical Anthropology.* 1995;**96**:235–250.
97. Reed KE. Early hominid evolution and ecological change through the African Plio-Pleistocene. *Journal of Human Evolution.* 1997;**32**:289–322.
98. McKee J.The autocatalytic nature of hominid evolution in African Plio-Pleistocene environments. In Bromage T and Schrenk F, editors. *African Biogeography, Climate Change, and Human Evolution.* New York: Oxford University Press. 1999; 57–75.

99. Lee-Thorp JA, Sponheimer M, Luyt J. Tracking changing environments using stable carbon isotopes in fossil tooth enamel: an example from the South African hominin sites. *Journal of Human Evolution.* 2007;**53**:595–601.
100. Bamford M. Pliocene fossil woods from an early hominid cave deposit, Sterkfontein, South Africa. *South African Journal of Science.* 1999;**95**:231–237.
101. Benefit B, McCrossin M. Diet, species diversity and distribution of African fossil baboons. *Kroeber Anthropological Society Papers.* 1990;**71**:79–93.
102. Lee-Thorp JA, Sponheimer M, Passey BH, de Ruiter DJ, Cerling TE. Stable isotopes in fossil hominin tooth enamel suggest a fundamental dietary shift in the Pliocene. *Philosophical Transactions of the Royal Society B: Biological Sciences.* 2010;**365**:3389–3396.
103. Sponheimer M, Passey BH, de Ruiter DJ, Guatelli-Steinberg D, Cerling TE, Lee-Thorp JA. Isotopic evidence for dietary variability in the early hominin Paranthropus robustus. *Science.* 2006;**314**:980–982.
104. Sillen A. Strontium-calcium ratios (Sr/Ca) of *Australopithecus robustus* and associated fauna from Swartkrans. *Journal of Human Evolution.* 1992;**23**:495–516.
105. Sponheimer M, de Ruiter D, Lee-Thorp J, Späth A. Sr/Ca and early hominin diets revisited: new data from modern and fossil tooth enamel. *Journal of Human Evolution.* 2005;**48**:147–156.
106. Balter V, Braga J, Télouk P, Thackeray JF. Evidence for dietary change but not landscape use in South African early hominins. *Nature.* 2012;**489**:558–560.
107. Lee-Thorp J. The demise of "Nutcracker Man." *Proceedings of the National Academy of Sciences.* 2011;**108**:9319–9320.
108. Ungar PS, Grine FE, Teaford MF. Dental microwear and diet of the Plio-Pleistocene hominin Paranthropus boisei. *PLoS One.* 2008;**3**:e2044.
109. Du Brul EL. Early hominid feeding mechanisms. *American Journal of Physical Anthropology.* 1977;**47**:305–320.
110. Cowlishaw G, Dunbar RI. *Primate Conservation Biology.* Chicago: University of Chicago Press; 2000.
111. Macho GA. Baboon feeding ecology informs the dietary niche of Paranthropus boisei. *PLoS One.* 2014;**9**:e84942.
112. Stewart KM. Environmental change and hominin exploitation of C4-based resources in wetland/savanna mosaics. *Journal of Human Evolution.* 2014;**77**:1–16.
113. Backwell LR, d'Errico F. Evidence of termite foraging by Swartkrans early hominids. *Proceedings of the National Academy of Sciences.* 2001;**98**:1358–1363.

114. Lesnik JJ. Termites in the hominin diet: A meta-analysis of termite genera, species and castes as a dietary supplement for South African robust australopithecines. *Journal of Human Evolution.* 2014;**71**:94–104.
115. Darwin C. *The Descent of Man and Selection in Relation to Sex.* London: John Murray; 1871.
116. Bateman AJ. Intra-sexual selection in Drosophila. *Heredity (Edinb).* 1948;**2**(Pt. 3):349–368.
117. Robert T. Parental investment and sexual selection. In Campbell B, editor. *Sexual Selection and the Descent of Man.* Chicago: Aldine. 1972;136–179.
118. Plavcan JM, van Schaik CP, Kappeler PM. Competition, coalitions and canine size in primates. *Journal of Human Evolution.* 1995;**28**:245–276.
119. Dixson AF. *Primate Sexuality: Comparative Studies of the Prosimians, Monkeys, Apes and Human Beings,* 2nd ed. Oxford: Oxford University Pres; 2012.
120. Lovejoy CO. The origin of man. *Science.* 1981;**21**:341–350.
121. Lovejoy CO. Reexamining human origins in light of Ardipithecus ramidus. *Science.* 2009;**326**:74–e8.
122. Lucas P, Corlett R, Luke D. Sexual dimorphism of tooth size in anthropoids. *Human Evolution.* 1986;**1**:23–39.
123. Lucas P. An analysis of canine size and jaw shape in some Old and New World non-human primates. *Journal of Zoology.* 1981;**195**:437–448.
124. Hylander WL. Functional links between canine height and jaw gape in catarrhines with special reference to early hominins. *American Journal of Physical Anthropology.* 2013;**150**:247–259.
125. Mayr E. Cause and effect in biology. *Science* 1961;**134**:1501–1506.
126. Plavcan JM. *Sexual Dimorphism in the Dentition of Extant Anthropoid Primates.* Ann Arbor: University Microfilms; 1990.
127. Plavcan JM. Inferring social behavior from sexual dimorphism in the fossil record. *Journal of Human Evolution.* 2000;**39**:327–344.
128. Plavcan JM. Sexual dimorphism in primate evolution. *American Journal of Physical Anthropology.* 2001;**116**(S33):25–53.
129. Kelley J. Phylogeny and sexually dimorphic characters: canine reduction in Ouranopithecus. In De Bonis L, Koufos GD, and Andrews, editors. *Hominoid Evolution and Climatic Change in Europe: Volume 2: Phylogeny of the Neogene Hominoid Primates of Eurasia.* Cambridge: Cambridge University Press. 2001; 269–283.
130. Clutton-Brock TH, Harvey PH, Rudder B. Sexual dimorphism, socionomic sex ratio and body weight in primates. *Nature.* 1977;**269**:797–800.

131. Harvey PH, Kavanagh M, Clutton-Brock T. Canine tooth size in female primates. *Nature*. 1978;**276**:817–818.
132. Leutenegger W, Cheverud J. Correlates of sexual dimorphism in primates: ecological and size variables. *International Journal of Primatology*. 1982;**3**:387–402.
133. Cheverud JM, Dow MM, Leutenegger W. The quantitative assessment of phylogenetic constraints in comparative analyses: sexual dimorphism in body weight among primates. *Evolution*. 1985;**39**:1335–1351.
134. Rensch B. The laws of evolution. In Tax S, editor. *Evolution after Darwin*, Vol. 1. Chicago: Chicago University Press. 1960; 95–116.
135. Gingerich PD, Smith BH. Allometric scaling in the dentition of primates and insectivores. In Jungers WL, editor. *Size and Scaling in Primate Biology*. New York: Plenum. 1984; 257–272.
136. Plavcan JM, van Schaik CP. Canine dimorphism. *Evolutionary Anthropology*. 1993;**2**:208–214.
137. Leutenegger W, Kelly JT. Relationship of sexual dimorphism in canine size and body size to social, behavioral, and ecological correlates in anthropoid primates. *Primates*. 1977;**18**:117–136.
138. Plavcan JM, van Schaik CP. Intrasexual competition and canine dimorphism in anthropoid primates. *American Journal of Physical Anthropology*. 1992;**87**:461–477.
139. Plavcan JM, Van Schaik CP. Interpreting hominid behavior on the basis of sexual dimorphism. *Journal of Human Evolution*. 1997;**32**:345–374.
140. Dobson SD. Letter to the editor: canine displays are not aggressive signals: a comment on Plavcan and Ruff (2008). *American Journal of Physical Anthropology*. 2010;**143**:325–326.
141. McGraw WS, Plavcan JM, Adachi-Kanazawa K. Adult female Cercopithecus diana employ canine teeth to kill another adult female C. diana. *International Journal of Primatology*. 2002;**23**:1301–1308.
142. Milton K. Multimale mating and absence of canine tooth dimorphism in woolly spider monkeys (Brachyteles arachnoides). *American Journal of Physical Anthropology*. 1985;**68**:519–523.
143. Strier KB. Causes and consequences of nonaggression in the woolly spider monkey, or muriqui (*Brachyteles arachnoides*). In Silverberg J and Gray J, editors. *Aggression and Peacefulness in Humans and other Primates*. New York: Oxford University Press. 1992; 100–115.
144. Kay RF, Plavcan JM, Glander KE, Wright PC. Sexual selection and canine dimorphism in New World monkeys. *American Journal of Physical Anthropology*. 1988;**77**:385–397.

145. Thorén S, Lindenfors P, Kappeler PM. Phylogenetic analyses of dimorphism in primates: evidence for stronger selection on canine size than on body size. *American Journal of Physical Anthropology*. 2006;**130**:50–59.
146. Plavcan JM. Understanding dimorphism as a function of changes in male and female traits. *Evolutionary Anthropology*. 2011;**20**:143–155.
147. Greenfield LO. Relative canine size, behavior and diet in male ceboids. *Journal of Human Evolution*. 1992;**23**:469–480.
148. Kinzey WG. Dietary and dental adaptations in the Pitheciinae. *American Journal of Physical Anthropology*. 1992;**88**:499–514.
149. Greenfield LO. Origin of the human canine: a new solution to an old enigma. *American Journal of Physical Anthropology*. 1992;**35**(S15):153–185.
150. Greenfield LO. Canine tip wear in male and female anthropoids. *American Journal of Physical Anthropology*. 1998;**107**:87–96.
151. Plavcan JM, Kelley J. Evaluating the "dual selection" hypothesis of canine reduction. *American Journal of Physical Anthropology*. 1996;**99**:379–388.
152. Alvesalo L, Varrela J. Permanent tooth sizes in 46, XY females. *American Journal of Human Genetics*. 1980;**32**:736.
153. Alvesalo L, Tammisalo E, Hakola P. Enamel thickness in 47, XYY males' permanent teeth. *Annals of Human Biology*. 1985;**12**:421–427.
154. Zingeser M, Phoenix C. Metric characteristics of the canine dental complex in prenatally androgenized female rhesus monkeys (Macaca mulatta). *American Journal of Physical Anthropology*. 1978;**49**(2):187–192.
155. Ribeiro D, Brook A, Hughes T, Sampson W, Townsend G. Intrauterine hormone effects on tooth dimensions. *Journal of Dental Research*. 2013:0022034513484934.
156. Heikkinen T, Harila V, Tapanainen JS, Alvesalo L. Masculinization of the eruption pattern of permanent mandibular canines in opposite sex twin girls. *American Journal of Physical Anthropology*. 2013;**151**:566–572.
157. Schwartz GT, Dean C. Ontogeny of canine dimorphism in extant hominoids. *American Journal of Physical Anthropology*. 2001;**115**:269–283.
158. Guatelli-Steinberg D, Ferrell RJ, Hubbard A, Schmidt S, Talabere T. Sexual dimorphism in lateral enamel formation in Cercocebus and Papio: time vs. rate. *American Journal of Physical Anthropology*. 2009;**140**: 216–233.
159. Schwartz GT, Miller ER, Gunnell GF. Developmental processes and canine dimorphism in primate evolution. *Journal of Human Evolution*. 2005;**48**:97–103.
160. Kelley J. Sex determination in Miocene catarrhine primates. *American Journal of Physical Anthropology*. 1995;**96**:391–417.

161. Kelley J, Plavcan JM. A simulation test of hominoid species number at Lufeng, China: implications for the use of the coefficient of variation in paleotaxonomy. *Journal of Human Evolution*. 1998;**35**:577–596.
162. Fleagle JG. *Primate Adaptation and Evolution*, 3rd ed. San Diego: Academic Press; 2013.
163. de Bonis L, Koufos GD. The face and the mandible of Ouranopithecus macedoniensis: description of new specimens and comparisons. *Journal of Human Evolution*. 1993;**24**:469–491.
164. Begun DR, Nargolwalla MC, Kordos L. European Miocene hominids and the origin of the African ape and human clade. *Evolutionary Anthropology*. 2012;**21**:10–23.
165. Daegling DJ, McGraw WS, Ungar PS, Pampush JD, Vick AE, Bitty EA. Hard-object feeding in sooty mangabeys (Cercocebus atys) and interpretation of early hominin feeding ecology. *PLoS One*. 2011;**6**:e23095.
166. Ward CV, Plavcan JM, Manthi FK. Anterior dental evolution in the *Australopithecus anamensis–afarensis* lineage. *Philosophical Transactions of the Royal Society B: Biological Sciences*. 2010;**365**:3333–3344.
167. Manthi FK, Plavcan JM, Ward CV. New hominin fossils from Kanapoi, Kenya, and the mosaic evolution of canine teeth in early hominins. *South African Journal of Science*. 2012;**108**:1–9.
168. Plavcan JM. Sexual size dimorphism, canine dimorphism, and male-male competition in primates. *Human Nature*. 2012;**23**:45–67.
169. Jolly CJ. The seed-eaters: a new model of hominid differentiation based on a baboon analogy. *Man*. 1970:5–26.
170. Jungers WL. On canine reduction in early hominids. *Current Anthropology*. 1978;**19**:155–156.
171. Gantt DG. Patterns of dental wear and the role of the canine in Cercopithecinae. *American Journal of Physical Anthropology*. 1979;**51**:353–359.
172. Kay RF. *Mastication, Molar Tooth Structure and Diet in Primates*. Ph.D. Dissertation, Yale University, 1973.
173. Delezene LK. Modularity of the anthropoid dentition: implications for the evolution of the hominin canine honing complex. *Journal of Human Evolution*. 2015;**86**:1–12.
174. Reno PL, Meindl RS, McCollum MA, Lovejoy CO. The case is unchanged and remains robust: *Australopithecus afarensis* exhibits only moderate skeletal dimorphism: a reply to Plavcan et al. (2005). *Journal of Human Evolution*. 2005;**49**:279–288.
175. Plavcan JM, Lockwood CA, Kimbel WH, Lague MR, Harmon EH. Sexual dimorphism in *Australopithecus afarensis* revisited: how strong is the case

for a human-like pattern of dimorphism? *Journal of Human Evolution.* 2005;**48**:313–320.

176. McLean CY, Reno PL, Pollen AA, Bassan AI, Capellini TD, Guenther C, et al. Human-specific loss of regulatory DNA and the evolution of human-specific traits. *Nature.* 2011;**471**:216–219.

177. Antón SC, Potts R, Aiello LC. Evolution of early *Homo*: an integrated biological perspective. *Science.* 2014;**345**:1236828.

178. Weston EM, Friday AE, Johnstone RA, Schrenk F. Wide faces or large canines? The attractive versus the aggressive primate. *Proceedings of the Royal Society of London B: Biological Sciences.* 2004;**271**(**Suppl 6**):S416–S419.

179. Dobzhansky TG. *Mankind Evolving: The Evolution of the Human Species.* New Haven and London: Yale University Press;1962.

180. Bogin BA. Evolutionary hypotheses for human childhood. *American Journal of Physical Anthropology.* 1997; **104**(**S25**): 63–89.

181. Leigh SR. Evolution of human growth. *Evolutionary Anthropology.* 2001;**10**:223–236.

182. Charnov EL, Berrigan D. Why do female primates have such long lifespans and so few babies? Or life in the slow lane. *Evolutionary Anthropology.* 1993;**1**:191–194.

183. Janson CH, van Schaik CP. Ecological risk aversion in juvenile primates: slow and steady wins the race. In Pereira ME and Fairbanks L, editors. *Juvenile Primates: Life history, Development, and Behavior.* New York: Oxford University Press.1993; 57–74.

184. Leigh SR. Ontogenetic correlates of diet in anthropoid primates. *American Journal of Physical Anthropology.* 1994;**94**:499–522.

185. Kuzawa CW, Chugani HT, Grossman LI, Lipovich L, Muzik O, Hof PR, et al. Metabolic costs and evolutionary implications of human brain development. *Proceedings of the National Academy of Sciences.* 2014;**111**:13010–13015.

186. Leigh SR, Blomquist GE. Life history. In Bearder SK, Campbell C, and MaKinnon K, Panger M, Bearder SK, and Panger M, editors. *Primates in Perspective.* New York: Oxford University Press. 2007; 396–407.

187. Deaner RO, Barton RA, van Schaik CP. Primate brains and life histories: renewing the connection. In Kappeler PM and Pereira MA, editors. *Primate Life Histories and Socioecology.* Chicago: University of Chicago Press. 2003;233–265.

188. Sacher GA, Staffeldt EF. Relation of gestation time to brain weight for placental mammals: implications for the theory of vertebrate growth. *American Naturalist.* 1974;**108**:593–615.

REFERENCES 259

189. Harvey PH, Clutton-Brock TH. Life history variation in primates. *Evolution.* 1985;**39**:559–581.
190. Smith BH. Dental development as a measure of life history in primates. *Evolution.* 1989;**43**:683–688.
191. Smith BH. Life history and the evolution of human maturation. *Evolutionary Anthropology.* 1992;**1**:134–142.
192. Dean MC, Lucas VS. Dental and skeletal growth in early fossil hominins. *Annals of Human Biology.* 2009;**36**:545–561.
193. Dart RA. The infancy of *Australopithecus*. In *The* Robert Broom Commemorative Volume Special Publication of The Royal Society of South Africa, Cape Town; 142–153. 1948.
194. Bower B. Hominid headway. *Science News.* 1987:408–409.
195. Smith BH. Dental development in *Australopithecus and early Homo. Nature.* 1986;**323**:327–330.
196. Smith TM, Tafforeau P, Le Cabec A, Bonnin A, Houssaye A, Pouech J, et al. Dental ontogeny in pliocene and early pleistocene hominins. *PLoS One.* 2015;**10**:e0118118.
197. Schultz AH. Eruption and decay of the permanent teeth in primates. *American Journal of Physical Anthropology.* 1935;**19**:489–581.
198. Anemone RL, Mooney MP, Siegel MI. Longitudinal study of dental development in chimpanzees of known chronological age: implications for understanding the age at death of Plio-Pleistocene hominids. *American Journal of Physical Anthropology.* 1996;**99**:119–133.
199. Schultz AH. *Age Changes in Primates and their Modification in Man.* Oxford: Pergamon Press; 1960.
200. Smith BH. Dental development and the evolution of life history in Hominidae. *American Journal of Physical Anthropology.* 1991;**86**:157–174.
201. Harvey PH, Read AF, Promislow DE. Life history variation in placental mammals: unifying the data with theory. In Harvey PH and Partridge L, editors. *Oxford Surveys in Evolutionary Biology.* 1989;**6**:15–31.
202. Robson SL, Wood B. Hominin life history: reconstruction and evolution. *Journal of Anatomy.* 2008;**212**:394–425.
203. Kelley J, Schwartz GT. Life-history inference in the early hominins *Australopithecus* and *Paranthropus*. *International Journal of Primatology.* 2012;**33**:1332–1363.
204. Smith TM, Machanda Z, Bernard AB, Donovan RM, Papakyrikos AM, Muller MN, et al. First molar eruption, weaning, and life history in living wild chimpanzees. *Proceedings of the National Academy of Sciences.* 2013;**110**:2787–2791.

205. Humphrey LT. Weaning behaviour in human evolution. *Seminars in Cell and Developmental Biology;* 2010: **21**: 453–461.
206. Macho GA. Primate molar crown formation times and life history evolution revisited. *American Journal of Primatology.* 2001;**55**:189–201.
207. Kelley J, Schwartz GT. Dental development and life history in living African and Asian apes. *Proceedings of the National Academy of Sciences.* 2010;**107**:1035–1040.
208. Dean MC. Tooth microstructure tracks the pace of human life-history evolution. *Proceedings of the Royal Society of London B: Biological Sciences.* 2006;**273**:2799–2808.
209. Hogg RT, Walker RS. Life-History Correlates of Enamel Microstructure in Cebidae (Platyrrhini, Primates). *The Anatomical Record.* 2011;**294**:2193–2206.
210. von Asper H. Uber die "Braune Retzinusgsche Parallelstreifung" im schmelz der menschlichen Zahne. *Schweiz V Schr Zahnheilk.* 1916;**26**:275–314.
211. Gysi A. Metabolism in adult enamel. *Dental Digest.* 1931;**37**:661–668.
212. Mimura F. The periodicity of growth lines seen in enamel. *Kobyo-shi.* 1939;**13**:454–455.
213. Bromage TG. Enamel incremental periodicity in the pig-tailed macaque: a polychrome fluorescent labeling study of dental hard tissues. *American Journal of Physical Anthropology.* 1991;**86**:205–214.
214. Lacruz RS, Hacia JG, Bromage TG, Boyde A, Lei Y, Xu Y, et al. The circadian clock modulates enamel development. *Journal of Biological Rhythms.* 2012;**27**:237–245.
215. Dean MC. Growth layers and incremental markings in hard tissues; a review of the literature and some preliminary observations about enamel structure in Paranthropus boisei. *Journal of Human Evolution.* 1987;**16**:157–172.
216. FitzGerald CM. Do enamel microstructures have regular time dependency? Conclusions from the literature and a large-scale study. *Journal of Human Evolution.* 1998;**35**:371–386.
217. Reid DJ, Dean MC. Variation in modern human enamel formation times. *Journal of Human Evolution.* 2006;**50**:329–346.
218. Halberg F. Biological rhythms. In Hedlund LW, Franz JM, and Kenny AD, editors. *Biological Rhythms and Endocrine Function.* New York: Plenum Press. 1975; 1–41.
219. Appenzeller O, Gunga H-C, Qualls C, Furlan R, Porta A, Lucas S, et al. A hypothesis: autonomic rhythms are reflected in growth lines of teeth in humans and extinct archosaurs. *Autonomic Neuroscience.* 2005;**117**:115–159.
220. Bromage T, Lacruz R, Hogg R, Goldman H, McFarlin S, Warshaw J, et al. Lamellar bone is an incremental tissue reconciling enamel rhythms, body

size, and organismal life history. *Calcified Tissue International.* 2009;**84**:388–404.
221. Bromage TG, Hogg RT, Lacruz RS, Hou C. Primate enamel evinces long period biological timing and regulation of life history. *Journal of Theoretical Biology.* 2012;**305**:131–144.
222. Mann AE. *Some Paleodemographic Aspects of the South African Australopithecines.* Dept. of Anthropology, University of Pennsylvania; 1975.
223. Bromage TG, Dean MC. Re-evaluation of the age at death of immature fossil hominids. *Nature.* 1985;**317**:525–527.
224. Beynon A, Wood B. Patterns and rates of enamel growth in the molar teeth of early hominids. *Nature.* 1987;**326**:493–496.
225. Beynon AD, Dean MC. Distinct dental development patterns in early fossil hominids. *Nature.* 1988;**335**:509–514.
226. Dean C, Leakey MG, Reid D, Schrenk F, Schwartz GT, Stringer C, et al. Growth processes in teeth distinguish modern humans from *Homo erectus* and earlier hominins. *Nature.* 2001;**414**:628–631.
227. Lacruz RS, Rozzi FR, Bromage TG. Variation in enamel development of South African fossil hominids. *Journal of Human Evolution.* 2006;**51**:580–590.
228. Broom R, Robinson J. Eruption of the permanent teeth in the South African fossil ape-men. *Nature.* 1951;**167**:443.
229. Dean M. The eruption pattern of the permanent incisors and first permanent molars in *Australopithecus (Paranthropus) robustus*. *American Journal of Physical Anthropology.* 1985;**67**:251–257.
230. Conroy GC. Alleged synapomorphy of the M1/I1 eruption pattern in robust australopithecines and *Homo*: evidence from high-resolution computed tomography. *American Journal of Physical Anthropology.* 1988;**75**:487–492.
231. Conroy GC, Vannier MW. Dental development in South African australopithecines. Part II: Dental stage assessment. *American Journal of Physical Anthropology.* 1991;**86**:137–156.
232. Conroy GC, Vannier MW. Dental development of the Taung skull from computerized tomography. *Nature.* 1987;**329**:625–627.
233. Mann A, Lampl M, Monge J. Patterns of ontogeny in human evolution: evidence from dental development. *American Journal of Physical Anthropology.* 1990;**33** (**S11**):111–150.
234. Beynon A, Dean M. Hominid dental development. *Nature.* 1991;**351**:196.
235. Macho GA, Wood BA. The role of time and timing in hominid dental evolution. *Evolutionary Anthropology.* 1995;**4**:17–31.
236. Dean M, Reid D. Perikymata spacing and distribution on hominid anterior teeth. *American Journal of Physical Anthropology.* 2001;**116**:209–215.

237. Phillips-Conroy JE, Jolly CJ. Dental eruption schedules of wild and captive baboons. *American Journal of Primatology*. 1988;**15**:17–29.

238. Thompson JL, Krovitz GE, Nelson AJ. Patterns of Growth and Development in the genus *Homo*: Cambridge: Cambridge University Press; 2003.

239. Godfrey LR, Samonds KE, Jungers WL, Sutherland MR. Dental development and primate life histories. In Kappeler PM and Pereira ME, editors. *Primate Life histories and Socioecology*. Chicago: University of Chicago Press. 2003;177–203.

240. Montagu A. The "Cerebral Rubicon": brain size and the achievement of hominid status. *American Anthropologist*. 1961;**63**:377–378.

241. Collard M, Wood B. Defining the Genus *Homo*. In Henke W, Rothe H, and Tattersall I, editors. *Handbook of Paleoanthropology*. Berlin Heidelberg: Springer. 2007; 1575–1610.

242. Kimbel WH, Walter RC, Johanson DC, Reed KE, Aronson JL, Assefa Z, et al. Late Pliocene *Homo* and Oldowan tools from the Hadar Formation (Kada Hadar Member), Ethiopia. *Journal of Human Evolution*. 1996;**31**:549–561.

243. Kimbel WH, Johanson DC, Rak Y. Systematic assessment of a maxilla of *Homo* from Hadar, Ethiopia. *American Journal of Physical Anthropology*. 1997;**103**:235–262.

244. Villmoare B, Kimbel WH, Seyoum C, Campisano CJ, DiMaggio EN, Rowan J, et al. Early *Homo* at 2.8 Ma from Ledi-Geraru, Afar, Ethiopia. *Science*. 2015;**347**:1352–1355.

245. Johanson DC, Masao FT, Eck GG, White TD, Walter RC, Kimbel WH, et al. New partial skeleton of *Homo habilis* from Olduvai Gorge, Tanzania. *Nature*. 1987;**327**:205–209.

246. Schrenk F, Bromage TG, Betzler CG, Ring U, Juwayeyi YM. Oldest *Homo* and Pliocene biogeography of the Malawi rift. *Nature*. 1993;**365**:833–836.

247. Wood B. *Koobi Fora Research Project*, Vol. 4. Oxford: Clarendon; 1991.

248. Blumenschine RJ, Peters CR, Masao FT, Clarke RJ, Deino AL, Hay RL, et al. Late Pliocene *Homo* and hominid land use from western Olduvai Gorge, Tanzania. *Science*. 2003;**299**:1217–1221.

249. Leakey MG, Spoor F, Dean MC, Feibel CS, Anton SC, Kiarie C, et al. New fossils from Koobi Fora in northern Kenya confirm taxonomic diversity in early *Homo*. *Nature*. 2012;**488**:201–204.

250. Beurton PJ. Ernst Mayr through time on the biological species concept–a conceptual analysis. *Theory in Biosciences*. 2002;**121**:81–98.

251. Wood B, Collard M. The changing face of genus *Homo*. *Evolutionary Anthropology*. 1999;**8**:195–207.

252. Tobias PV. The species *Homo habilis*: example of a premature discovery. *Annales Zoologici Fennici*. 1991;**28**:371–380.
253. Antón SC. Natural history of *Homo erectus*. *American Journal of Physical Anthropology*. 2003;**122**(S37):126–170.
254. Brain CK, Sillent A. Evidence from the Swartkrans cave for the earliest use of fire. *Nature*. 1988;**336**:464–466.
255. Alperson-Afil N, Goren-Inbar N. Out of Africa and into Eurasia with controlled use of fire: evidence from Gesher Benot Ya'aqov, Israel. *Archaeology, Ethnology and Anthropology of Eurasia*. 2006;**28**:63–78.
256. Berna F, Goldberg P, Horwitz LK, Brink J, Holt S, Bamford M, et al. Microstratigraphic evidence of in situ fire in the Acheulean strata of Wonderwerk Cave, Northern Cape province, South Africa. *Proceedings of the National Academy of Sciences*. 2012;**109**:E1215–E1220.
257. Mayr E, editor, Taxonomic categories in fossil hominids. *Cold Spring Harbor Symposia on Quantitatve Biology*. 1950;**15**:109–118.
258. Black D. On a lower molar hominid tooth from the Chou Kou Tien deposit. *Geological Survey of China*; 1927.
259. Black D. The brain cast of Sinanthropus–a review. *Journal of Comparative Neurology*. 1933;**57**:361–368.
260. Carter K, Worthington S. Morphologic and demographic predictors of third molar agenesis a systematic review and meta-analysis. *Journal of Dent Research*. 2015:0022034515581644.
261. Woo J-K. Mandible of the Sinanthropus–type discovered at Lantien, Shensi–Sinanthropus lantianensis. *Vertebrata PalAsiatica*. 1964;**1**:1–17.
262. Frayer DW, Wolpoff MH, Thorne AG, Smith FH, Pope GG. Theories of modern human origins: the paleontological test. *American Anthropologist*. 1993;**95**:14–50.
263. Crummett TL. *The Evolution of Shovel Shaping: Regional and Temporal Variations in Human Incisor Morphology*. University of Michigan; 1994.
264. Crummett T. The three dimensions of shovel-shaping. *Aspects of Dental Biology: Palaeontology, Anthropology and Evolution International Institute for the Study of Man, Florence*. 1995:305–313.
265. Blumberg JE, Hylander WL, Goepp RA. Taurodontism: a biometric study. *American Journal of Physical Anthropology*. 1971;**34**:243–255.
266. Swisher C, Rink W, Antón SC, Schwarcz HP, Curtis GH, Widiasmoro AS. Latest *Homo erectus* of Java: potential contemporaneity with *Homo sapiens* in southeast Asia. *Science*. 1996;**274**:1870–1874.

267. Asfaw B, Gilbert WH, Beyene Y, Hart WK, Renne PR, WoldeGabriel G, et al. Remains of *Homo erectus* from Bouri, Middle Awash, Ethiopia. *Nature.* 2002;**416**:317–320.
268. Lordkipanidze D, de León MSP, Margvelashvili A, Rak Y, Rightmire GP, Vekua A, et al. A complete skull from Dmanisi, Georgia, and the evolutionary biology of early *Homo. Science.* 2013;**342**:326–331.
269. Rightmire GP, Lordkipanidze D, Vekua A. Anatomical descriptions, comparative studies and evolutionary significance of the hominin skulls from Dmanisi, Republic of Georgia. *Journal of Human Evolution.* 2006;**50**:115–141.
270. De Castro JB, Arsuaga JL, Carbonell E, Rosas A, Martınez I, Mosquera M. A hominid from the Lower Pleistocene of Atapuerca, Spain: possible ancestor to Neandertals and modern humans. *Science.* 1997;**276**(5317):1392–1395.
271. Carbonell E, de Castro JMB, Parés JM, Pérez-González A, Cuenca-Bescós G, Ollé A, et al. The first hominin of Europe. *Nature.* 2008;**452**:465–469.
272. Bermúdez de Castro J, Martinon-Torres M, Carbonell E, Sarmiento S, Rosas A, Van der Made J, et al. The Atapuerca sites and their contribution to the knowledge of human evolution in Europe. *Evolutionary Anthropology.* 2004;**13**:25–41.
273. de Castro JMB, Rosas A, Nicolás E. Dental remains from Atapuerca-TD6 (Gran Dolina site, Burgos, Spain). *Journal of Human Evolution.* 1999;**37**:523–566.
274. Stringer C. The status of *Homo heidelbergensis* (Schoetensack 1908). *Evolutionary Anthropology.* 2012;**21**:101–107.
275. de Castro JB. Dental remains from Atapuerca/Ibeas (Spain) II. Morphology. *Journal of Human Evolution.* 1988;**17**:279–304.
276. Rightmire GP. Human evolution in the Middle Pleistocene: the role of *Homo heidelbergensis. Evolutionary Anthropology.* 1998;**6**:218–227.
277. Wolpoff MH. Cranial remains of middle Pleistocene European hominids. *Journal of Human Evolution.* 1980;**9**:339–358.
278. Arsuaga J, Martínez I, Arnold L, Aranburu A, Gracia-Téllez A, Sharp W, et al. Neandertal roots: cranial and chronological evidence from Sima de los Huesos. *Science.* 2014;**344**:1358–1363.
279. Green RE, Krause J, Briggs AW, Maricic T, Stenzel U, Kircher M, et al. A draft sequence of the Neandertal genome. *Science.* 2010;**328**:710–722.
280. Endicott P, Ho SY, Stringer C. Using genetic evidence to evaluate four palaeoanthropological hypotheses for the timing of Neanderthal and modern human origins. *Journal of Human Evolution.* 2010;**59**:87–95.
281. Tattersall I. *The Last Neanderthal: The Rise, Success, and Mysterious Extinction of Our Closest Human Relatives.* Boulder, CO: Westview Press; 1999.

282. Wolpoff MH, Caspari R. *Race and Human Evolution*. New York: Simon and Schuster; 1997.
283. Wolpoff MH. The Krapina dental remains. *American Journal of Physical Anthropology*. 1979;**50**:67–113.
284. Bailey SE. Dental morphological affinities among late Pleistocene and recent humans. *Dental Anthropology*. 2000;**14**:1–8.
285. Bailey SE. A closer look at Neanderthal postcanine dental morphology: the mandibular dentition. *The Anatomical Record*. 2002;**269**:148–156.
286. Brace CL, Hinton RJ, Brown T, Green R, Harris EF, Jacobson A, et al. Oceanic tooth-size variation as a reflection of biological and cultural mixing [and comments and reply]. *Current Anthropology*. 1981;**22**:549–569.
287. Demes B. Another look at an old face: biomechanics of the Neanderthal facial skeleton reconsidered. *Journal of Human Evolution*. 1987;**16**:297–303.
288. Clement AF, Hillson SW, Aiello LC. Tooth wear, Neanderthal facial morphology and the anterior dental loading hypothesis. *Journal of Human Evolution*. 2012;**62**:367–376.
289. Antón S. Mechanical and other perspectives on Neandertal craniofacial morphology. In: *Integrative Paths to the Past: Palaeoanthropological Advances in Honor of F Clark Howell*. Englewood Cliffs, NJ: Prentice Hall. 1994:677–695.
290. O'Connor CF, Franciscus RG, Holton NE. Bite force production capability and efficiency in Neanderthals and modern humans. *American Journal of Physical Anthropology*. 2005;**127**:129–151.
291. Bailey SE. A morphometric analysis of maxillary molar crowns of Middle-Late Pleistocene hominins. *Journal of Human Evolution*. 2004;**47**:183–198.
292. Gorjanovic-Kramberger K. *Die Kronen und Wurzeln der Mahlzähne des Homo primigenius und ihre genetische Bedeutung*. 1907.
293. Xing S, Martinón-Torres M, Bermúdez de Castro JM, Wu X, Liu W. Hominin teeth from the early Late Pleistocene site of Xujiayao, Northern China. *American Journal of Physical Anthropology*. 2015;**156**:224–240.
294. Callaway E. Neanderthals made some of Europe's oldest art. *Nature*. 2014;**29**:2.
295. Hublin J-J, Spoor F, Braun M, Zonneveld F, Condemi S. A late Neanderthal associated with Upper Palaeolithic artefacts. *Nature*. 1996;**381**:224–226.
296. Benazzi S, Douka K, Fornai C, Bauer CC, Kullmer O, Svoboda J, et al. Early dispersal of modern humans in Europe and implications for Neanderthal behaviour. *Nature*. 2011;**479**:525–528.
297. Zilhão J. Neandertals and moderns mixed, and it matters. *Evolutionary Anthropology*. 2006;**15**(5):183–195.

298. McDougall I, Brown FH, Fleagle JG. Stratigraphic placement and age of modern humans from Kibish, Ethiopia. *Nature.* 2005;**433**:733–736.
299. Bailey SE, Hublin JJ. What does it mean to be dentally "modern"? In Scott JR and Irish JD, editors. *Anthropological Perspectives on Tooth Morphology: Genetics, Evolution, Variation.* Cambridge: Cambridge University Press. 2013; 222–248.
300. Reich D, Green RE, Kircher M, Krause J, Patterson N, Durand EY, et al. Genetic history of an archaic hominin group from Denisova Cave in Siberia. *Nature.* 2010;**468**:1053–1060.
301. Brown P, Sutikna T, Morwood MJ, Soejono RP, Saptomo EW, Due RA. A new small-bodied hominin from the Late Pleistocene of Flores, Indonesia. *Nature.* 2004;**431**:1055–1061.
302. Roberts RG, Westaway KE, Zhao J-x, Turney CS, Bird MI, Rink WJ, et al. Geochronology of cave deposits at Liang Bua and of adjacent river terraces in the Wae Racang valley, western Flores, Indonesia: a synthesis of age estimates for the type locality of *Homo floresiensis. Journal of Human Evolution.* 2009;**57**:484–502.
303. Hershkovitz I, Kornreich L, Laron Z. Comparative skeletal features between *Homo floresiensis* and patients with primary growth hormone insensitivity (Laron Syndrome). *American Journal of Physical Anthropology.* 2007;**134**:198–208.
304. Aiello LC. Five years of *Homo floresiensis. American Journal of Physical Anthropology.* 2010;**142**:167–179.
305. Brown P, Maeda T. Liang Bua *Homo floresiensis* mandibles and mandibular teeth: a contribution to the comparative morphology of a new hominin species. *Journal of Human Evolution.* 2009;**57**:571–596.
306. Argue D, Morwood M, Sutikna T, Saptomo E. *Homo floresiensis*: a cladistic analysis. *Journal of Human Evolution.* 2009;**57**:623–639.
307. Morwood MJ, Jungers WL. Conclusions: implications of the Liang Bua excavations for hominin evolution and biogeography. *Journal of Human Evolution.* 2009;**57**:640–648.
308. Baab KL, McNulty KP, Harvati K. *Homo floresiensis* contextualized: a geometric morphometric comparative analysis of fossil and pathological human samples. *PLoS One.* 2013;**8**:e69119.
309. Wolpoff MH, Wu X, Thorne AG. Modern *Homo sapiens* origins: a general theory of hominid evolution involving the fossil evidence from East Asia. In Smith FH and Spencer F, editors. *The Origins of Modern Humans: A World Survey of the Fossil Evidence.* New York: Alan R. Liss. 1984; 411–483.
310. Wolpoff MH. *Paleoanthropology.* Boston: McGraw-Hill; 1999.

311. Wolpoff MH, Hawks J, Caspari R. Multiregional, not multiple origins. *American Journal of Physical Anthropology.* 2000;**112**:129–136.
312. Cann RL, Stoneking M, Wilson A. Mitochondrial DNA and human evolution. *Nature.* 1987;**325**:31–36.
313. Cann HM, De Toma C, Cazes L, Legrand M-F, Morel V, Piouffre L, et al. A human genome diversity cell line panel. *Science.* 2002;**296**:261.
314. Vigilant L, Stoneking M, Harpending H, Hawkes K, Wilson AC. Africa populations and the evolution of human mitochondrial DNA. *Science.* 1991;**253**:1503–1507.
315. Liu H, Prugnolle F, Manica A, Balloux F. A geographically explicit genetic model of worldwide human-settlement history. *The American Journal of Human Genetics.* 2006;**79**:230–237.
316. Weaver TD, Roseman CC, Stringer CB. Close correspondence between quantitative- and molecular-genetic divergence times for Neandertals and modern humans. *Proceedings of the National Academy of Sciences.* 2008;**105**:4645–4649.
317. Reyes-Centeno H, Ghirotto S, Détroit F, Grimaud-Hervé D, Barbujani G, Harvati K. Genomic and cranial phenotype data support multiple modern human dispersals from Africa and a southern route into Asia. *Proceedings of the National Academy of Sciences.* 2014;**111**:7248–7253.
318. Relethford J. Genetic evidence and the modern human origins debate. *Heredity.* 2008;**100**:555–563.
319. Ramachandran S, Deshpande O, Roseman CC, Rosenberg NA, Feldman MW, Cavalli-Sforza LL. Support from the relationship of genetic and geographic distance in human populations for a serial founder effect originating in Africa. *Proceedings of the National Academy of Sciences.* 2005;**102**:15942–15947.
320. Templeton A. Out of Africa again and again. *Nature.* 2002;**416**:45–51.
321. Eriksson A, Manica A. Effect of ancient population structure on the degree of polymorphism shared between modern human populations and ancient hominins. *Proceedings of the National Academy of Sciences.* 2012;**109**:13956–13960.
322. Prüfer K, Racimo F, Patterson N, Jay F, Sankararaman S, Sawyer S, et al. The complete genome sequence of a Neanderthal from the Altai Mountains. *Nature.* 2014;**505**:43–49.
323. Meyer M, Fu Q, Aximu-Petri A, Glocke I, Nickel B, Arsuaga J-L, et al. A mitochondrial genome sequence of a hominin from Sima de los Huesos. *Nature.* 2014;**505**:403–406.

324. Organ C, Nunn CL, Machanda Z, Wrangham RW. Phylogenetic rate shifts in feeding time during the evolution of *Homo*. *Proceedings of the National Academy of Sciences*. 2011;**108**:14555–14559.
325. Ungar PS. Dental evidence for the reconstruction of diet in African early *Homo*. *Current Anthropology*. 2012;**53**(S6):S318–S329.
326. Brace CL, Rosenberg KR, Hunt KD. Gradual change in human tooth size in the late Pleistocene and post-Pleistocene. *Evolution*. 1987;**41**:705–720.
327. Pobiner B. Evidence for meat-eating by early humans. *Nature Education Knowledge*. 2013;**4**(6):1.
328. Domínguez-Rodrigo M, Pickering TR, Semaw S, Rogers MJ. Cutmarked bones from Pliocene archaeological sites at Gona, Afar, Ethiopia: implications for the function of the world's oldest stone tools. *Journal of Human Evolution*. 2005;**48**:109–121.
329. Potts R, Shipman P. Cutmarks made by stone tools on bones from Olduvai Gorge, Tanzania. *Nature*. 1981;**291**:577–580.
330. Shipman P, Fisher DC, Rose JJ. Mastodon butchery: microscopic evidence of carcass processing and bone tool use. *Paleobiology*. 1984;**10**:358–365.
331. Shipman P. Studies of hominid–Faunal interactions at Olduvai Borge. *Journal of Human Evolution*. 1986;**15**:691–706.
332. Ferraro JV, Plummer TW, Pobiner BL, Oliver JS, Bishop LC, Braun DR, et al. Earliest archaeological evidence of persistent hominin carnivory. *PLoS One*. 2013; e62174.
333. Joordens JC, d'Errico F, Wesselingh FP, Munro S, De Vos J, Wallinga J, et al. *Homo erectus* at Trinil on Java used shells for tool production and engraving. *Nature*. 2015;**518**:228–231.
334. Skinner MM, Alemseged Z, Gaunitz C, Hublin J-J. Enamel thickness trends in Plio-Pleistocene hominin mandibular molars. *Journal of Human Evolution*. 2015; **85**: 35–45.
335. Pickering TR, Domínguez-Rodrigo M, Heaton JL, Yravedra J, Barba R, Bunn HT, et al. Taphonomy of ungulate ribs and the consumption of meat and bone by 1.2-million-year-old hominins at Olduvai Gorge, Tanzania. *Journal of Archaeological Science*. 2013;**40**:1295–1309.
336. Tobias PV. *Olduvai Gorge volume 4: The Skulls, Endocasts and Teeth of Homo Habilis*. Cambridge: Cambridge University Press; 1991.
337. Ungar P. Dental topography and diets of *Australopithecus afarensis* and early *Homo*. *Journal of Human Evolution*. 2004;**46**:605–622.
338. Ungar PS, Sponheimer M. The diets of early hominins. *Science*. 2011;**334**:190–193.

339. Ungar PS, Grine FE, Teaford MF. Diet in early *Homo*: a review of the evidence and a new model of adaptive versatility. *Annual Review of Anthropology*. 2006;**35**:209–228.
340. Potts R. Environmental and behavioral evidence pertaining to the evolution of early *Homo*. *Current Anthropology*. 2012;**53**(S6):S299–S317.
341. Spoor F, Gunz P, Neubauer S, Stelzer S, Scott N, Kwekason A, et al. Reconstructed *Homo habilis* type OH 7 suggests deep-rooted species diversity in early Homo. *Nature*. 2015;**519**:83–86.
342. McHenry HM, Coffing K. *Australopithecus* to *Homo*: transformations in body and mind. *Annual Review of Anthropology*. 2000:**29**:125–146.
343. Smith TM, Olejniczak AJ, Zermeno JP, Tafforeau P, Skinner MM, Hoffmann A, et al. Variation in enamel thickness within the genus *Homo*. *Journal of Human Evolution*. 2012;**62**:395–411.
344. Eng CM, Lieberman DE, Zink KD, Peters MA. Bite force and occlusal stress production in hominin evolution. *American Journal of Physical Anthropology*. 2013;**151**:544–557.
345. Stedman HH, Kozyak BW, Nelson A, Thesier DM, Su LT, Low DW, et al. Myosin gene mutation correlates with anatomical changes in the human lineage. *Nature*. 2004;**428**:415–418.
346. Darwin C. *On the Origin of Species by Means of Natural Selection*. London: Murray. 1859.
347. Lahti DC, Johnson NA, Ajie BC, Otto SP, Hendry AP, Blumstein DT, et al. Relaxed selection in the wild. *Trends in Ecology and Evolution*. 2009;**24**:487–496.
348. Brace CL. The probable mutation effect. *American Naturalist*. 1964:**98**: 453–455.
349. Kieser JA. *Human Adult Odontometrics: The Study of Variation in Adult Tooth Size*. Cambridge: Cambridge University Press; 1990.
350. McKee JK. A genetic model of dental reduction through the probable mutation effect. *American Journal of Physical Anthropology*. 1984;**65**:231–241.
351. Workman MS, Leamy LJ, Routman EJ, Cheverud JM. Analysis of quantitative trait locus effects on the size and shape of mandibular molars in mice. *Genetics*. 2002;**160**:1573–1586.
352. Polychronis G, Halazonetis DJ. Shape covariation between the craniofacial complex and first molars in humans. *Journal of Anatomy*. 2014;**225**:220–231.
353. Wolff J. Das gesetz der transformation der knochen. *DMW-Deutsche Medizinische Wochenschrift*. 1892;**19**:1222–1224.
354. Corruccini RS, Beecher RM. Occlusal variation related to soft diet in a nonhuman primate. *Science*. 1982;**218**:74–76.

355. Calcagno JM, Gibson KR. Human dental reduction: natural selection or the probable mutation effect. *American Journal of Physical Anthropology*. 1988;**77**:505–517.
356. Walker A, Leakey RE. The Nariokotome *Homo Erectus*. Skeleton: Harvard University Press; 1993.
357. Lordkipanidze D, Vekua A, Ferring R, Rightmire GP, Agusti J, Kiladze G, et al. Anthropology: the earliest toothless hominin skull. *Nature*. 2005;**434**:717–718.
358. De Castro JMB, Nicolas ME. Posterior dental size reduction in hominids: the Atapuerca evidence. *American Journal of Physical Anthropology*. 1995;**96**:335–356.
359. Pérez-Pérez A, Bermúdez de Castro J, Arsuaga JL. Nonocclusal dental microwear analysis of 300,000-year-old *Homo heilderbergensis* teeth from Sima de los Huesos (Sierra de Atapuerca, Spain). *American Journal of Physical Anthropology*. 1999;**108**:433–457.
360. Jernvall J, Jung HS. Genotype, phenotype, and developmental biology of molar tooth characters. *American Journal of Physical Anthropology*. 2000;**113**(**S31**):171–190.
361. Hunter JP, Guatelli-Steinberg D, Weston TC, Durner R, Betsinger TK. Model of tooth morphogenesis predicts carabelli cusp expression, size, and symmetry in humans. *PLoS One*. 2010;5(7):e11844.
362. Moormann SM, Guatelli-Steinberg D, Hunter JP. Metmerism, morphogenesis and the expression of Carabelli and other dental traits in humans. *American Journal of Physical Anthropology*. 2012;**150**:400–408.
363. Gómez-Robles A, de Castro JMB, Martinón-Torres M, Prado-Simón L, Arsuaga JL. A geometric morphometric analysis of hominin upper second and third molars, with particular emphasis on European Pleistocene populations. *Journal of Human Evolution*. 2012;**63**:512–526.
364. Dirks W, Bowman JE. Life history theory and dental development in four species of catarrhine primates. *Journal of Human Evolution*. 2007;**53**:309–320.
365. Hawkes K, O'Connell JF, Jones NB, Alvarez H, Charnov EL. Grandmothering, menopause, and the evolution of human life histories. *Proceedings of the National Academy of Sciences*. 1998;**95**:1336–1339.
366. Burkart JM, Hrdy SB, Van Schaik CP. Cooperative breeding and human cognitive evolution. *Evolutionary Anthropology*. 2009;**18**:175–186.
367. Burkart J, Allon O, Amici F, Fichtel C, Finkenwirth C, Heschl A, et al. The evolutionary origin of human hyper-cooperation. *Nature Communications*. 2014;5.

368. Dean MC. Retrieving chronological age from dental remains of early fossil hominins to reconstruct human growth in the past. *Philosophical Transactions of the Royal Society B.* 2010;**365**:3397–3410.
369. Dean MC, Liversidge HM. Age estimation in fossil hominins: comparing dental development in early *Homo* with modern humans. *Annals of Human Biology.* 2015;**42**:413–427.
370. Caspari R, Lee S-H. Older age becomes common late in human evolution. *Proceedings of the National Academy of Sciences U S A.* 2004;**101**:10895–10900.
371. Miles A. The dentition in the assessment of individual age in skeletal material. In *Dental Anthropology: Volume V: Society for the Study of Human Biology.* Oxford: Pergamon Press. 1963; 191–209.
372. Lacruz RS, Dean MC, Ramirez-Rozzi F, Bromage TG. Megadontia, striae periodicity and patterns of enamel secretion in Plio-Pleistocene fossil hominins. *Journal of Anatomy.* 2008;**213**:148–158.
373. Smith BH, Crummett TL, Brandt KL. Ages of eruption of primate teeth: a compendium for aging individuals and comparing life histories. *American Journal of Physical Anthropology.* 1994;**37(S19)**:177–231.
374. Dean MC, Smith BH. Growth and Development of the Nariokotome Youth, KNM-WT 15000. In Grine F, Fleagle J, Leakey R, editors.*The First Humans – Origin and Early Evolution of the Genus* Homo*. Vertebrate Paleobiology and Paleoanthropology.* Netherlands: Springer. 2009; 101–120.
375. Nissen HW, Riesen AH. The eruption of the permanent dentition of chimpanzee. *American Journal of Physical Anthropology.* 1964;**22(3)**:285–294.
376. Tanner JM. *Growth at Adolescence.* Springfield: Thomas; 1962.
377. de Castro JMB, Martinón-Torres M, Prado L, Gómez-Robles A, Rosell J, López-Polín L, et al. New immature hominin fossil from European Lower Pleistocene shows the earliest evidence of a modern human dental development pattern. *Proceedings of the National Academy of Sciences.* 2010;**107**:11739–11744.
378. Hrdy SB. Evolutionary context of human development: the cooperative breeding model. In Hrdy SB, editor. *Family Relationships: An Evolutionary Perspective.* New York: Oxford University Press. 2007; 39–68.
379. Piperata BA. Variation in maternal strategies during lactation: the role of the biosocial context. *American Journal of Human Biology.* 2009;**21**:817–827.
380. Valeggia C, Ellison PT. Lactational amenorrhoea in well-nourished Toba women of Formosa, Argentina. *Journal of Biosocial Science.* 2004;**36**:573–595.
381. Piperata BA, Guatelli-Steinberg D. Offsetting the costs of reproduction: the role of social support in human evolution. *American Journal of Physical Anthropology.* 2011;**144(S52)**:239.

382. Gurven M, Walker R. Energetic demand of multiple dependents and the evolution of slow human growth. *Proceedings of the Royal Society of London B: Biological Sciences*. 2006;**273**:835–841.
383. Hamilton WD. The moulding of senescence by natural selection. *Journal of Theoretical Biology*. 1966;**12**:12–45.
384. Langen TA. Prolonged offspring dependence and cooperative breeding in birds. *Behavioral Ecology*. 2000;**11**:367–377.
385. Aiello LC, Wells JC. Energetics and the evolution of the genus *Homo*. *Annual Review of Anthropology*. 2002:323–338.
386. Isler K, van Schaik CP. How our ancestors broke through the gray ceiling. *Current Anthropology*. 2012;**53**(S6):S453–S465.
387. Cuozzo FP, Sauther ML. Severe wear and tooth loss in wild ring-tailed lemurs (Lemur catta): a function of feeding ecology, dental structure, and individual life history. *Journal of Human Evolution*. 2006;**51**:490–505.
388. Krings M, Stone A, Schmitz RW, Krainitzki H, Stoneking M, Pääbo S. Neandertal DNA sequences and the origin of modern humans. *Cell*. 1997;**90**: 19–30.
389. Higham T, Douka K, Wood R, Ramsey CB, Brock F, Basell L, et al. The timing and spatiotemporal patterning of Neanderthal disappearance. *Nature*. 2014;**512**:306–309.
390. Gómez-Robles A, Martinón-Torres M, De Castro JB, Margvelashvili A, Bastir M, Arsuaga JL, et al. A geometric morphometric analysis of hominin upper first molar shape. *Journal of Human Evolution*. 2007;**53**:272–285.
391. Martinón-Torres M, De Castro JB, Gómez-Robles A, Arsuaga JL, Carbonell E, Lordkipanidze D, et al. Dental evidence on the hominin dispersals during the Pleistocene. *Proceedings of the National Academy of Sciences*. 2007;**104**:13279–13282.
392. Bocquet-Appel J-P, Degioanni A. Neanderthal demographic estimates. *Current Anthropology*. 2013;**54**(S8):S202–S213.
393. Weaver TD, Roseman CC, Stringer CB. Were neandertal and modern human cranial differences produced by natural selection or genetic drift? *Journal of Human Evolution*. 2007;**53**:135–145.
394. Stringer C, Humphrey L, Compton T. Cladistic analysis of dental traits in recent humans using a fossil outgroup. *Journal of Human Evolution*. 1997;**32**:389–402.
395. Brace CL. Refocusing on the Neanderthal problem. *American Anthropologist*. 1962;**64**: 729–741.
396. Brace CL, Nelson H, Korn N. *Atlas of Fossil Man*. New York: Holt, Rinehart and Winston; 1971.

397. Xing S, Martinón-Torres M, de Castro JMB, Zhang Y, Fan X, Zheng L, et al. Middle Pleistocene hominin teeth from Longtan Cave, Hexian, China. *PLoS One*. 2014;9(12):e114265.
398. Gómez-Robles A, de Castro JMB, Arsuaga J-L, Carbonell E, Polly PD. No known hominin species matches the expected dental morphology of the last common ancestor of Neanderthals and modern humans. *Proceedings of the National Academy of Sciences*. 2013;110:18196-18201.
399. Shea JJ. Spear points from the Middle Paleolithic of the Levant. *Journal of Field Archaeology*. 1988;15:441-450.
400. Jacob-Friesen K. Eiszeitliche elefantenjäger in der Lüneburger Heide. *Jahrbuch des Römisch-Germanischen Zentralmuseums Mainz*. 1956;3:1-22.
401. Boëda E, Geneste J-M, Griggo C, Mercier N, Muhesen S, Reyss J, et al. A Levallois point embedded in the vertebra of a wild ass (*Equus africanus*): hafting, projectiles and Mousterian hunting weapons. *Antiquity*. 1999;73:394-402.
402. Richards MP, Pettitt PB, Trinkaus E, Smith FH, Paunović M, Karavanić I. Neanderthal diet at Vindija and Neanderthal predation: the evidence from stable isotopes. *Proceedings of the National Academy of Sciences*. 2000;97:7663-7666.
403. Richards MP, Trinkaus E. Isotopic evidence for the diets of European Neanderthals and early modern humans. *Proceedings of the National Academy of Sciences*. 2009;106:16034-16039.
404. Bocherens H, Drucker DG, Billiou D, Patou-Mathis M, Vandermeersch B. Isotopic evidence for diet and subsistence pattern of the Saint-Césaire I Neanderthal: review and use of a multi-source mixing model. *Journal of Human Evolution*. 2005;49:71-87.
405. O'Connell TC, Hedges RE. Investigations into the effect of diet on modern human hair isotopic values. *American Journal of Physical Anthropology*. 1999;108:409-425.
406. Bocherens H. Neanderthal dietary habits: review of the isotopic evidence. In Hublin J-J and Richards MP, editors. *The Evolution of Hominin Diets*. Dordrecht: Springer. 2009; 241-250.
407. Stiner MC, Munro ND. Approaches to prehistoric diet breadth, demography, and prey ranking systems in time and space. *Journal of Archaeological Method and Theory*. 2002;9:181-214.
408. Kuhn S, Stiner M. What's a Mother to Do? *Current Anthropology*. 2006;47:953-981.
409. Hardy BL, Moncel M-H. Neanderthal use of fish, mammals, birds, starchy plants and wood 125-250,000 years ago. *PLoS One*. 2011;6(8):e23768.
410. Blasco R, Peris JF. Middle Pleistocene bird consumption at level XI of Bolomor cave (Valencia, Spain). *Journal of Archaeological Science*. 2009;36:2213-2223.

411. Henry AG, Brooks AS, Piperno DR. Microfossils in calculus demonstrate consumption of plants and cooked foods in Neanderthal diets (Shanidar III, Iraq; Spy I and II, Belgium). *Proceedings of the National Academy of Sciences.* 2011;**108**:486–491.
412. Hardy K, Buckley S, Collins MJ, Estalrrich A, Brothwell D, Copeland L, et al. Neanderthal medics? Evidence for food, cooking, and medicinal plants entrapped in dental calculus. *Naturwissenschaften.* 2012;**99**:617–626.
413. Newton PN, Nishida T. Possible buccal administration of herbal drugs by wild chimpanzees, Pan troglodytes. *Animal Behaviour.* 1990;**39**:798–801.
414. Fiorenza L, Benazzi S, Tausch J, Kullmer O, Bromage TG, Schrenk F. Molar macrowear reveals Neanderthal eco-geographic dietary variation. *PLoS One.* 2011;**6**(3):e14769.
415. El Zaatari S, Grine FE, Ungar PS, Hublin J-J. Ecogeographic variation in Neandertal dietary habits: evidence from occlusal molar microwear texture analysis. *Journal of Human Evolution.* 2011;**61**:411–424.
416. Bar-Yosef O. Eat what is there: Hunting and gathering in the world of Neanderthals and their neighbours. *International Journal of Osteoarchaeology.* 2004;**14**:333–342.
417. Ungar PS, Fennell KJ, Gordon K, Trinkaus E. Neandertal incisor beveling. *Journal of Human Evolution.* 1997;**32**:407–421.
418. Molnar S. Tooth wear and culture: a survey of tooth functions among some prehistoric populations. *Current Anthropology.* 1972; **13**:511–526.
419. Heim J-L. *Les Hommes Fossiles de la Ferrassie. 1. Le Gisement, Les Squelettes Adultes (Crâne et Squelette du Tronc).* Masson; 1976.
420. Trinkaus E. *The Shanidar Neandertals.* New York: Academic Press; 1983.
421. Fox CL, Frayer DW. Non-dietary Marks in the Anterior Dentition of the Krapina Neanderthals. *International Journal of Osteoarchaeology.* 1997;**7**:133–149.
422. Krueger K, Ungar P. Incisor microwear textures of five bioarcheological groups. *International Journal of Osteoarchaeology.* 2010;**20**:549–560.
423. Krueger KL. Reconstructing diet and behavior in bioarchaeological groups using incisor microwear texture analysis. *Journal of Archaeological Science: Reports.* 2015;**1**:29–37.
424. Krueger KL, Ungar PS, Guatelli-Steinberg D, Hublin JJ, A. P-P, Trinkaus E. Anterior dental microwear textures show environment-driven variability in Neandertal beahvior (in review). *Journal of Human Evolution.*
425. de Lumley M-A. L'Homme de l'Hortus. *Etude Quaternary.* 1973;**2**:311–550.
426. Brace CL. Egg on the face, *f* in the mouth, and the overbite. *American Anthropologist.* 1986; **88**:695–697.

427. Lozano-Ruiz M, De Castro JB, Martinón-Torres M, Sarmiento S. Cutmarks on fossil human anterior teeth of the Sima de los Huesos site (Atapuerca, Spain). *Journal of Archaeological Science*. 2004;**31**:1127–1135.
428. Lozano M, de Castro JMB, Carbonell E, Arsuaga JL. Non-masticatory uses of anterior teeth of Sima de los Huesos individuals (Sierra de Atapuerca, Spain). *Journal of Human Evolution*. 2008;**55**:713–728.
429. Lozano M, Mosquera M, de Castro JMB, Arsuaga JL, Carbonell E. Right handedness of *Homo heidelbergensis* from Sima de los Huesos (Atapuerca, Spain) 500,000 years ago. *Evolution and Human Behavior*. 2009;**30**:369–376.
430. Frayer DW, Lozano M, Bermúdez de Castro JM, Carbonell E, Arsuaga JL, Radovčić J, et al. More than 500,000 years of right-handedness in Europe. Laterality: asymmetries of body. *Brain and Cognition*. 2012;**17**:51–69.
431. Benítez-Burraco A, Longa VM. Right-handedness, lateralization and language in Neanderthals: a comment on Frayer et al. (2010). *Journal of Anthropological Science*. 2012;**90**:187–192.
432. D'Anastasio R, Wroe S, Tuniz C, Mancini L, Cesana DT, Dreossi D, et al. Micro-biomechanics of the Kebara 2 hyoid and its implications for speech in Neanderthals. *PLoS One*. 2013: e82261.
433. Volpato V, Macchiarelli R, Guatelli-Steinberg D., Fiore I, Bondioli L., Frayer D W. Hand to mouth in a Neandertal: right-handedness in Regourdou 1. *PloS One*. 2013;**7**(8): e43949.
434. Estalrrich A, Rosas A. Handedness in Neandertals from the El Sidrón (Asturias, Spain): evidence from instrumental striations with ontogenetic inferences. *PLoS One*. 2013;**8**(5):e62797.
435. Froehl A, Churchill S. Energetic competition between Neandertals and anatomically modern humans. *PaleoAnthropology*. 2009;**96**:116.
436. Goodman AH, Rose JC. Assessment of systemic physiological perturbations from dental enamel hypoplasias and associated histological structures. *American Journal of Physical Anthropology*. 1990;**33**(S11):59–110.
437. Barrett CK, Guatelli-Steinberg D, Sciulli PW. Revisiting dental fluctuating asymmetry in neandertals and modern humans. *American Journal of Physical Anthropology*. 2012;**149**:193–204.
438. Goodman AH, Martinez C, Chavez A. Nutritional supplementation and the development of linear enamel hypoplasias in children from Tezonteopan, Mexico. *The American Journal of Clinical Nutrition*. 1991;**53**:773–781.
439. Guatelli-Steinberg D, Benderlioglu Z. Brief communication: Linear enamel hypoplasia and the shift from irregular to regular provisioning in Cayo Santiago rhesus monkeys (Macaca mulatta). *American Journal of Physical Anthropology*. 2006;**131**:416–419.

440. Smith TM, Tafforeau P, Reid DJ, Pouech J, Lazzari V, Zermeno JP, et al. Dental evidence for ontogenetic differences between modern humans and Neanderthals. *Proceedings of the National Academy of Sciences.* 2010;**107**:20923–20928.
441. Hillson S, Bond S. Relationship of enamel hypoplasia to the pattern of tooth crown growth: A discussion. *American Journal of Physical Anthropology.* 1997;**104**:89–103.
442. Guatelli-Steinberg D, Larsen CS, Hutchinson DL. Prevalence and the duration of linear enamel hypoplasia: a comparative study of Neandertals and Inuit foragers. *Journal of Human Evolution.* 2004;**47**:65–84.
443. Ponce de León MS, Golovanova L, Doronichev V, Romanova G, Akazawa T, Kondo O, et al. Neanderthal brain size at birth provides insights into the evolution of human life history. *Proceedings of the National Academy of Sciences.* 2008;**105(37)**:13764–13768.
444. Ramirez Rozzi FV, Bermúdez de Castro JM. Surprisingly rapid growth in Neanderthals. *Nature.* 2004;**428**:936–939.
445. Guatelli-Steinberg D, Reid DJ, Bishop TA, Larsen CS. Anterior tooth growth periods in Neandertals were comparable to those of modern humans. *Proceedings of the National Academy of Sciences.* 2005;**102**:14197–14202.
446. Macchiarelli R, Bondioli L, Debenath A, Mazurier A, Tournepiche J-F, Birch W, et al. How Neanderthal molar teeth grew. *Nature.* 2006;**444**:748–751.
447. Smith TM, Toussaint M, Reid DJ, Olejniczak AJ, Hublin J-J. Rapid dental development in a middle Paleolithic Belgian Neanderthal. *Proceedings of the National Academy of Sciences.* 2007;**104**:20220–20225.
448. Smith TM, Harvati K, Olejniczak AJ, Reid DJ, Hublin J-J, Panagopoulou E. Brief communication: dental development and enamel thickness in the Lakonis Neanderthal molar. *American Journal of Physical Anthropology.* 2009;**138**:112–118.
449. Smith TM, Tafforeau P, Reid DJ, Pouech J, Lazzari V, Zermeno JP, et al. Dental evidence for ontogenetic differences between modern humans and Neanderthals. *Proceedings of the National Academy of Sciences U S A.* 2010;**107**:20923–20928.
450. Tompkins RL. Relative dental development of Upper Pleistocene hominids compared to human population variation. *American Journal of Physical Anthropology.* 1996;**99**:103–118.
451. Shackelford LL, Stinespring Harris AE, Konigsberg LW. Estimating the distribution of probable age-at-death from dental remains of immature human fossils. *American Journal of Physical Anthropology.* 2012;**147**:227–253.

452. Thompson JL, Nelson AJ. The place of Neandertals in the evolution of hominid patterns of growth and development. *Journal of Human Evolution.* 2000;**38**:475–495.
453. Martín-González JA, Mateos A, Goikoetxea I, Leonard WR, Rodríguez J. Differences between Neandertal and modern human infant and child growth models. *Journal of Human Evolution.* 2012;**63**:140–149.
454. Trinkaus E. Late Pleistocene adult mortality patterns and modern human establishment. *Proceedings of the National Academy of Sciences.* 2011;**108**:1267–1271.
455. Dale L. Hutchinson, Clark Spencer Larsen, Inui Choi. Stressed to the max? Physiological perturbation in the Krapina Neandertals. *Current Anthropology.* 1997;**38**:904–914.
456. Lavelle C, Moore W. The incidence of agenesis and polygenesis in the primate dentition. *American Journal of Physical Anthropology.* 1973;**38**:671–679.
457. Weaver TD, Roseman CC. New developments in the genetic evidence for modern human origins. *Evolutionary Anthropology.* 2008;**17**:69–90.
458. Lahr MM, Foley R. Multiple dispersals and modern human origins. *Evolutionary Anthropology.* 1994;**3**:48–60.
459. Reyes-Centeno H, Hubbe M, Hanihara T, Stringer C, Harvati K. Testing modern human out-of-Africa dispersal models and implications for modern human origins. *Journal of Human Evolution.* 2015;**87**:95–106.
460. Rasmussen M, Guo X, Wang Y, Lohmueller KE, Rasmussen S, Albrechtsen A, et al. An Aboriginal Australian genome reveals separate human dispersals into Asia. *Science.* 2011;**334**:94–98.
461. Hubbard AR, Guatelli-Steinberg D, Irish JD. Do nuclear DNA and dental nonmetric data produce similar reconstructions of regional population history? An example from modern coastal Kenya. *American Journal of Physical Anthropology.* 2015;**157**:295–304.
462. Turner CG. Late Pleistocene and Holocene population history of East Asia based on dental variation. *American Journal of Physical Anthropology.* 1987;**73**:305–321.
463. Turner CG. The dental bridge between Australia and Asia: following Macintosh into the East Asian hearth of humanity. *Archaeology in Oceania.* 1992;**27**:143–152.
464. Irish JD. Ancestral dental traits in recent Sub-Saharan Africans and the origins of modern humans. *Journal of Human Evolution.* 1998;**34**:81–98.
465. Liu W, Jin C-Z, Zhang Y-Q, Cai Y-J, Xing S, Wu X-J, et al. Human remains from Zhirendong, South China, and modern human emergence in East Asia. *Proceedings of the National Academy of Sciences.* 2010;**107**:19201–19206.

466. Bae CJ, Wang W, Zhao J, Huang S, Tian F, Shen G. Modern human teeth from Late Pleistocene Luna Cave (Guangxi, China). *Quaternary International.* 2014;**354**:169–83.
467. Shen G, Wu X, Wang Q, Tu H, Feng Y-x, Zhao J-x. Mass spectrometric U-series dating of Huanglong Cave in Hubei Province, central China: evidence for early presence of modern humans in eastern Asia. *Journal of Human Evolution.* 2013;**65**:162–167.
468. Liu W. The dental continuity of humans in China from Pleistocene to Holocene, and the origins of Mongoloids. *Proceedings of the 30th International Geological Congress.* 1997;**21**:24–32.
469. Hrdlička A. Shovel-shaped teeth. *American Journal of Physical Anthropology.* 1920;**3**:429–465.
470. Smith TM, Tafforeau P, Reid DJ, Grün R, Eggins S, Boutakiout M, et al. Earliest evidence of modern human life history in North African early *Homo sapiens*. *Proceedings of the National Academy of Sciences.* 2007;**104**:6128–6133.
471. Hublin J-J. Northwestern African Middle Pleistocene hominids and their bearing on the emergence of *Homo sapiens*. *Human Roots.* 2001:99–121.
472. Hublin J-J. Recent human evolution in northwestern Africa. *Philosophical Transactions of the Royal Society of London B: Biological Sciences.* 1992;**337**:185–191.
473. Trinkaus E, Athreya S, Churchill S, Demeter F, Henneberg M, Kondo O, et al. Modern human versus Neandertal evolutionary distinctiveness. *Current Anthropology.* 2006;**47**:597–620.
474. Guatelli-Steinberg D, Reid DJ. Brief communication: the distribution of perikymata on Qafzeh anterior teeth. *American Journal of Physical Anthropology.* 2010;**141**:152–157.
475. Macchiarelli R, Bondioli L. Post-Pleistocene reductions in human dental structure: a reappraisal in terms of increasing population density. *Human Evolution.* 1986;**1**:405–417.
476. y'Edynak G. Culture, diet, and dental reduction in Mesolithic forager-fishers of Yugoslavia. *Current Anthropology.* 1978; **19**:616–618.
477. Friedewald VE, Kornman KS, Beck JD, Genco R, Goldfine A, Libby P, et al. The *American Journal of Cardiology* and *Journal of Periodontology* editors' consensus: periodontitis and atherosclerotic cardiovascular disease. *Journal of Periodontology.* 2009;**80**:1021–1032.
478. Saini R, Saini S, Saini SR. Periodontal diseases: a risk factor to cardiovascular disease. *Annals of Cardiac Anaesthesia.* 2010;**13**:159.
479. Pereira TV, Salzano FM, Mostowska A, Trzeciak WH, Ruiz-Linares A, Chies JA, et al. Natural selection and molecular evolution in primate PAX9

gene, a major determinant of tooth development. *Proceedings of the National Academy of Sciences*. 2006;**103**:5676–5681.
480. Brook A. A unifying aetiological explanation for anomalies of human tooth number and size. *Archives of Oral Biology*. 1984;**29**:373–378.
481. Kavanagh KD, Evans AR, Jernvall J. Predicting evolutionary patterns of mammalian teeth from development. *Nature*. 2007;**449**:427–432.
482. Bernal V, Gonzalez PN, Perez SI. Developmental processes, evolvability, and dental diversification of New World monkeys. *Evolutionary Biology*. 2013;**40**:532–541.
483. De Castro JMB. Third molar agenesis in human prehistoric populations of the Canary Islands. *American Journal of Physical Anthropology*. 1989;**79**:207–215.
484. Grine F, Gwinnett A, Oaks J. Early hominid dental pathology: interproximal caries in 1.5 million-year-old Paranthropus robustus from Swartkrans. *Archives of Oral Biology*. 1990;**35**:381–386.
485. Trinkaus E, Smith RJ, Lebel S. Dental caries in the Aubesier 5 Neandertal primary molar. *Journal of Archaeological Science*. 2000;**27**:1017–1021.
486. Lukacs JR. Oral health in past populations: context, concepts and controversies. In Grauer A, editor. *A Companion to Paleopathology*. Chichester UK: Wiley-Blackwell. 2012; 553–581.
487. Gilmore CC. A comparison of antemortem tooth loss in human hunter-gatherers and non-human catarrhines: implications for the identification of behavioral evolution in the human fossil record. *American Journal of Physical Anthropology*. 2013;**151**:252–264.
488. Cohen MN, Armelagos GJ. Paleopathology at the origins of agriculture: editor's summation. In Cohen MN and Aremelagos GJ, editors. *Paleopathology at the Origis of Agriculture*. New York: Academic Press. 1984; 585–601.
489. Lukacs JR. Dental paleopathology and agricultural intensification in South Asia: New evidence from Bronze Age Harappa. *American Journal of Physical Anthropology*. 1992;**87**:133–150.
490. Kelley MA, Levesque DR, Weidl E. Contrasting patterns of dental disease in five early northern Chilean groups. In Kelley MA and Larsen CS, editors. *Advances in Dental Anthropology*. New York: Wiley-Liss. 1991; 203–213.
491. Beckett S, Lovell NC. Dental disease evidence for agricultural intensification in the Nubian C? Group. *International Journal of Osteoarchaeology*. 1994;**4**:223–239.
492. Adler CJ, Dobney K, Weyrich LS, Kaidonis J, Walker AW, Haak W, et al. Sequencing ancient calcified dental plaque shows changes in oral microbiota with dietary shifts of the Neolithic and Industrial revolutions. *Nature Genetics*. 2013;**45**:450–455.

493. Seiler R, Spielman AI, Zink A, Rühli F. Oral pathologies of the Neolithic Iceman, c.3,300 BC. *European Journal of Oral Science.* 2013:1–5.
494. Humphrey LT, De Groote I, Morales J, Barton N, Collcutt S, Ramsey CB, et al. Earliest evidence for caries and exploitation of starchy plant foods in Pleistocene hunter-gatherers from Morocco. *Proceedings of the National Academy of Sciences.* 2014;**111**:954–959.
495. Oxenham M, Tayles N. *Bioarchaeology of Southeast Asia.* Cambridge: Cambridge University Press; 2006.
496. Lukacs JR. Fertility and agriculture accentuate sex differences in dental caries rates. *Current Anthropology.* 2008;**49**:901–914.
497. Larsen CS. Biological changes in human populations with agriculture. *Annual Review of Anthropology.* 1995;**24**:185–213.
498. Lukacs JR, Largaespada LL. Explaining sex differences in dental caries prevalence: saliva, hormones, and "life-history" etiologies. *American Journal of Human Biology* 2006;**18**:540–555.
499. Muhler JC, Shafer WG. Experimental dental caries VII. The effect of various androgens and estrogens on dental caries in the rat. *Journal of Dental Research.* 1955;**34**(5):661–665.
500. Laine M, Tenovuo J, Lehtonen O-P, Ojanotko-Harri A, Vilja P, Tuohimaa P. Pregnancy-related changes in human whole saliva. *Archives of Oral Biology.* 1988;**33**:913–917.
501. Salvolini E, Giorgio R, Curatola A, Mazzanti L, Fratto G. Biochemical modifications of human whole saliva induced by pregnancy. *British Journal of Obstetrics and Gynecology.* 1998;**105**:656–660.
502. Christensen K, Gaist D, Jeune B, Vaupel JW. "A tooth per child?" *The Lancet.* 1998;**352**:1387.
503. Gibbons A. An evolutionary theory of dentistry. *Science.* 2012:336.
504. Corruccini RS. Anthropological aspects of orofacial and occlusal variations and anomalies. In Kelley MA and Larsen CS, editors. *Advances in Dental Anthropology.* New York: Wiley-Liss. 1991:295–323.
505. Potts R. Environmental hypotheses of hominin evolution. *American Journal of Physical Anthropology.* 1998;**107**(**S27**):93–136.
506. Guatelli-Steinberg D. Macroscopic and microscopic analyses of linear enamel hypoplasia in Plio-Pleistocene South African hominins with respect to aspects of enamel development and morphology. *American Journal of Physical Anthropology.* 2003;**120**:309–322.
507. Guatelli-Steinberg D. Analysis and significance of linear enamel hypoplasia in Plio-Pleistocene hominins. *American Journal of Physical Anthropology.* 2004;**123**:199–215.

508. Guatelli-Steinberg D. Recent Studies of Dental Development in Neandertals: Implications for Neandertal Life Histories. *Evolutionary Anthropology.* 2009;**18**:9–20.
509. Liu W, Martinón-Torres M, Cai Y-j, Xing S, Tong H-w, Pei S-w, et al. The earliest unequivocally modern humans in southern China. *Nature.* 2015; **526**:696–699.
510. Berger LR, Hawks J, de Ruiter DJ, Churchill SE, Schmid P, Delezene LK, et al. *Homo naledi*, a new species of the genus *Homo* from the Dinaledi Chamber, South Africa. *eLife.* 2015:4.
511. Hlusko LJ. Integrating the genotype and phenotype in hominid paleontology. *Proceedings of the National Academy of Sciences U S A.* 2004;**101**:2653–2657.
512. Humphrey LT, Dean MC, Jeffries TE, Penn M. Unlocking evidence of early diet from tooth enamel. *Proceedings of the National Academy of Sciences.* 2008;**105**:6834–6839.
513. Austin C, Smith TM, Bradman A, Hinde K, Joannes-Boyau R, Bishop D, et al. Barium distributions in teeth reveal early-life dietary transitions in primates. *Nature.* 2013;**498**:216–219.
514. Cuozzo FP, Ungar PS, Sauther ML. Primate dental ecology: how teeth respond to the environment. *American Journal of Physical Anthropology.* 2012;**148**:159–162.
515. Smith TM, Guatelli-Steinberg D. Developmental variation of the primate dentition: The 2011 AAPA symposium in honor of Don Reid. *Evolutionary Anthropology.* 2011;**20**:161–163.
516. Little AC, Jones BC, DeBruine LM. Facial attractiveness: evolutionary based research. *Philosophical Transactions of the Royal Society B: Biological Sciences.* 2011;**366**:1638–1659.
517. Hendrie CA, Brewer G, Evans AR. Evidence to suggest that teeth act as human ornament displays signalling mate quality. *PLoS One.* 2012;**7**:e42178.
518. Zumbroich TJ. The ethnobotany of teeth blackening in Southeast Asia. *Ethnobotany Research and Applications.* 2009;**7**:381–398.
519. Martens M. Tooth transfigurement in Indonesia. Sulang Language Data and Working Papers: Topics in Lexicography, no. 17.
520. Willis M, Harris L, Hergenrader P. On traditional dental extraction: case reports from Dinka and Nuer en route to restoration. *British Dental Journal.* 2008;**204**:121–124.

Index

abrasive diets, 37, 39
Adler, Christina, 227
age at first reproduction, 84, 92
agriculture, 220, 222, 227, 228, 231, 238, 279, 280
Aiello, Leslie, 132
Ala240Pro mutation, 223
allomother, 172, 174, 207
Ameloblasts, 93
AMHS, 126, 134, 137, 171, 176, 211, 237
anatomically modern, 8, 55, 114, 123, 127, 130, 134, 135, 137, 156, 159, 171, 176, 178, 181, 185, 186, 200, 203, 208, 209, 211, 212, 213, 214, 215, 216, 217, 218, 219, 220, 230, 236, 237, 242, 275
anisotropy, 40, 41, 49, 54, 191
antemortem tooth loss, 226, 229, 241, 279
  AMTL, 226, 229, 230
anthropoids, 18, 65, 67, 71, 74, 79, 162, 254, 256
Antón, Susan, 113, 235
Ardipithecus kadabba, 16
Ardipithecus ramidus, 16, 18, 19, 46, 47, 52, 57, 61, 62, 63, 64, 76, 78, 79, 80, 81, 82, 234, 247, 252, 254
  Ar. ramidus, 18, 47, 234
  Ardi, 16, 18, 20, 61
Argue, Debbie, 132
Armelagos, George, 226
Arsuaga, Juan Luis, 125
Austin, Christine, 240
Australians, 135, 213, 214, 215, 230
Australopithecus afarensis, 18, 20, 21, 22, 47, 49, 56, 57, 66, 76, 79, 80, 81, 82, 100, 101, 102, 106, 132, 247, 248, 252, 257, 268
  Au. afarensis, 20, 21, 22, 146
  Lucy, 20
Australopithecus africanus, 18, 22, 23, 28, 30, 32, 43, 46, 49, 50, 51, 52, 57, 58, 102, 106, 226

Au. africanus, 22, 23, 50, 144, 146
Australopithecus anamensis, 18, 47, 52, 56, 57, 76, 247, 252, 257
  Au. anamensis, 20, 21, 47, 49, 80, 146
Australopithecus bahrelghazali, 21, 47
Australopithecus deyiremeda, 21, 28
Australopithecus garhi, 22, 139, 248
  Au. garhi, 23
Australopithecus sediba, 23, 28, 39, 49, 51, 57, 248, 249
  Au. sediba, 23
aye-aye, 33, 56

baboons, 12, 13, 52, 54, 55, 68, 69, 79, 253, 262
bacteria, 39, 149, 188, 223, 225, 227, 228, 231
Barium-Calcium, 240
bark, 33, 36, 51, 58, 71
Barrett, Chris, 198
Bar-Yosef, Omar, 190
Begun, David, 75
Benderlioglu, Zeynep, 196
Berger, Lee, 238
Bermúdez de Castro, José, 170, 212
Berrigan, David, 85, 200
biological species concept, 116, 262
bipedalism, 15, 16, 61, 63, 77
bite force, 43, 72, 129, 142, 145, 146, 151, 156
Black, Davidson, 118
Blomquist, Greg, 169, 201
Bocherens, Hervi, 185, 187
Bogin, Barry, 157
Bond, Sandra, 197
bonobos, 14, 32, 66
Boule, Marcelin, 177
bovids, 38, 48, 56, 185
Bower, Bruce, 87
Boyd, Kevin, 242
Brace, Loring, 138, 146, 192, 220, 231
Bromage, Timothy, 95, 97
Broom, Robert, 24, 259

INDEX 283

brown capuchins, 40
browsers, 49, 51
buccal, 5, 7, 124, 132, 192, 239, 274
Burkart, Judith, 172

C3 pathway, 44
C4 foods, 45, 46, 52, 53, 56, 79, 82
C4 pathway, 45
calculus. *See* dental calculus
Callitrichines, 225
canine reduction, 63, 77, 78, 79, 80, 234, 256, 257
Cantius, 74
Carabelli, 153, 239, 270
Carbon-13, 185
caries, 226, 227, 228, 229, 242, 243, 279, 280,
Cartmill, Matt, 218
Caspari, Rachel, 160, 207
Catopithecus, 74
cavernous sinus thrombosis, 223
cavities, 119, 226, 227, 229
Charnov, Eric, 85, 200
childhood, 4, 8, 44, 73, 84, 85, 86, 87, 149, 157, 173, 185, 206, 209, 230, 242, 258
chimpanzees, 4, 14, 16, 28, 31, 32, 46, 47, 49, 52, 57, 61, 66, 76, 79, 88, 91, 97, 101, 104, 105, 139, 143, 158, 160, 162, 163, 167, 170, 171, 172, 175, 188, 205, 230, 232, 233, 234, 235, 246, 251, 259, 274
Churchill, Steven, 194
cichlid, 36, 250
circadian rhythm, 93, 95, 103
cladistic, 13, 25, 26, 117, 132, 181, 214, 215, 266
cladogram, 13, 26, 28, 182
Clement, Anna, 128
Coffing, Katie, 144
Cohen, Mark, 226
complexity, 40, 41, 47, 49, 50, 54, 143, 155, 186, 189, 235
Constantino, Paul, 43, 146, 248, 249, 251
cooking, 32, 138, 139, 140, 141, 145, 147, 151, 220, 231, 249, 274
Cooking Hypothesis, 140
cooperative breeders, 172
cooperative breeding, 173, 174, 176, 271, 272
Corruccini, Robert S., 150
cross-striations, 93, 94, 95, 103, 201
Cucina, Andrea, 229

Cuozzo, Frank, 174, 241
Cuvier, Georges, 4

Daegling, David, 32, 43
Daoxian, 237
Dart, Raymond, 14, 18, 22, 31, 63, 87
Darwin, Charles, 14, 59, 60, 61, 63, 67, 77, 82, 126, 138, 146, 211, 244, 254, 255, 269
Dawkins, Richard, 11
De Lumley, Marie-Antoinette, 191
Dean, Christopher, 102, 160, 164, 165, 166, 197, 203, 241
deciduous teeth, 87, 88, 89, 102, 106, 240
decussating enamel, 47
Delezene, Lucas, 80
Denisovan, 131, 136
dental calculus, 3, 35, 39, 44, 51, 58, 187, 188, 189, 209, 228, 231, 236, 274
dental development, 87, 88, 89, 91, 98, 100, 101, 102, 103, 104, 105, 106, 108, 160, 162, 163, 164, 165, 169, 170, 171, 173, 199, 204, 205, 206, 207, 209, 210, 218, 219, 230, 234, 235, 236, 237, 242, 259, 261, 270, 271, 276
dental morphology, 4, 39, 56, 109, 125, 131, 136, 142, 181, 182, 183, 208, 213, 214, 215, 217, 230, 237, 238, 265, 273
dental paleoanthropology, 232, 238
dental reduction, 138, 146, 147, 150, 151, 152, 156, 211, 212, 220, 221, 222, 223, 224, 231, 238, 269, 270, 278
dentine, 34, 93, 95, 119, 121, 166, 243
derived traits, 13, 24, 125, 214, 217
developmental pathways., 65, 158, *See also* ontogenetic pathways
diastema, 16, 22
dietary divergence, 137, 142
Dietary Hypothesis, 30, 43, 58, 137, 234
distal, 5, 7, 17
Dmanisi, 119, 121, 150, 174, 175, 226, 264
DNA, 11, 14, 29, 116, 123, 125, 131, 134, 135, 136, 178, 180, 181, 183, 213, 227, 228, 231, 237, 258, 267, 272, 277
Dobzhanksy, Theodosius, 86
Dominy, Nathaniel J., 48
dual selection hypothesis, 71, 80

East African Rift valley, 24, 36
ecological risk aversion hypothesis, 85
El Sidrón, 194, 275

El Zaatari, Sireen, 189
enamel matrix, 93, 94, 95, 100
enamel prisms, 47, 93, 164, 240
enamel thickness, 36, 37, 145, 164, 195, 247, 250, 269, 276
Energetic Budget Effect, 148
Eng, Carolyn, 145
Eriksson, Anders, 178
eruption, 73, 87, 88, 89, 90, 91, 92, 98, 100, 102, 104, 105, 106, 108, 160, 162, 163, 166, 171, 175, 176, 204, 206, 218, 236, 256, 259, 261, 262, 271
Eskimos, 190, 191, 192
evolutionary psychology, 243, 244
Expensive Tissue Hypothesis, 31

fallback foods, 34, 37, 241
female choice, 60, 64, 80
Fernando Ramirez-Rozzi, 203
Fiore, Ivana, 194
Fiorenza, Luca, 189
fire, 3, 118, 137, 138, 141, 151, 152, 156, 235, 263
first molar eruption, 91, 92, 93, 101, 104, 105, 108, 162
fluctuating asymmetry, 195, 196, 198, 275
Frayer, David, 193, 263, 274, 275
Froehl, Andrew, 194

gape, 65, 72, 75, 79, 81, 82, 234, 254
gene flow, 135, 179, 181, 182, 213, 222
generalists, 33, 36, 233
genetic drift, 152, 156, 180, 181, 212, 222, 272
Gesher Benot Ya'akov, 141
gibbons, 64, 69
Gigantopithecus, 75
Gilmore, Cassandra, 229
gingival emergence, 105, 106, 166
glossopetrae, 1, 246
Godfrey, Laurie, 106
Gómez-Robles, Aida, 182
gorillas, 28, 46, 59, 66, 91, 92, 97, 106, 246
Gran Dolina, 123, 170, 264
Grandmother Hypothesis, 159, 207
grazers, 49, 51
Green, Richard, 135, 178
Greenfield, Leonard, 64, 71, 80
Grine, Fred, 33, 43, 50, 54

Hamilton, WD, 173
hard foods, 33, 34, 37, 38, 42, 43, 47, 50, 54, 55, 56, 144, 235, 241
hard vs. tough foods, 34
hard-object feeding, 35, 37, 50
Hardy, Karen, 188
Havers-Halberg, 97
Hawkes, Kristin, 159, 171, 173
Hawks, John, 140
Henry, Amanda, 51, 187
Hillson, Simon, 197
histology, 160, 164
Hlusko, Leslea, 239
Homo antecessor, 117, 123, 162, 165, 170, 171, 176, 180, 181, 183, 199
Homo erectus, ix, 24, 26, 63, 113, 115, 117, 118, 119, 120, 121, 124, 128, 133, 137, 138, 140, 141, 143, 144, 145, 146, 147, 148, 149, 150, 151, 152, 155, 156, 162, 165, 166, 167, 169, 170, 171, 173, 174, 175, 176, 180, 181, 182, 183, 199, 216, 230, 234, 235, 238, 261, 263, 264, 268, 270
Homo floresiensis, 109, 126, 132, 133, 266
Homo habilis, 53, 113, 114, 115, 116, 117, 118, 119, 121, 133, 137, 139, 144, 145, 146, 148, 149, 150, 151, 155, 162, 163, 164, 165, 170, 181, 234, 238, 262, 263, 268, 269
Homo heidelbergensis, 123, 124, 125, 133, 134, 136, 137, 140, 151, 153, 155, 156, 179, 180, 183, 212, 264, 275
Homo naledi, 238, 239, 281
Homo rudolfensis, 28, 115, 116, 117
Homo sapiens, 8, 101, 117, 126, 135, 169, 171, 181, 263, 266, 278
homoplasy, 12, 65, 75, 102
honing complex, 16, 63, 75, 257
honing facet, 75
howler monkeys, 40
Hrdy, Sarah, 173
Huanglong Cave, 216, 278
Hubbard, Amelia, 213
Hublin, Jean-Jacques, 131, 217
Humphrey, Louise, 227, 240
Hunter, John, 153, 239
Hutchinson, Dale, 197
Hylander, William, 64, 72
hypocone, 180
hypsodont, 37, 38

impaction, 149, 150, 223, 229
Industrial Revolution, 228, 229, 231
infection, 149, 197, 223, 226
Inhibitory Cascade Model, 224, 225
Irish, Joel, 28, 213, 215

Jebel Irhoud, 217, 218, 219

Kay, Richard, 68
Kenyanthropus platyops, 21, 28, 47, 49, 116
Kieser, Jules, 147, 148, 221
Koobi Fora, 115, 141, 262
Krapina Neanderthals, 181, 197, 214, 274
Kreuger, Kristin, 191
Kromdrai, 50
Kuhn, Steven, 186
Kuzawa, Chris, 85

Lacruz, Rodrigo, 95, 101
Lahti, David, 147
Lambert, Joanna, 36
Larsen, Clark Spencer, 197, 228, 277
lateral enamel, 98, 100, 256
Le Gros Clark, Sir Wilfrid, 117
Le Moustier, 130, 206
Leakey, Louis, 24, 113, 114, 117
Leakey, Meave, 115
learning, 84, 86, 87, 158, 159, 173, 207, 235
Lee Sang-Hee, 160, 207
Lee Thorp, Julia, 48
Leigh, Steve, 69, 85, 169, 201
life history, 8, 84, 85, 86, 88, 89, 90, 91, 92, 93, 97, 102, 104, 106, 108, 156, 157, 158, 159, 160, 162, 164, 169, 171, 175, 179, 199, 200, 201, 204, 207, 209, 219, 232, 236, 237, 241, 259, 260, 261, 272, 276, 278
life history mode, 169, 175, 219
life history modes, 176, 200
lifespan, 37, 92, 97, 158, 170, 208
linear enamel hypoplasia, 195, 196, 197, 198, 233, 236, 276, 280, 281
linear enamel hypoplasias, 195
lingual, 5, 7, 119, 120, 153, 239
Liu, Wu, 217
Liversidge, Helene, 105, 160, 165, 241
longevity, 8, 56, 157, 159, 160, 169, 170
long-period increments, 95
Lovejoy, Owen, 19, 62, 77
Lucas, Peter, 37, 42, 64, 72, 234

Lufengpithecus, 74
Lukacs, John, ix, 228
Luna Cave, 216, 278

M1 eruption, 101, 104, 105, 108, 109, 171, 237
macaques, 69, 240
Macchiarelli, Roberto, 194, 204, 222
Macho, Gabrielle, 54, 55, 92
macrowear, 189, 236, 274
Makapansgat, 49, 249
Malawi, 115, 262
male-male competition, 60, 64, 67, 68, 78, 81, 234, 257
mandrills, 69
mangabey, 36
Manica, Andrea, 178
Mann, Alan, 87, 98
Manthi, Fredrick, 76
marmosets, 71, 172
Martín-González, Jesús, 206
Martinón-Torres, Maria, 181
maturation stage, 93
Mayr, Ernst, 116, 178
McGraw, Scott, ix, 36
McHenry, Henry, 144
meat-eating, 31, 138, 139, 142, 155, 268
mechanically challenging foods, 36, 75, 78, 79, 82, 145, 149, 234
Megadontia Quotient, 144
Melanesians, 135, 215
mesial, 5, 7, 17, 80
microwear, ix, 37, 40, 41, 42, 43, 45, 47, 49, 50, 51, 54, 55, 142, 143, 152, 155, 191, 233, 235, 236, 248, 250, 251, 252, 253, 270, 274
microwear texture analysis, 40, 50, 191
Miles, AEW, 160
mitchondria, 134
mitochondrial DNA, 136
mtDNA, 136
modularity, 158
Molnar, Steven, 190
monogamous, 64, 67, 68, 78, 81
monogamy, 77, 78, 80, 81, 87
Moormann, Stephanie, 239
multi-male groups, 67, 68
Multiregional Continuity, 133
MYH 16, 145

Narikotome Boy, 169, 173, 174, 175, 235
Nariokotome Boy, 26, 167, 168
National Evolutionary Synthesis Center, 231, 242
natural selection, 36, 84, 93, 133, 134, 147, 158, 159, 181, 219, 224, 229, 270, 272
Neander Valley, 126
Neanderthal anterior teeth, 128, 129, 190, 191, 237
Neanderthal molars, 129
Neanderthal teeth, 128, 179, 180, 184, 189, 192, 196, 199, 201, 203, 204, 205, 226
neonatal line, 107
New World monkeys, 71, 225, 255, 279
Nitrogen-15, 184
Nutcracker Man, 24, 25, 32, 53, 114, 253

Obama, President Barak, 20
Old World monkeys, 66, 72
Oldowan tools, 114, 139
Olduvai Gorge, 24, 113, 114, 139, 143, 262, 268
ontogenetic pathway, 73
orangutans, 43, 59, 66, 91, 92, 105, 106
Orrorin tugenensis, 16
Otzi, 227
Ouranopithecus, 74, 75, 254, 257
outgroups, 14
Oxenham, Marc, 227
OY ratio, 169, 170

Paranthropus aethiopicus, 24
Paranthropus boisei, 22, 24, 25, 26, 53, 54, 55, 56, 57, 58, 100, 115, 143, 234, 248, 252, 253, 260
Paranthropus robustus, 24, 30, 32, 43, 46, 49, 50, 51, 52, 54, 57, 58, 98, 102, 106, 143, 226, 234, 235, 253, 279
parsimony, 13, 28
pathology, 4, 150, 151, 212, 226, 238, 279
Patterning Cascade Model, 153, 154, 238, 239
PAX 9 gene, 223, 225
Peking Man, 118
perikymata, 98, 99, 100, 101, 103, 104, 163, 164, 167, 197, 198, 201, 203, 219, 237
periodicity, 94, 95, 97, 99, 100, 104, 107, 108, 164, 167, 204, 218, 260, 271
periodontitis, 223, 226, 227, 243
periodontium, 223
phenetic, 12,

phylogeny, 8, 14, 23, 133, 136, 248, 249
physiological stress, 4, 179, 195, 198, 199, 209, 210, 236
phytoliths, 37, 39, 42, 51, 187
Pickering, Travis, 143
Piperata, Barbara, 172
placental mammals, 86, 89, 258, 259
plaque. *See* dental calculus
Plavcan, Michael, 60, 66, 69, 78
polygynous, 67, 81
posterior teeth, 56, 115, 124, 137, 138, 144, 165, 190, 235
Potts, Rick, 144, 233
primitive traits, 12
Probable Mutation Effect, 146, 156, 220, 221, 231
PME, 146, 147, 221, 222
prosimians, 60, 65, 106
Proteopithecus, 74
pulp, 119, 226

Qafzeh, 127, 181, 219, 220, 230, 231, 237, 278

Recent African Origin, 134
Regourdou 1194, 275
Reid, Donald, ix, 197, 242
relaxed selection, 78, 146, 147, 151, 152, 156, 212, 220, 221, 235
Rensch's rule, 66, 74
retromolar space, 127
Richard Wrangham, 32
right-handed, 193, 194, 237
ring-tailed lemurs, 65, 241, 272
Robinson, John T., 30

Sahelanthropus tchadensis, 16
Sauther, Michelle, 174, 241
Schultz, Adolph H., 88
Schultz's Rule, 88, 160
Sciulli, Paul, ix, 198
Scladina, 206
secretory stage, 93
sedges, 45, 51, 53, 54, 55, 57, 251
septicemia, 150, 223
sexual dimorphism, 8, 60, 64, 65, 66, 67, 68, 69, 70, 71, 72, 73, 74, 76, 78, 80, 81, 82, 234, 254, 255
sexual maturity, 84, 85, 92, 97, 158, 199, 200, 207, 209

sexual selection, 59, 65, 67, 69, 71, 77, 78, 82, 243, 254
sexually monomorphic, 82
Shackelford, Laura, 205, 237
Shipman, Pat, 139
shovel-shaped, 119, 120, 128, 133, 180, 216, 217
shovel-shaped incisors, 119, 120, 133, 180, 216, 217
Sima de Los Huesos, 125, 126, 136, 151, 152, 179, 180, 193, 212, 264, 267, 270, 275
Sivapithecus, 75
Smith, Fred, 218
Smith, Holly, 89, 102, 106, 158, 162, 163, 166
Smith, Patricia, 221
Smith, Tanya, 107, 163, 197, 203, 205, 218
Sorrentino, John, 242
sperm competition, 68, 81
Sponheimer, Matt, 46, 52, 56, 57
stable carbon isotopes, 44, 50, 253
stable isotopes, 184, 251, 273
starch grains, 187
Starrett, Alyssa, ix, 5, 7, 15, 17, 19, 20, 25, 26, 33, 38, 48, 62, 70, 76, 101, 121, 122, 127, 128, 129, 150, 161, 168, 180
Steinberg, Dan, ix, 196
Steno, 1, 2, 246
Sterkfontein, 50, 51, 251, 253
Stewart, Kathlyn, 55, 57
Stiner, Mary, 186
Strait, David, 32
striae of Retzius, 94, 95, 96, 99, 103, 164, 201, 204
Strontium-Calcium, 240
stuff and cut, 192
suids, 38, 56
Sundadonty, 213
Swartkrans, 50, 51, 57, 98, 253, 263, 279
Switek, Brian, 1
synchrotron, 95, 96, 99, 107, 121, 164, 205, 218, 234

Tai forest, 50
Taung Child, 15, 18

taurodont, 119, 121, 124, 129, 180
Tayles, Nancy, 227
Templeton, Alan, 135
testosterone, 72, 73, 83, 228
Texture fill volume, 191
Theropithecus oswaldi, 53
thick enamel, 24, 34, 35, 36, 37, 38, 56, 241, 250
third molar agenesis, 119, 217, 223, 224, 225,
Tigara, 198, 199, 203, 236
tough foods, 3, 34, 42, 49, 54, 56, 72, 138, 143
trace elements, 44, 46, 155
Trinkaus, Erik, 208
tropical grasses, 39, 45, 48, 57
Turkana Basin, 47, 142, 252
Turner, Christy G, 213

underground storage organs, 32, 43, 50, 51, 141
USOs, 32, 43
Ungar, Peter, 49, 54, 142, 143, 148, 235, 241
Upper Paleolithic, 179, 186, 189, 198, 203, 207, 208

Variability Selection Hypothesis, 144, 233
Vega Lizama, Elma, 229
Volpato, Virgine, 194

Ward, Carol, 76
weaning, 84, 89, 91, 92, 97, 106, 157, 158, 169, 173, 199, 240, 259
White, Peter, 221
wisdom teeth, 20, 211
Wonderwerk Cave, 141, 263
woolly spider monkeys, 68, 81, 255

Xing, Song, ix, 120, 180

ZY chromosome, 72
Y'Edynak, Gloria, 222

Zhiren Cave, 216
Zhoukoudian, 118, 119, 120, 125, 180, 181

Printed in the United States
By Bookmasters